THE
IMAGE OF MAN
IN C. S. LEWIS

THE
IMAGE OF MAN
IN C. S. LEWIS

william luther white

ABINGDON PRESS   Nashville and New York

THE IMAGE OF MAN IN C. S. LEWIS

Standard Book Number: 687-18673-0

Library of Congress Catalog Card Number: 76-84722

SET UP, PRINTED, AND BOUND BY THE
PARTHENON PRESS, AT NASHVILLE,
TENNESSEE, UNITED STATES OF AMERICA

Acknowledgments

The primary research for this volume was undertaken for a Ph.D. dissertation, done at Northwestern University and Garrett Theological Seminary in 1968. A special word of gratitude is due Dr. Philip S. Watson, under whose guidance this project has been brought to completion, and Dr. William Hordern, under whose encouragement the topic was initially chosen. My deep appreciation extends also to the professors who have served as advisors in my minor areas—Dr. Henry E. Kolbe in Christian ethics and Dr. Richard Ellmann in English literature. The fully documented dissertation is listed with University Microfilms, Ann Arbor, Michigan (No. 69-1965).

My expression of thanks would be incomplete without acknowledging my debt to two of America's foremost Lewis scholars—Prof. Chad Walsh and Prof. Clyde S. Kilby. Though my conclusions sometimes differ from theirs, I have benefited greatly from the insights these men have presented in books, articles, letters, and conversations.

Nor can I neglect to mention the persons who have sacrificed the most for this project—my wife Patricia and our two children. The words of William Faulkner, given in tribute to some of his favorite characters, are perhaps the most appropriate imaginable here: "They endured."

Foreword

Many admirers of C. S. Lewis have gone through three stages, if I can generalize from my own experience. I first came on his books about twenty-five years ago, at a time when I was revolting—intellectually and emotionally—against a flat and barren agnosticism. I found in Lewis an uncompromising exponent of no-nonsense theology, expressed with a rigor of mind and a graciousness of style, plus a soaring imagination.

Later, much later, the doubts came. After I had put myself in print with an adulatory book about the Oxford don, I began rereading him, and a vague uneasiness developed. There was unquestionably something shrill and sharp-edged about his writings at times, the treatment of morality in particular. Too much rule-book advice, too many either/or legalisms. I also began to be troubled at what seemed a willful disregard of the present and its main thinkers in favor of the past. I began to wonder whether he was playing a role, rather like some American aesthete extolling the beauties of a vanished feudal order. This uneasy reexamination of Lewis also led me to notice the unabashed delight that some extreme fundamentalists took in his work; though he was certainly never a formal member of their fellowship, they seemed to issue him guest-privilege cards on an astonishing scale. Could it be, I asked myself, that the very brilliance of his writing was at the service of a backward-looking way of facing the primal questions of God, man, society, and the meaning of the Christian faith? All these questions eddied in my mind, even while I found my affection and respect for Lewis the man steadily increasing each time I had a chance to visit him in Oxford.

But there is a third stage. This comes when one takes fully into account the fact that Lewis was by training and temperament a literary scholar and poet, and that he practiced a highly sophisticated use of language, metaphor and myth in particular. He knew, and indeed he frequently stated, that univocal language—the assertions of mathematics or formal logic—cannot express religious concepts. No words are adequate to God; all simple, unambiguous assertions are forms of idol-carving. Only the language of poetry—the metaphor, the myth—can properly hint at the literally unsayable, while at the same time, by its very nature, carrying a built-in warning that no literal, one-for-one statement is intended. I came to see Lewis' magnificent achievement more clearly. In book after book—supremely in the interplanetary novels and the Narnia series—he creates the metaphors and myths that can truly say the real but unsayable.

THE IMAGE OF MAN IN C. S. LEWIS is an exceedingly welcome and useful book for anyone who is at the third stage in his consideration of Lewis. Dr. White is well equipped to undertake this task of exploration and reevaluation. Well versed in theology and with a fine literary sensitivity, he also has the blessed ability to read what Lewis actually says without reading his own presuppositions into it. The Lewis that emerges is one who, indeed, is in many ways more attuned to past ages than to the brawling and sprawling present, but who at the same time is curiously modern. This Lewis acknowledged the religious meaning of the eclipse of God for many moderns long before *Time* magazine had featured God's demise. Most important of all, Lewis appears as a more poetic Bultmann, emphasizing the necessarily metaphorical and mythical nature of language, and attacking with radical consistency any attempt to box God up in the language of formal logic or static theology. Indeed, I suppose one might say that Lewis' more imaginative (and greatest) books have something of a Zen-like quality to them; they are like vast *kōans* that press the mysterious button enabling the imagination to grasp beyond words that ultimate meaning underlying and overarching the plain worlds of common sense and formal logic. Where Lewis differs from many students of religious language is his unceasing insistence that such discourse has a real objective correlative. You cannot strip away figures of speech and arrive at the nothingness of common sense. Rather, the language of faith points in a broken but essential way to a realm of utter being that can be hinted at by no other tongue.

It is the merit of Dr. White's study that he spells these matters out in convincing detail, and in the process liberates Lewis from both his blinder admirers and his unthinking enemies. The Lewis revealed here is one far more complex than the theologian hailed or denounced by opposing theological factions. He is a thinker whose way of thought and mode of expression lines him up with the poets as much as with the theologians, and whose vision of the ultimate is characterized by strands of thought that cut athwart the usual categories of liberal and conservative theology. Supremely, Lewis is seen as a writer who gave to modern man one of the most luminous presentations of the Christian understanding of man himself.

Lewis' works are full of seminal insights, some of which he tosses out casually and never develops systematically. Most of all, he represents a theory of religious language and the superbly successful practice of that theory. THE IMAGE OF MAN IN C. S. LEWIS provides a clear and accurate introduction to the Lewis who is gradually being discovered as the over-simplifications of his assorted readers are cleared away. It may well be that this present book, by leading others to a new understanding of Lewis, will have important theological consequences. I am convinced that the major hang-up in current theology is the problem of religious language. Until that is solved, the theological scene will be nothing more than a frenzy of one rootless fad after another. Lewis, by virtue of being a literary scholar and a poet before he turned theologian, has expounded and demonstrated an approach to the language of religion that scholars will disregard to their loss. They have no excuse for disregarding it. Dr. White's admirable book is ready at hand.

CHAD WALSH
Beloit College

Contents

Introduction

We live for a day.
What are we?
What are we not?
A man is a dream about a shadow.[1]

Although C. S. Lewis as yet has received little critical attention from professional theologians, there are several reasons why theologians might be quite interested in him. He was, for one thing, intensely concerned about the problem of religious language throughout most of his life. The problem of "God-talk" has attracted great interest in theological circles in recent years. But Lewis was sensitive to some of the major issues involved in this discussion when he published an allegory of his own religious pilgrimage back in 1933. He retained a lively concern in the area until the year of his death. One of his final articles is related to Bishop J. A. T. Robinson's *Honest to God*. There is a sense in which Lewis did in fact what many theologians have advocated in theory: while others debated demythologizing, and remythologizing, Lewis was busy creating new Christian myths which have the power to attract, delight, and influence multitudes.

Theologians might also be curious about the thought of a brilliant twentieth-century intellectual who made the difficult journey from atheism to Christianity. From the time he was a lad in preparatory school until he was a young professor at Oxford, Lewis was an avowed atheist. What he has to report, therefore, about faith and doubt, feeling and intellect, might be of considerable relevance to other Christians, skeptics, and would-be believers in this secular age.

Beyond this, Lewis is one of the best-known English authors of the

[1] C. S. Lewis. From *Poems*, ed. Walter Hooper (New York: Harcourt, Brace & World, 1965), p. 16.

twentieth century. He has been both much praised and much criticized. With nearly fifty highly readable volumes to his credit, he is certainly one of the most prolific writers in our generation. He is generally recognized as one of the most respected apologists for the Christian faith in our century. When George Stephenson reviewed *The Great Divorce* in 1946, he prophesied that Lewis would before long gain the Shakespearean reputation for being "full of quotations." Considering the frequency with which Lewis is found quoted today in books, lectures, and sermons, it may appear that this prophecy was not wholly unwarranted.

Austin Farrer, the Warden of Keble College, Oxford, claims a double success for Lewis as an advocate of the Christian faith. As a master of rational argument he could demolish underbrush which might otherwise stifle belief. But he also knew that reason would not, of itself, create belief. He advanced beyond the preparatory stage and led his readers into "a mental world of great richness, great vigour and clarity, and in every corner illuminated by his Christian belief." Lewis thus provided a positive demonstration of the force of Christian ideas—both rationally and imaginatively.

Perhaps the chief reason for his persistent neglect by professional theologians is found in Lewis' amateur status. He took no seminary courses. He earned no theological degrees. Yet he was by no means unacquainted with such thinkers as Buber, Otto, Nygren, Aquinas, and Augustine. Recognized as one of the century's most articulate Christians, it is certain that his theological influence will exceed that of many theologians owning certified degrees. As critic Chad Walsh has said, Lewis is "peculiarly capable of reaching and influencing the people who will influence the masses day after tomorrow. If Christianity revives in England and America . . . it will bear strong traces of the Gospel according to C. S. Lewis." [2]

Of ten Ph.D. dissertations devoted in whole or in part to Lewis, it is perhaps a curious fact that all ten studies have been done in the area of language and literature, and none in the field of theology. With but a single exception the same condition prevails with regard to the authors of the major books on Lewis. The primary scholarship of Chad Walsh, Clyde S. Kilby, and Roger Lancelyn Green is in the field of English literature. The first important exception to this monopoly is the volume by Richard B. Cunningham, published in 1967.

None of these authors has attempted to discuss all of Lewis' books. Cunningham comes closest to doing so, but his special interest is in the

[2] *C. S. Lewis: Apostle to the Skeptics* (New York: The Macmillan Co., 1949), pp. 171-72.

apologetic works. Since Chad Walsh's study in 1949, twenty-seven volumes have been published under Lewis' name. Prof. Kilby's book is concerned especially with the "Christian" works. Roger Green's brief volume concentrates on Lewis' science fiction and children's stories.

Both the content of Lewis' Christian affirmation and the vitality of his literary expression demand further analysis. The following pages concentrate upon Lewis' "anthropology," examining his doctrine of man as it is developed in his theological and critical works and exploring the extent to which this image is reflected in his imaginative writings. The author is celebrated more for his literary craft than for his theological innovation; therefore major attention will be focused upon the mythology which Lewis created and the literary forms he used to communicate his concept of man to the contemporary world. Lewis' actual practice will be related to certain current theories of religious language and theories of literature.

Major topics to be considered regarding the nature of man include the theological ideas of Creation, Fall, and Redemption—those basic doctrines which, Lewis once said, "any child in a Christian family learns before he is twelve." In less theological terminology, we might say that we shall discuss what man was intended to be, what man has become, and what man may yet become. This framework for reviewing a Christian interpretation of man will also furnish an opportunity to investigate the fresh images which Lewis developed as he attempted to portray the essential truths of some ancient doctrines. We may expect to find new interpretations of the *imago Dei* when Lewis treats man's origin, novel symbols of "bent" men when he discusses man's present condition, and fresh models of "new" men when he considers man's potential and destiny.

There are other questions in which we will be interested in this study. Does Lewis present a balanced, coherent, and consistent view of human nature in his expository works? How do his views compare at various points with some of the noted theologians of our day? What are his ideas on Christian ethics? Is he able to express his convictions about man in his imaginative material without becoming offensively didactic? How is his artistic creativity related to his theological affirmations?

It is generally agreed among literary critics that unassimilated ideology has no artistic merit. A work of literature is distinctly different from a string of doctrinal statements. If ideas are used at all in a work of art, they must be incorporated into its very texture so that they cease to be concepts and are transformed into characters, symbols, and myths.

15

Insofar as Lewis is artistically successful in effecting this transformation, his imaginative genre is "more myth than allegory." Hence, it cannot be reduced simply to didactic content.

Still one may inquire what general view of man is portrayed in an author, as in Lewis' science fiction, children's stories, and theological fantasies. The problem of interpreting this imaginative material will be approached in three supplementary ways: (a) through personal judgment, informed by a background of contemporary theology, literary theory, and a general knowledge of Lewis' works; (b) through knowledge of the author's own critical ideas, expressed in a dozen volumes; and (c) through a survey of theological and literary criticism on Lewis, available in a few books and unpublished dissertations and in many book reviews and journal articles. This combination of methods should prevent our going astray very often in interpreting Lewis' imaginative material.

Literary critic Edmund Fuller opens his *Man in Modern Fiction* with a discussion of three basic "images of man" which are reflected in contemporary literature. "Inescapably," says Fuller,

our literature and other arts reflect these divisions about the nature of man, and where they are not understood, there is difficulty or bewilderment in appraising the reflections in fiction of these conflicts in the minds of men about themselves, their nature, their potentialities, their limitations, their origins, their objectives, and, perhaps above all, their obligations.[3]

According to Fuller, modern writers tend to exhibit either a theistic, an atheistic, or a "God-residue" view of human nature. Most of our centuries-old literary heritage, he says, is based upon the assumption that there is a God and that man's relationship with him is a matter of some importance. Man has been seen essentially as a created being, with either an actual or a potential relationship to his Creator. Though imperfect, man is thought capable of redemption.

But many contemporary writers, Fuller continues, work on the assumption that there is no God and no possibility of a divine-human relationship. Man is viewed as a curious biological accident, produced by random forces in a morally neutral universe. Some writers oscillate between these two clear-cut positions, in what Fuller calls the God-residue category. Sensitive to the concerns of ethical humanism, these authors suppose that God does not really exist in any significant way but that man should continue to live as though He did.

[3] (Vintage Books; New York: Random House, 1958) , p. 7.

No writer, of course, can be required to believe (or to disbelieve) in God. But in analyzing the "vision of life" an author presents, it is well to be aware of these differing fundamental attitudes toward human nature and the possibility (or impossibility) he sees for a relationship to that power which has brought man into existence. C. S. Lewis unquestionably falls into Fuller's first category, at least in all but his very earliest work.

In singling out a specific area of Lewis' theology for further investigation, it is especially appropriate to select his doctrine of man. While it has perhaps received less attention than some other aspects of his religious thought, it appears to me to be the most dominant part of his theology. John D. Haigh wrote, "One great fact distinguishes Lewis' fiction from the typical nineteenth or twentieth century [novel]—it deals with Man rather than men." Lewis concentrates upon essential elements of the psyche rather than upon individual characterizations or sociological trends. He has more in common, says Haigh, with Spenser, Milton, or Bunyan than with Fielding, Dickens, or Forster. While he does not restrict himself to allegory to depict the inner world, his preoccupation with man produces a narrative form which differs markedly from the psychosociological novel stemming from Fielding and Richardson.

While intending to concentrate on Lewis' anthropology, it will be impossible not to lapse occasionally into other aspects of his theology. In *The Failure of Theology in Modern Literature*, John Killinger emphasizes (following John Calvin, he notes) that the Christian doctrine of God and doctrine of man are inseparably linked. Man is not understandable apart from God.

He was created in the image of God, and his nature and condition are discernible only in relation to that image. He is not a law unto himself; he is a dependent creature. There have been two major facts in his history: the Fall, by which the *imago Dei* was marred; and Redemption, by which the image is restored, now in part and later in full.[4]

Despite the essential interrelatedness of the two doctrines, however, it is not my plan to undertake any lengthy discussion of Lewis' doctrine of God. I will likewise give but slight consideration to his concepts of Christ, the Trinity, and other important doctrines. To attempt a discussion of Lewis' entire theology, and to provide adequate illustration from his imaginative works, would prolong one study unduly.

[4] (Nashville: Abingdon Press, 1963) , p. 59.

This is perhaps the place to record the other limitations of this particular project. I will be considering all forty-nine of Lewis' books, but it is not essential for my purposes to survey all of Lewis' articles, book reviews, and letters which have been published in widely scattered periodicals in England, America, and on the Continent across the past fifty years. While I will discuss this mass of material in more detail later, my primary concern is with the concept of human nature projected in Lewis' major work, most of which is readily available to the public.

Except in passing, I will say little about the sources behind Lewis' theology. I will not attempt to trace his theological "development," and I will offer no extended biographical treatment. (Jeffrey J. Hart is reported to be working currently on a biography of Lewis.) Nor do I plan to provide in these pages summaries of Lewis' books. Prof. Kilby's book provides excellent brief statements on many of the books, and additional outlines can be found in several dissertations. I hesitate to venture further in this direction for two reasons.

First, what Corbin S. Carnell says about Lewis' space trilogy applies equally to his other works of fiction: "No outline conveys anything of the strange beauty and power of these novels." [5] Lewis once spoke wistfully in a sermon of "the scent of a flower we have not found, the echo of a tune we have not heard, news from a country we have never yet visited." Then he confessed to his congregation that he was attempting by such language to "weave a spell." In much of his imaginative work Lewis is far more intent upon "weaving a spell" than he is upon delineating characters or developing a plot. For just this reason, it is especially difficult to represent his work in summary. Possibly the critic who abstracts and analyzes a piece of literature always distorts the original to some extent. But one may come to feel that this is particularly true in the case of Lewis' work. When we isolate and wrench from the context a few elements for attention or discussion, we are no longer dealing with the completed "living" thing which the artist created, but with only a pale shadow of it. The contrast, I think, is similar to that between the collection of dead butterflies pinned in Eustace' box (in *The Voyage of the Dawn Treader*) and a meadow filled with the radiant colors and flitting wings of butterflies in motion.

My second objection to elaborate summarizing of Lewis' work is a related one. The summarizer tends inevitably to sift out those things which most catch his attention and to leave behind the other elements.

[5] "The Dialectic of Desire: C. S. Lewis' Interpretation of *Sehnsucht*" (Ph.D. diss., University of Florida, 1960), p. 96.

Should I, while preparing a study on the doctrine of man, attempt to summarize these works, I would distort them in one particular, unfortunate way. They would come to appear far more "theological" and didactic than they actually are. I think it best to leave the summarizing to others and to draw simply upon Lewis' material as it becomes pertinent to my course of discussion. I make no claims, therefore, for exhausting the meaning and significance of that small library which Lewis has authored.

Lastly, I will attempt no final estimate of the literary merit of Lewis' works. Nor will I discuss in any detail the structure of Lewis' fiction or trace his literary relationships. John D. Haigh shows himself a learned and able scholar when he undertakes this task in a Ph.D. dissertation, done at Leeds University, England. It may be, as Haigh concludes, that Lewis is not a "major" English writer but remains a capable writer of the "second rank" with a limited—though authentic and unique—contribution to literature. "Within its chosen field," Haigh writes, "Lewis' fiction displays a unique combination of powerful intuitions with a clear didactic purpose, of Orthodox Christian beliefs with a speculative imagination." In any case, most critics seem to agree with Mark Longaker and Edwin C. Bolles that Lewis "has assured himself a place in the history of English letters." [6] Whether that place in literature is primary or secondary is not my present concern. It is sufficient simply to consider Lewis an important writer of our time, whose doctrinal explanation and imaginative expression of the idea of human nature are worthy of attention.

Since the references to Lewis' books are numerous in the following pages, shortened forms of titles will be used generally after the first mention in the text. The following list is provided as a convenient reference to the abbreviated titles commonly used in this study:

A Toast	*Screwtape Proposes a Toast*
Abolition	*The Abolition of Man*
Allegory	*The Allegory of Love*
Caspian	*Prince Caspian*
Criticism	*Experiment in Criticism*
Dawn Treader	*The Voyage of the Dawn Treader*
Divorce	*The Great Divorce*
Faces	*Till We Have Faces*

[6] *Contemporary English Literature* (New York: Appleton-Century-Crofts, 1953), p. 453.

19

Grief	*A Grief Observed*
Hideous Strength	*That Hideous Strength*
Horse and Boy	*The Horse and His Boy*
Last Night	*The World's Last Night*
Letters	*Letters of C. S. Lewis*
Lion	*The Lion, the Witch and the Wardrobe*
Macdonald	*George Macdonald: An Anthology*
Malcolm	*Letters to Malcolm: Chiefly on Prayer*
Pain	*The Problem of Pain*
Paper	*They Asked for a Paper*
Preface	*A Preface to Paradise Lost*
Psalms	*Reflections on the Psalms*
Reflections	*Christian Reflections*
Regress	*The Pilgrim's Regress*
Rehabilitations	*Rehabilitations and Other Essays*
Screwtape	*The Screwtape Letters*
Silent Planet	*Out of the Silent Planet*
Sixteenth Century	*English Literature in the Sixteenth Century, Excluding Drama*
Studies in Literature	*Studies in Medieval and Renaissance Literature*
Surprised	*Surprised by Joy*
Torso	*Arthurian Torso*
Transposition	*Transposition and Other Addresses*

I

C. S. Lewis — The Man and His Reputation

Books, books, books!

My father bought all the books he read and never got rid of any of them. There were books in the study, books in the drawing room, books in the cloakroom, books (two deep) in the great bookcase on the landing, books in a bedroom, books piled as high as my shoulder in the cistern attic, books of all kinds reflecting every transient stage of my parents' interest, books readable and unreadable, books suitable for a child and books most emphatically not. Nothing was forbidden me. In the seemingly endless rainy afternoons I took volume after volume from the shelves. I had always the same certainty of finding a book that was new to me as a man who walks into a field has of finding a new blade of grass.

—Surprised by Joy, p. 14

For Americans who love the fine arts and the achievements of culture, November 22, 1963, was a day when giants fell. President John F. Kennedy was felled that day by an assassin's bullet in Dallas, Texas. Aldous Huxley died at his home in Hollywood. And C. S. Lewis, in declining health for several months, died of a heart attack at his home near Oxford.

Lewis blended a keen intellect and a lively imagination to produce some of the most perceptive Christian literature of the present day. Edmund Fuller hailed him as "the most imaginative and versatile of Christian apologists." Sydney J. Harris praised his dry wit, sharp satire, graceful style, and deadly marksmanship.

With vitality and gusto Lewis produced what a *TLS* review called "an astonishingly large output." Counting the material published posthumously, Lewis is credited with forty-nine major titles between the years of 1919 and 1967. He once referred to his collection of work as "a very mixed bag" of imaginative, religious, and critical writings. There are thirteen volumes of literary criticism, nineteen volumes of theology and philosophy, and seventeen volumes of imaginative material. The imaginative works include seven fantasies, seven Narnia stories, and three volumes of verse. The interested reader will find a list of specific titles under each classification in Appendix 2 of the present study.

Lewis was—and is—a controversial author. His biting wit and creative imagination won for him both admirers and enemies. His style and content are so distinctive that it is unusual for anyone to like Lewis only a little; generally speaking, he is either much loved or greatly disliked. Some reviewers, like Kathleen Nott and Alistair Cooke, appear outraged by everything Lewis stood for. Others, like Leonard Bacon, find Lewis provocative and delightful despite some of his ideas. Yet others, like Alec Vidler, accord Lewis extravagant praise. Vidler, who was Dean of King's College, Cambridge, thought Lewis' work superior to Chesterton's. For whatever it is worth, it would be accurate to report that of reviews of Lewis' works indexed by the *Book Review Digest,* favorable reviews outnumber unfavorable reviews by a ratio of about five to one. Lewis is very widely—although by no means universally—appreciated.

Perhaps Lewis was *too* prolific a writer. This, at least, is W. H. Auden's complaint. Auden finds his books delightful and instructive but says he would have preferred for Lewis to produce fewer and better books. Lewis did have an unusual gift for instantaneous phrase. He wrote out all his books in longhand and rewrote very little. According to Chad Walsh and Nevill Coghill, he generally made whatever changes he found necessary on his original manuscript and then turned the copy over to a professional typist to prepare for the publisher. Whether his books would have improved markedly with more rewriting, or whether they might have lost some of their original spontaneity, we cannot know. There are indeed some passages which reflect hasty construction. But we shall never know which titles would have been sacrificed entirely had Lewis deemed it necessary to labor long over every volume he published.

Biographical material on Lewis is available in several books. Therefore, I will mention here but a few of the major events of his life. The opening chapters of the books by Walsh, Green, Kilby, and Cunningham can be consulted for further details.[1] Warren Lewis, a noted historian and a lifelong close friend of his brother, provides an important memoir as the

---

[1] Walsh, *Apostle;* Roger Lancelyn Green *C. S. Lewis* (London: The Bodley Head, 1963); Clyde S. Kilby, *The Christian World of C. S. Lewis* (Grand Rapids: Eerdmans Publishing Co., 1964); Richard B. Cunningham, *C. S. Lewis: Defender of the Faith.* (Philadelphia: Westminster Press, 1967).

introduction to *Letters of C. S. Lewis*. Walter Hooper, Lewis' private secretary for several years, gives additional information in the preface to *Poems*. The 1965 volume *Light on C. S. Lewis*, edited by his publisher Jocelyn Gibb, carries chapters concerning the impression Lewis made on nine of his acquaintances in the university and literary world. A very important source of biographic information from Lewis' own hand is the spiritual autobiography of his early life, *Surprised by Joy*. The allegory *Pilgrim's Regress* also alludes to Lewis' own religious pilgrimage. For convenient reference I have arranged several of the major events in Lewis' life in "A Chronology" which will be found as Appendix 3 in the present volume.

Clive Staples Lewis was born November 29, 1898, in Belfast, Northern Ireland, the son of a court solicitor and a clergyman's daughter. Education was held in high esteem in the family. His mother—herself a college graduate—was teaching French and Latin to "Jack" before he was eight years old. The family enjoyed relative economic prosperity, and Lewis remembered those early years as a time of tranquil security and settled happiness.

Everything was different for the two Lewis boys following their mother's death from cancer in 1908. Their father was unable emotionally to adjust to his loss, and the brothers were compelled to become increasingly dependent upon each other. At the age of nine Jack was sent to Hertfordshire, England, to begin his education—across the Irish Sea and three hundred miles from home. There followed a series of English private schools—quite dreadful for the most part—which Lewis describes in detail in *Surprised by Joy*. At the age of sixteen he was sent to Surrey to be groomed for university entrance. He became a private pupil of the fierce dialectician W. T. Kirkpatrick, retired headmaster of Lurgan College, Ireland, where Lewis' father had once studied. Lewis never thereafter escaped from the influence of "The Great Knock" and his exacting teaching methods.

Lewis was accepted as an Oxford student in 1917. But he soon found himself in the Army and in the trenches on the French front. Wounded slightly (by an English shell), he was hospitalized briefly. In December of 1918 he was discharged from the Army. Lewis returned to his studies at Oxford, and in 1919 he published his first book, a volume of verse. Undertaking two courses of study (classics and English literature), he eventually earned his B.A. and M.A. degrees. Upon graduation in 1924 he was given a temporary appointment at Oxford as a lecturer in philosophy. The following year he was elected a fellow of Magdalen College,

Oxford, and was appointed tutor in English literature—a position which he was to retain for thirty years.

In 1929, after a few years' teaching experience, Lewis declared himself a "reluctant" convert to theism and then to the Christian faith, which he had abandoned eighteen years earlier. His reputation as a creative scholar was established by the publication of *The Allegory of Love* in 1936. His fame as an author of Christian apologetics spread widely after the publication of *The Screwtape Letters* (actually his ninth book) in 1942.

Lewis became professor of Medieval and Renaissance English at Cambridge University, and a fellow of Magdalene College, in 1954. A bachelor for nearly sixty years, he married Helen Joy Davidman Gresham in a hospital-bedside ceremony in 1957. Both Mrs. Gresham and her former husband had once been atheists and devoted Communists. Lewis' books were partially instrumental in their conversion to Christianity prior to the collapse of their marriage. Joy, herself a talented writer, worked as Lewis' secretary for several years before marrying him. Her health improved temporarily following their wedding, and there is every indication that the couple enjoyed a very meaningful marital relationship for a little over three years. Joy died of cancer in 1960. Lewis' health was already in rapid decline, with complications of bone disease, prostate trouble, and a heart condition. He died of a heart attack on November 22, 1963, a week short of his sixty-fifth birthday.

Lewis' contribution to the field of theology was recognized formally in Scotland in 1946 when St. Andrews University presented him with an honorary Doctor of Divinity degree, a rare distinction for a layman without theological training. In 1955, Lewis was honored by election to membership in the British Academy (for the promotion of historical, philosophical, and philological studies). Additional literary honors which came to him included the 1937 Sir Israel Gollancz Memorial Prize for *The Allegory of Love* and the 1957 Carnegie Medal for *The Last Battle*. The Gollancz Prize is awarded bienially for published work connected with Old English or early English language and literature. The Carnegie Medal is the award of the Library Association for the most outstanding children's book published by a British subject during the preceding year. This English award is the equivalent of the Newbery Medal in America.

It is reported almost universally in works about Lewis that he received the Hawthornden Prize of 1936. This appears to be one of those small myths of scholarship which has embedded itself so solidly in tradition that it is everywhere taken as unquestioned fact. Some early writer on Lewis probably confused the Gollancz award with the Hawthornden

Prize, and this error has been repeated in countless places since. According to *Literary and Library Prizes,* Lewis did not receive the Hawthornden Prize for 1936 or for any other year. He did receive the Gollancz Prize for *The Allegory of Love.* The Lewis entry in *Who's Who,* which presumably would have been verified by Lewis himself, also mentions the Gollancz but not the Hawthornden Prize.

With the bare facts of biography now filled in, it is appropriate to turn to a consideration of Lewis' reputation as a scholar, teacher, popular author, public figure, and unique individual.

Whatever persons may feel about his apologetic or imaginative work, few question that Lewis was a brilliant scholar and first-rate literary critic. J. A. W. Bennett, Lewis' successor at Cambridge, has called him a "Johnsonian Colossus" in learning, noting that Lewis upon occasion had taught philosophy and political theory at Oxford as well as literature. Lewis' ability to read with ease in five or six languages greatly enhanced his literary contribution. As has been mentioned already, his mother began teaching him Latin and French before he was eight. He continued the study of these languages in his teens and added Greek, German, and Italian. He maintained that any student who is not thoroughly familiar with Anglo-Saxon remains forever a child in English studies. Lewis' deep learning is immediately evident in his four major scholarly works; *The Allegory of Love, A Preface to Paradise Lost, The Discarded Image,* and the massive *English Literature in the Sixteenth Century*—a volume in the Oxford History of English Literature series. John Lawlor, English professor at the University of Keele, asserts that few men have ever read so widely before the publication of a first book as did Lewis for his *Allegory,* and M. C. Bradbrook claims that this volume "permanently altered the general way of reading medieval poetry." Nevill Coghill, an Oxford colleague of Lewis, thinks no other modern scholar can equal Lewis in total critical achievement. What Bergen Evans said about *Studies in Words* could apply as well to several of Lewis' critical books: "Rarely is so much learning displayed with so much grace and charm."

Lewis charmed students in the classroom as well as in his publications. He had a wide reputation as one of the best—if not the very best—lecturers at Oxford in his day. He was often compelled to announce that students in literature had the privilege of being seated first. Other students and visitors were welcome as long as space permitted. Roger Lancelyn Green, author and former student of Lewis, reports that many students attended the same course of Lewis' lectures more than once, out of fascination for his style and content.

25

Especially during World War II, Lewis became something of a celebrity beyond the precincts of Oxford. For two or three years his voice on the radio was one of the most familiar in England. The series of BBC broadcasts which he did at this time were heard regularly by an estimated audience of 600,000. These talks were later printed in *Mere Christianity*. Lewis occasionally preached at Oxford's University Church, and it is said that he and Archbishop William Temple were the only two men able to fill the sanctuary to capacity.

While he is acknowledged as a brilliant scholar and exciting lecturer, Lewis' wider fame depends upon his less-academic books. Nathan A. Scott, Jr., professor of theology and literature at the University of Chicago, said that "this distinguished don of Oxbridge doubtless captured a larger audience of literate and thoughtful people than any other expositor of the Christian faith has been able to win in our time." Charles Moorman called Lewis a sort of "cocktail-party *advocatus Christi.*" Lewis defended the Christian faith with urbanity and wit to readers who often lacked sympathy for it. He attacked popular skepticism with sophisticated Christianity, said Moorman, and attempted "to justify the ways of God to skeptical man."

Although complete sales figures on Lewis' books are not available, there is some evidence that statements like those quoted above are not without foundation. A London obituary announced that Lewis' paperback sales alone were in the vicinity of one million in England. This figure includes over 250,000 copies of *The Screwtape Letters*, over 270,000 copies of *Mere Christianity*, and almost 120,000 copies of *The Problem of Pain*. Half a million copies of *Screwtape* have been sold in the United States, and Lewis' best-known work continues to sell here at the rate of more than 50,000 copies annually. Time Reading Program, a book distribution plan of Time, Inc., which offers readers "the most worthwhile books of modern times," has chosen two Lewis titles recently—*Till We Have Faces* in 1966 and *Screwtape* in 1968. John D. Haigh reports that *Screwtape* has been translated now into fifteen languages. Several other books as well have gone into a number of foreign translations.

While Lewis is known especially for *Screwtape*, few literary authorities —including Lewis himself—consider this to be his finest imaginative work. The candidates for top position generally include *Perelandra* (a part of the science-fiction triology) and *Till We Have Faces*. The lush and exotic scenes of the imagined-planet Perelandra have already inspired the interpretation of other artists in poetry, painting, and music. These enthralling isles are a creation that, as Robert Frost might say, men

26

come back and back to. The English composer Donald Swann and his librettist David March have completed the ambitious undertaking of making *Perelandra* into an opera.

According to a *Saturday Review* article by Leonard Bacon, *Perelandra* so portrays the author's poetic imagination in full blast that it should never have been written in prose, however excellent. It is probably fortunate, however, that Lewis did not attempt this in poetry. While he longed to think of himself as a poet, most critics agree that Lewis was not a very good poet.

Chad Walsh prophesied that the science-fiction trilogy "will be one of the few myths of the century that will firmly grip the imagination of future writers and provide them with a treasure trove of symbols." But when *Till We Have Faces* was published in 1956, Walsh called it "the most significant and triumphant work that Lewis has yet produced." My own judgment coincides with that of Walsh, and with that of John Lawlor, that the lesser-known *Faces* represents Lewis' highest achievement in narrative.

In addition to the persons who purchased Lewis' books, an increasing number of students in the 1960's have found chapters or excerpts from Lewis' works in textbooks and anthologies. A dozen recent examples have come to my attention in the fields of literature, philosophy, and religion. With the recent upsurge of interest in his work which is being reflected in the *Essay and General Literature Index,* it appears that many college students are going to be familiar with the name of C. S. Lewis for years to come.

What sort of man was Lewis personally? How do his friends remember him? Lewis himself warned against interpreting imaginative literature in light of the author's "personality." But it is nevertheless a legitimate interest to wonder what kind of impression a noted writer made upon those who knew him best. And we are also interested here in Lewis for more than his fiction; his understanding of human nature would undoubtedly be related in some way to the basic facts of his own life. I will attempt to describe briefly some of the characteristics mentioned most often by those who were close to Lewis.

Lewis gave the impression of being unusually self-confident in all he undertook. In fact, his writings are sometimes charged with being smug. Nevill Coghill found in the Lewis style "an indefeasible core of Protestant certainties, the certainties of a simple, unchanging, entrenched ethic that knows how to distinguish, unarguably, between Right and Wrong, Natural and Unnatural, High and Low, Black and White."

Though he held his views confidently, his closest acquaintances uniformly deny that Lewis had any touch of arrogance, even after he had achieved considerable fame. He is remembered, on the contrary, for exceptional courtesy, both in conversation and in print. Owen Barfield, who knew Lewis across forty years, once marvelled that, in light of Lewis' fame, he could not recall "a single remark, a single word or silence, a single look, the lightest flicker of an eyelid or hemi-demi-semitone of alteration in the pitch of his voice, which would go to suggest that he felt his opinion entitled to more respect than that of old friends."

Despite his politeness Lewis sometimes exhibited a candor which would be taken for gruffness. Kilby says that Lewis was willing to break through the charm of "deceptive delicacy." He was convinced that genuine love dispenses with modesty. John Lawlor points out that Lewis valued his time very highly and was never in a mood to squander it. Chad Walsh testifies that Lewis was impatient with vagueness and half-formed ideas. Yet when he pushed a person to the wall in a discussion, and left him pinned there, says Walsh, the maneuver was performed so smoothly and "in such a friendly, manly way" that it seemed almost a compliment and an act of respect.

Lewis' reputation for rational argument is widely celebrated. He was known as a formidable opponent in controversy, a "black belt" among novices. Despite his respect for truth Lewis would occasionally use his immense dialectical skill to batter an opponent into silence. He had learned this skill at the hands of "the Great Knock" before his college days. It was said of Kirkpatrick that the most casual remark was usually taken by him as a summons to disputation. Lewis appreciated and honored rational opposition. He undoubtedly considered this particular method the most stimulating and productive possible for discussions with students and colleagues. John Lawlor felt that talking with Lewis was like wielding a peashooter against a howitzer: "One quickly felt that for him dialectic supplied the place of conversation." Owen Barfield noted that to discuss with Lewis was something like trying to run beside an automobile in top gear. Austin Farrer called Lewis "a bonny fighter" in the argumentative business and claimed that nobody could put him down. Lewis, he said, would attend Oxford's Socratic Club "snuffing the imminent battle and saying 'Aha!' at the sound of the trumpet." Nevill Coghill refers to conversations with Lewis which fairly "sparkled and exploded."

Barfield records a "puzzlement" about Lewis, however, even after knowing him for most of his adult life. Did Lewis perhaps take too much delight in this kind of gladiatorial combat, too much delight in holding unusual opinions, too much glee in defending unpopular positions?

28

Perhaps he did. Lewis noted in *Surprised* that bad times, both at home and at school, drove him and his brother Warren to be fast companions in boyhood and that this relationship had probably biased his outlook on all of life. "To this day," he said, "the vision of the world which comes most naturally to me is one in which 'we two' or 'we few' (and in a sense 'we happy few') stand together against something stronger and larger." The isolated position of England in 1940 came as no shock to Lewis: it was the kind of thing he had grown to expect.

Although Lewis was willing to defend his Christian beliefs in debate, the poet Kathleen Raine notes that he did not attempt to proselytize or persuade others in private life. John Lawlor, a dialectical materialist and a cofounder of a socialist society while an Oxford student, also maintains that Lewis never imposed his Christianity upon others or allowed his beliefs to obtrude during tutorials.

Chad Walsh was struck with Lewis' "plain unselfconsciousness." He discovered with regret, during a visit, that Lewis kept no scrapbook of reviews. Walsh may not have known then that Lewis did not even save copies of everything he wrote. Walter Hooper, his secretary in later years, said that Lewis tossed most of his own books and articles into the W.P.B. (wastepaper basket) and promptly forgot what he had written. His phenomenal memory, Hooper claimed, recorded almost everything *except* his own writings. Sometimes he would hear lines quoted from one of his earlier poems and inquire who was the author. Owen Barfield tells of making Lewis the subject of a long poem. Lewis could still quote several lines from the work years later, but he had forgotten the poem's original connection with himself.

Incidents such as these sound suspiciously like raw material for legend. But the characteristic of unselfconsciousness is so widely and consistently mentioned among those who knew Lewis that it would be an omission not to record it. The explanation offered by Barfield may be the correct one:

At a certain stage in his life he deliberately ceased to take any interest in himself except as a kind of spiritual alumnus taking his moral finals. . . . What began as deliberate choice became at length (as he had no doubt always intended it should) an ingrained and effortless habit of soul. Self-knowledge, for him, had come to mean recognition of his own weaknesses and shortcomings and nothing more. Anything beyond that he sharply suspected, both in himself and in others, as a symptom of spiritual megalomania. At best, there was so much else, in letters and in life, that he found much *more* interesting![2]

[2] "Introduction," *Light on C. S. Lewis*, ed. Jocelyn Gibb (London: Geoffrey Bles, 1965), p. xvi.

Even so, admits Barfield, "he stood before me as a mystery as solidly as he stood beside me as a friend." [3]

Simon Barrington-Ward thought that even such works of Lewis as *Surprised by Joy, Letters to Malcolm,* and *A Grief Observed* reflect a certain distance and impersonality. He suggested that the explanation may lie in a horror of sentimentality which Lewis carried over from his childhood. There might be some difficulty in reconciling this hypothesis with Lewis' plea to educators in *The Abolition of Man* for proper recognition of the importance of sentiment and emotion. Barrington-Ward is not the only critic, however, to discover a characteristic of reticence in Lewis' work. Other readers (myself included) consider the particular works mentioned by Barrington-Ward to be unusually warm and personal. Perhaps we have here a conflict in taste and temperament which cannot be further resolved.

There is a puzzle about a certain Mrs. Moore in Lewis' life. The solution to this mystery may lie in the same general direction as the problem of Lewis' striking unselfconsciousness. His brother and other friends were astonished at the sonlike relationship to Mrs. Moore which Jack "inflicted" upon himself for more than thirty years. According to the memoir of W. H. Lewis, Mrs. Moore was an extremely unsuitable companion for his brother—a narrow-minded, self-centered, domineering and possessive autocrat who seemed to thrive on crises and chaos. She constantly interfered with Jack's work and demanded his aid with innumerable household chores. Several of C. S. Lewis' letters make clear that he was often furious with Mrs. Moore for her excessive expectations. Why then did he maintain this peculiar relationship across three decades —helping this female tyrant with spring-cleaning, marmalade-making, and mowing the lawn? What possible motive was there for bearing the worry and expense involved, and for remaining, as Warren claims, in "restrictive and distracting servitude for many of his most fruitful years" ?

Warren Lewis offers but a single hint, of which he does not appear very confident. Mrs. Moore lost her son Paddy in the war. Might the relationship have grown from a wartime promise which Lewis made to a comrade who failed to return home? [4] Or did Lewis make himself some promise about this unfortunate situation? Apparently no one knows. Lewis was seldom inclined to discuss his private affairs with anyone, and never his acts of charity. He once mentioned in a letter to a friend the vocation "imposed" upon him of caring for a semiparalyzed old

[3] *Ibid.,* p. xxi.
[4] "Memoir," *Letters,* p. 12.

lady: "the duty of looking after one's people rests on us all," he explained. In another letter he noted that most people find it easier to express charity by giving money than by offering time and toil. Could he have had in mind Mrs. Moore when he wrote about the need to "willingly accept what we suffer for others and offer it to God on their behalf"?

One acquainted with Lewis' theology and his intense desire to practice Christianity personally will not think it impossible that he deliberately undertook this relationship as a spiritual discipline. If he had not looked after the unlovable Mrs. Moore, who indeed would have? Nevill Coghill is persuaded, from the few incidents which he discovered by accident, that Lewis' benefactions were immense. His generosity was generally expressed personally and privately. Like all others, however, Coghill is compelled to conclude: "Much of Lewis' life was hidden from me; he almost never spoke about himself."

Lewis was a voracious reader throughout his life. He has been accused of having "a thirst for print" upon arising in the morning. In books like *Allegory* and *Sixteenth Century,* and even in his casual letters, he demonstrated comfortable familiarity with a great multitude of authors. While his knowledge of literature was prodigious, he did not parade his knowledge for its own sake. As the need arose, he could call upon an enormous background of reading experience.

Not only was Lewis' early home experience steeped in books, books, books. Away at preparatory school, he spent as much time as he possibly could in the school library, partially as an escape from sports and harsh social life. Lewis inherited from his father a physical defect which made him clumsy at skills demanding manual dexterity; he had but a single joint in his thumbs. Minor though the problem might appear, it cast dark shadows across Lewis' childhood and drove him to writing because he was so unsuccessful at nearly everything else he attempted. Lewis was not simply joking when he once wrote that he had chosen his vocation in a cultured profession because of the brute fact that he had few or no talents for any other career. Even before Lewis had entered Oxford, Kirkpatrick recommended to his father that he had better prepare the boy for a literary life since he was adapted for nothing else. A typical letter from soldier Lewis to his father in 1918 began, "I have been up in the trenches for a few days," and concluded, "Do you know of any life of George Eliot published in a cheap edition? If you can find one, I should like to read it."

His final year as an Oxford student was haunted with the fear that he might not be able to get a teaching job and that he would face both professional and literary failure. When he did receive employment at Oxford, Lewis was compelled to continue reading in connection with his work. It appears that he spent most of his school holidays in various libraries. Without the cares and responsibilities of home and family and with few distracting hobbies, it is possible for a human being to master a great many books in half a century: C. S. Lewis (burdened only with Mrs. Moore) came close to demonstrating just how many. Reading, writing, and talking about reading and writing were the essence of his life.

In view of his remarkably comprehensive literary conquests an attempt to trace influences on his thinking can become complex indeed. The interested reader is referred to John D. Haigh's dissertation for a discussion of literary influences on Lewis, and to Corbin S. Carnell's dissertation for a discussion of theological influences.[5] I will mention but a few of the major theological sources here.

It would be difficult to exaggerate the influence of Plato and Augustine upon Lewis' thought. He once wrote, "to lose what I owe to Plato and Aristotle would be like the amputation of a limb. Hardly any lawful price seems to me too high for what I have gained by being made to learn Latin and Greek." The influence of Thomas Aquinas and William Law are found at many points. Lewis confessed that the personal debt he owed to George Macdonald's *Unspoken Sermons* was "almost as great as one man can owe to another." If he learned to appreciate "holiness" from Macdonald, Lewis learned to appreciate "the numinous" from Rudolf Otto's *Das Heilige*. A non-Christian author who had an important influence on Lewis at one stage was William Butler Yeats. Lewis was especially struck by the fact that Yeats rejected philosophical materialism, though for other than Christian reasons. Anders Nygren's *Agape and Eros*, G. K. Chesterton's *The Everlasting Man*, and Edwyn Bevan's *Symbolism and Belief* were very important to Lewis. He often acknowledged Charles Williams as an important contemporary influence upon his thought and life. Beyond those already mentioned, Carnell discusses the influence upon Lewis of Richard Hooker and Thomas Traherne, and the devotional works *The Imitation of Christ* and *Theologia Germanica*. Lewis did not appreciate the work of Teilhard de Chardin, Søren Kierkegaard, Paul Tillich, or Rudolf Bultmann. Anyone familiar with the later Karl Barth will feel that Lewis' occasional remarks about

---

[5] Haigh, "The Fiction of C. S. Lewis" (Ph.D. diss., Leeds University, England, 1962) ; Carnell, "The Dialectic of Desire," esp. chap. III.

"Barthanism" as "a flattening out of all things into common insignificance before the inscrutable Creator" are somewhat oversimplified and unfair. Perhaps the early Barth merited criticism of this type, but we should note that the later Karl Barth was not himself "Barthian" in this regard: his position was considerably changed by the time of his 1956 essay *The Humanity of God.* Lewis was a better authority on the great old theologians than on their contemporary counterparts.

Lewis was sociable in a personal way, but he was not interested in superficial gregariousness. His chief pleasures were hiking with friends and "sitting up till the small hours in someone's college rooms, talking nonsense, poetry, theology, metaphysics over beer, tea and pipes." Elaborating upon the nature of rational friendship, Lewis once expounded the unusual theory that genuine friendship is uninquisitive. Real friends, he said, are not interested in each other's "affairs"—such things as whether a man is married or single or how he earns his living. In a circle of true friends, "no one cares twopence about anyone else's family, profession, class, income, race, or previous history." Such matters arise naturally in conversation, but only incidentally—perhaps to furnish an illustration or analogy. The only question for rational friends is: "Do you see the same truth?" Friendship is "an affair of disentangled, or stripped, minds."

Lewis' concept of friendship was probably embodied in *The Inklings,* a small, fluctuating circle of literary friends bound together by a common interest in writing and in discussing the nature of language and myth. J. R. R. Tolkien, Owen Barfield, and Charles Williams were among the more prominent members of the group. Every Tuesday morning, from eleven o'clock till one, they gathered in a small Oxford pub. On Thursday evenings they assembled again in Lewis' college rooms. Tolkien's *Lord of the Rings* and Williams' *All Hallows Eve* owe something to the stimulation of this small circle of close friends, as do Lewis' *The Great Divorce,* his Narnia chronicles, and his books of science fiction.

Why did this group choose to call themselves *The Inklings?* While I have never seen in print an explanation, I think the name must have been selected to reflect the combined literary and religious interests of the group. Lewis opens *The Pilgrim's Regress* with a quotation from Plato concerning that which every soul seeks, not knowing what it is but having an "inkling" that it is. And in *The Problem of Pain* he speaks of that faint and uncertain "inkling" of something which one is born desiring. The circle, sensitive as they were to the ambiguities of language, surely found for themselves a very symbolic and characteristic name.

A recent letter from J. R. R. Tolkien lends support to this theory of a double meaning behind the circle's name.[6]

Lewis is quite often referred to in print as the author of some forty books. It becomes clear upon investigation that there is more than one reason for this lack of precision in count. The beginning student of Lewis will encounter three minor difficulties which make an exact tally of his major works more complex than at first might be supposed.

For one thing, several brief works which were published originally as slim volumes were gathered and reprinted later in collections. This happened in the case of *Hamlet: The Prince or the Poem?*, *The Literary Impact of the Authorized Version*, and *De Descriptione Temporum*. Should these works still be listed separately, or should they be counted only in terms of the larger works of which they have become a part? It seems to me wiser and simpler to follow the latter course. The one exception which I make to this procedure is with *Mere Christianity*. This particular volume combines in a revised and amplified edition, with a new introduction, three books which had previously enjoyed important and independent histories (*The Case for Christianity*, *Christian Behaviour*, and *Beyond Personality*). Hence we are required, I believe, to list these four volumes separately.

A second problem which complicates slightly the determination of the Lewis corpus arises from the fact that a single book may have been published under more than one title. The English *Broadcast Talks* was printed in the United States as *The Case for Christianity*. The English *Transposition and Other Addresses* became in this country *The Weight of Glory and Other Addresses*. Lewis' second major work of science fiction had two titles even in England: it was published as *Perelandra* in 1943 and as *Voyage to Venus* in 1953.

Yet another factor which has interfered with the complete enumeration of Lewis' works is his use of pseudonyms. It has long been known that Lewis' two earliest volumes were published under the name of *Clive Hamilton*. Only after his death, however, was it revealed that he had also published under the name of N. W. Clerk, in the case of *A Grief Observed*. Furthermore, many of his poems are in print under the pseudonym *Nat Whilk*—Anglo-Saxon for "I know not whom." (This name, incidentally, is probably a clue to the identity of that feigned

---

[6] In a letter to the author, Prof. J. R. R. Tolkien states that the name was a pleasantly ingenious pun, "suggesting people with vague or half-formed intimations and ideas plus those who dabble in ink." This letter from Professor Tolkien, dated September 11, 1967, is presented in full in Appendix 5 of the present study. Both Tolkien and Lewis were original members of *The Inklings*.

scholarly authority "Natvilcius" who is quoted in an extensive footnote at the beginning of *Perelandra*. Some of Lewis' poems are printed simply over the initials of *N. W.* And he once used the initials *A. B.* in some published letters. While this list may appear confusing to the person who meets the collection of names for the first time, there is no reason to believe that additional pseudonyms will be discovered.

Because of this pseudonym problem, erroneous information about Lewis' earliest published work has appeared in a number of scholarly references. Both *Twentieth Century Authors* and *Current Biography* name his first book as *Dymer*, published in 1926. For some reason, Lewis himself failed to ensure that *Who's Who* carried the correct material on this matter, and that source may account for the errors which have sprung up elsewhere. Actually, Lewis' first book was *Spirits in Bondage*, published under the pseudonym of Clive Hamilton in 1919.

Walter Hooper, now Chaplain of Wadham, contributed a bibliography of Lewis' extensive publications as the final chapter for *Light on C. S. Lewis*. While Hooper does not claim that his 1965 list is definitive, I think it certainly approximates that ideal. My own research has not uncovered a single item by Lewis which was not already included in this bibliography. The interested reader may consult this source, therefore, to explore the total scope of Lewis' writing beyond those forty-odd books for which he is best known. Hooper's bibliography records the following materials by Lewis which have not yet been reproduced in larger works: (a) nine prefaces; (b) eighty-eight essays and pamphlets; (c) five poems; (d) thirty-four book reviews, and (e) fifty-seven published letters.

As I count them, C. S. Lewis is the author of forty-nine major works. The full list, given in order according to original publication dates, will be found in Appendix 1 of the present study. There are seven differences between my list and the one which appears in Walter Hooper's bibliography. I do not list *Beyond the Bright Blur* separately since this material was incorporated immediately in *Letters to Malcolm*. Because of their major importance for Lewis, however, I consider *George Macdonald* and *Arthurian Torso* in the primary list rather than in a secondary category. The four remaining volumes—*Christian Reflections, Of Other Worlds, Letters to an American Lady,* and *Spenser's Images of Life*—have been published since Hooper's list appeared in 1965. According to Hooper, Lewis left behind very little unpublished material at his death.

II

Myth, Metaphor, and Religious Meaning

Our halting metaphor:

He whom I bow to only knows to whom I bow
When I attempt the ineffable name, murmuring Thou;
And dream of Pheidian fancies and embrace in heart
Meanings, I know, that cannot be the thing thou art.
All prayers always, taken at their word, blaspheme,
Invoking with frail imageries a folk-lore dream;
And all men are idolaters, crying unheard
To senseless idols, if thou take them at their word,
And all men in their praying, self-deceived, address
One that is not (so saith that old rebuke) unless
Thou, of mere grace, appropriate, and to thee divert
Men's arrows, all at hazard aimed, beyond desert.
Take not, oh Lord, our literal sense, but in thy great,
Unbroken speech our halting metaphor translate.

— *Regress,* pp. 144-45

A sensitivity to the ways in which language is customarily used in theology and literature can prevent the kind of misunderstanding which so often has impaired the work of Lewis critics in the past. Specific examples of misinterpretation will be discussed in Chapter IV. It is nearly axiomatic in contemporary theology that much "God-talk" has nonliteral meaning. Imaginative literature also, of course, has a symbolic, nonliteral significance.

The works of Owen Barfield (one of the Oxford *Inklings*), Ernst Cassirer, and Susanne Langer reflect the revived intellectual interest in myth in the twentieth century. Myth is no longer looked upon as child-like philosophy; the images of symbolic language are recognized, rather, as man's attempts to grasp his relationship with the world.

Lewis was keenly aware of the nature of language. He consciously and deliberately made use of his understanding of metaphor and myth, whether writing theology or composing novels. The fundamentalist or humanist reader who neglects to notice this fact in Lewis fails to catch his full meaning. Although references to the nature of religious language are widespread in Lewis' work, there are three places especially where he gives the subject concentrated attention. The chapter "Horrid Red Things" in *Miracles* is his most seminal discussion of the topic, although these pages are badly organized. Another statement of his views is found in "Is Theology Poetry?" an address to Oxford's Socratic Club which is now available in *Screwtape Proposes a Toast*. The third important discussion of religious language is "Bluspels and Flalansferes," now found in *Rehabilitations*. Key passages from *Mere Christianity* and *The Problem of Pain* will also be mentioned in the discussion which follows. Lewis repeatedly recommends to his readers two books in this field, Owen Barfield's *Poetic Diction* and Edwyn Bevan's *Symbolism and Belief* (the 1933/34 Gifford lectures at the University of Edinburgh).

Myth, says Lewis, "does not essentially exist in *words* at all." Myth represents ultimate, absolute reality. What most delights and nourishes men in myth is a "particular pattern of events." Only secondarily does a great myth exist in words.[1] A myth is always something different from the literary accounts in which it is expressed. For Lewis, myth used in literature represents a shadowy or distorted reflection of reality, which nevertheless conveys some of the meaning and power of the primary myth itself.[2] As Kilby says, Lewis defines myth "by its very power to convey essence rather than outward fact, reality rather than semblance, the genuine rather than the accidental." It is evident that Lewis' concept of myth is shaped by a Platonic interpretation of literature.

Lewis maintains that God has endowed man with conscience and has sent the human race "good dreams." As an illustration of this idea, he mentions in *Mere Christianity* "those queer stories scattered all through the heathen religions about a god who dies and comes to life again and, by his death, has somehow given new life to men." Commenting further upon this concept in a footnote in *Miracles*, Lewis speaks of myth as neither misunderstood history nor diabolical illusion (as some have thought) but as "a real though unfocussed gleam of divine truth falling

---

[1] "Preface," *Macdonald*, p. 15.

[2] See Charles W. Moorman, "Space Ship and Grail: The Myths of C. S. Lewis," *College English*, XVIII (May 1957), 401-5.

on human imagination." Even when myth becomes fact (as in Christ), he says, it also remains myth; "The story of Christ demands from us, and repays, not only a religious and historical but also an imaginative response."

Why does Christian theology contain elements similar to some found in primitive or savage religions? Christianity does not claim that other religions are 100 percent erroneous, says Lewis, but that while a special illumination has been vouchsafed to Jews and Christians, there is some divine illumination given to all men. "It is not the difference between falsehood and truth. It is the difference between a real event on the one hand and dim dreams of premonitions of that same event on the other."

Lewis is not satisfied to consider myth simply as the symbolic representation of "non-historical" truth. At one level, he says, myth operates as nonincarnate history. At another level, however, myth may become historic fact—as in the Incarnation. Lewis appreciates the Socratic understanding of myth as a "not unlikely tale." The creation myth of Genesis, therefore, is truer than history; it concerns the essence of history which transcends all particular facts.

Lewis admits in *Miracles* that on the surface much religious language seems to presuppose "a conception of reality which the increase of our knowledge has been steadily refuting for the last two thousand years and which no honest man in his senses could return to to-day." It sounds like a suspiciously primitive—or even savage—picture of the universe, he notes, to talk about a God who has a "Son" and a locale called "Heaven."

Lewis states in *Four Loves* that even at his highest sanctity and intelligence man has no direct knowledge about God. We have only analogies. Lewis labors "these deprecations," he explains, because efforts to be clear and brief may sometimes suggest more confidence than one actually possesses. He notes in *Mere Christianity* that no illustration about God works perfectly: "In the long run God is no one but Himself and what He does is like nothing else." In *Sixteenth Century*, Lewis is discussing the existence of Platonic Forms in a "supercelestial place" when he remembers to add, "which is as much as to say, in no *Place* at all." This same notion is reflected in *Out of the Silent Planet* while Ransom is engaged in unraveling the theology of an alien planet and inquires where the "Old One" lives. He receives the reply, "He is not that sort . . . that he has to live anywhere."

In *Letters to Malcolm*, Lewis observes that God works constantly as an iconoclast. "Every idea of Him we form, He must in mercy shatter." He reports that Thomas Aquinas once said of his own elaborate theology,

"It reminds me of straw." Speaking of the creation myths of various cultures in *Reflections on the Psalms,* Lewis frankly admits, "All our language about such things, that of the theologian as well as that of the child, is crude."

That the language of theology is inadequate to describe the reality of God, Lewis simply takes for granted. But there is more to be said on the matter. One cannot abandon the need to speak of God just because the results are certain to be limited. On this subject, as on many others, Lewis had learned from the books of that dissenting minister George Macdonald. Someone might protest that the description of a "rusty moth-eaten heart" is "only a figure," said Macdonald. And this is readily acknowledged. But, he continued, "Is the reality intended, less or more than the figure?"

For Lewis, as for Macdonald, the reality represented in myth and metaphor is more—not less—than a figure of speech. Lewis is impatient with those Christians who become so entangled in their sophisticated knowledge of religious language that they neglect the realities which the theological symbols imperfectly represent. This is his criticism of clergymen who are more concerned about the spirit of the age than about the Christian faith, more interested in civilization than in spiritual life. In *The Great Divorce* a "Bright Person" exclaims about Heaven to such a man: "You shall see the face of God!" "Ah," replies the clergyman, "but we must all interpret those beautiful words in our own way! For me there is no such thing as a final answer." "Do you not even believe that He exists?" asked the Bright One. "Exists? What does Existence mean? You *will* keep on implying some sort of static, ready-made reality which is, so to speak, 'there,' and to which our minds have simply to conform. These great mysteries cannot be approached in that way." Lewis' objection, it appears, is not to the idea that the ultimate nature of "existence" and "reality" are mysterious. They are, of course. But one cannot afford to use the language-game as an escape from decision-making and responsibility. Mysterious or no, life goes on. And the direction which a life takes has eternal consequences.

Another illustration of this idea is found in the *Pilgrim's Regress* allegory. John seeks from Mr. Broad some specific directions for his journey. "That is a beautiful idea," says Mr. Broad; "the seeking is the finding." "Do you mean that I must cross the canyon or that I must not?" John repeats. The only response he can gain from Mr. Broad is, "These great truths need re-interpretation in every age." Such innocuous conclusions about man's religious quest are not so much inaccurate *per se* as they are patently insufficient. Lewis would agree, to be

39

sure, that reinterpretation is necessary and helpful. But it is no substitute for the basic decision about the Gospel, no substitute for the crossing of the canyon itself.

Analogies of the divine-human relationship are, for Lewis, "inadequate but useful." There is a difference between the myth which has been built into a systematic and fully believed theology and the myth told by primitive man to explain a ritual. Lewis doubts that the primitives have toward their myths "a relation of full credal affirmation such as one finds in Christianity and Islam." To say that conceptions of God are inadequate is not to say that they are "merely symbolic." Indeed, Lewis notes in *Reflections,* one could not know a representation to be only symbolic unless he had an independent knowledge of the thing represented for purposes of comparison. But no one can claim such an independent, metaphor-free knowledge of God.

Lewis addressed the Oxford Socratic Club in 1944 on the topic, "Is Theology Poetry?" In this presentation he discussed whether the systematic series of statements that Christians make about God and man's relations to him owe their attraction merely to their power of arousing and satisfying the human imagination. He noted that man, as a poetical animal, adorns everything he touches. But if Christian theology is merely poetry, he said, it is not even good poetry. The Greek, Irish, and Norse mythologies are not nearly so barren.

Theology, of course, shares with poetry the use of metaphors and symbols. The nonbeliever may suppose that the men who founded the faith were so naïve as to believe all theological statements literally, and that later Christians have retained the language through timidity or conservatism. Probably most first-century Christians (though not all), said Lewis in *A Toast,* were unconscious of the anthropomorphic imagery which they used. Yet any who went to Alexandria for a philosophical education "would have recognized the imagery at once for what it was, and would not have felt that his belief had been altered in any way that mattered."

"There is a kind of explaining which is not explaining away," Lewis insists. In understanding any doctrine it is important to distinguish between the core of the idea and the way in which this basic meaning is expressed. The means of expression may be inessential and capable of being changed without damaging the doctrine. The purpose of theological interpretation is not to jettison all nonnaturalistic elements. The core which remains may itself be supernatural or miraculous.

Some people conclude that whatever is meant metaphorically is hardly meant at all. Actually, reality has a positive structure which metaphor usefully though incompletely describes. To say "my heart is broken,"

40

for example, does not become a meaningless statement once the metaphor is recognized. Certainly this expression cannot be understood to mean "I feel very cheerful." While literally inadequate, the sentence does point in a recognizable direction. Likewise, says Lewis, Christian doctrines which are metaphorical intend something just as supernatural or shocking after the removal of the ancient imagery as before.

Lewis gives examples of his metaphor-plus understanding of religious language in *Pilgrim's Regress*. Mr. Wisdom instructs John that "the eastern and western things" which he has sought are neither real places nor mere illusions. After a moment of crisis when John has uttered a prayer for help, he concludes that it is absolutely necessary to use metaphors. The imagination and feelings require it. "The great thing," he concludes, "is to keep the intellect free from them: to remember that they *are* metaphors." The "Other" or the "Thou" need not be confused with the *mythical* Landlord of his childhood. But "however I think of it," John sighs, "I think of it inadequately." Later in the day, a Man (*the* Man) descends the gorge to remind John that his life has been saved all that day by his crying out to the metaphor-something. But, continues the Man, "If its help is not a metaphor, neither are its commands. If it can answer when you call, then it can speak without your asking." "I think I see, sir. . . . In some sense I have a Landlord after all?" For Lewis, that "metaphor-something" exists independent of human thinking and wishing.

Further on in *Regress*, Lewis emphasizes that neither religious mythology alone nor morality alone is an adequate basis for living. It is "History" who explains to John that both "the pictures" and "the rules" are dangerous when kept apart. It would be best to listen to Mother Kirk, who was brought into the country by the Landlord's Son and who allows no quarrel between rules and pictures. But people rarely do listen to her, History acknowledges. Even Pagan mythology contains a Divine call. In the Land of Pagus, where the schools were closed, the Landlord succeeded in getting many messages through, especially in the form of pictures. The ancient Shepherd People, however, were able to read, so they received rules from the Landlord instead of pictures. Yet "a Shepherd is only half a man, and a Pagan is only half a man." John, driven by "sweet desire," and Vertue, compelled by conscience, are expected to swear blood brotherhood. That is, religious longing and moral concern must combine to form the whole man. History urges both John and Vertue to seek reconciliation with the one who formerly reconciled the Shepherds and the Pagans—Mother Kirk.

The role of metaphor in ordinary language is greater than is often

41

recognized, says Lewis. To discuss anything not perceived by the senses, he points out in *Miracles,* men are driven to use language metaphorically. In abstract discussion a person may "grasp the argument," "see the point," or "follow you." "Complexes" and "repressions" are considered as though desires could be tied into bundles and pushed around. "Growth" and "development" are applied to institutions as though they were trees or flowers. Energy is "released" as if it were an animal in a cage. When psychologists speak of complexes, repressions, censors, and engrams, they are referring—whether they know it or not—to *tyings-up, shovings-back, Roman magistrates,* and *scratchings.* It is impossible to get rid of such mental pictures in discussing extrasensory reality. The only choice open is whether to substitute one set of images for another.

Owen Barfield, Lewis noted, stressed that all language has a figurative origin, even scientific terms like *organism, stimulus,* and *reference.* Do some metaphors grow so old that they die (as metaphors) and assume a life independent of their original meaning, he wondered. How much is human thought conditioned by metaphors employed unconsciously? Men, said Lewis in *Rehabilitations,* should choose imagery well, apprehend it precisely, and recognize that a metaphor is a metaphor and not a statement of fact. Thought becomes independent of metaphors only insofar as particular metaphors are optional—i.e., if the same basic idea is possible without them. Freedom from a certain metaphor may be only the freedom to choose between that metaphor and others.

"He who would increase the meaning and decrease the meaningless verbiage in his own speech and writing, must do two things," Lewis declares. "He must become conscious of the fossilized metaphors in his words; and he must freely use new metaphors, which he creates for himself." Lewis concludes his discussion on religious language in "Bluspels and Flalansferes" by affirming that "Reason is the natural organ of truth; but imagination is the organ of meaning."

In view of the fact that images are necessary, what sort of images are the most satisfactory for theological discourse? Some people have been troubled by "anthropomorphic" images of God, and have substituted images of another kind. They may think of God as "a great spiritual force"—drawing upon images of winds and tides, electricity and gravitation. Or they may speak of "the Being who moves and works through us all"—exchanging the fatherly image for one of gas and fluid.

Lewis takes the biblical images seriously, though not literally. He defends the manlike images used traditionally in Christian theology.

Man, after all, is the highest of the things we meet in sensuous experience. He has, at least, conquered the globe, honoured (though not followed) virtue, achieved knowledge, made poetry, music and art. If God exists at all it is not unreasonable to suppose that we are less unlike Him than anything else we know. (*Miracles,* p. 76)

Of course, there may be some intellectual difficulties with this type of language. In a letter to his brother, Lewis once suggested that the phrase "Our Father which art in Heaven" be compared with the words "The supreme being transcends space and time." The first statement, he noted, "goes to pieces if you begin to apply the literal meaning to it, but the second ends up meaning nothing concrete at all." What is gained, he asked in *Malcolm,* by substituting the image of a live wire, with power to shock, for that of an angered majesty, with wrath to judge? Lewis prefers religious analogies based upon deeply personal relationships. "All the liberalising and 'civilising' analogies," he concludes, "only lead us astray."

It is impossible to throw away religious analogies and to get behind them to pure literal truth. All that can be substituted for an analogical expression is a theological abstraction. Lewis recommends two rules for exegetics: 1) never take the images literally; and 2) when the purport of the images conflicts with the theological abstractions, trust the images. What is called "demythologizing" the Gospel can easily be "re-mythologizing" it by substituting a poorer imagery for a richer. After all,

abstract thinking is itself a tissue of analogies: a continual modelling of spiritual reality in legal or chemical or mechanical terms. Are these likely to be more adequate than the sensuous, organic, and personal images of Scripture —light and darkness, river and well, seed and harvest, master and servant, hen and chickens, father and child? (*Malcolm,* p. 52)

Lewis occasionally speaks of the myth in the Bible as that which has been "specially chosen by God from among countless myths to carry a spiritual truth. . . ." His conviction that biblical mythology is particularly related to divine inspiration is reflected also in *Regress.* Following John's baptism "a voice from beyond" said to him,

Child, if you will, it *is* mythology. It is but truth, not fact: an image, not the very real. But then it is My mythology. The words of Wisdom [Philosophy] are also myth and metaphor: but since they do not know themselves for what they are, in them the hidden myth is master, where it should be servant: and it is but of man's inventing. But this in My inventing, this is the veil under which I have chosen to appear even from the first until now. (P. 171)

43

What Lewis suggested in his books seems closely related to Paul Tillich's concept of "the broken myth" as he describes it in *Dynamics of Faith*. Said Tillich, all mythological elements in theology should be recognized as mythological. When it becomes clear that the character of a symbol is "to point beyond itself to something else," the primitive urge to interpret myth literalistically diminishes. "A myth which is understood as a myth, but not removed or replaced, can be called a 'broken myth.'" Mythological elements "should be maintained in their symbolic form and not be replaced by scientific substitutes. For there is no substitute for the use of symbols and myths: they are the language of faith." [3] For Lewis also, religious myths should be examined and analyzed, but they cannot be abandoned if man is to speak at all about the infinite. Rather, myth should be used consciously and deliberately, in the full knowledge that it is both inadequate and necessary.

The student of religious language will recognize a further resemblance between Lewis' thinking and some recent work of I. M. Crombie. Crombie claims that theology is anthropomorphic, but not fictitious. He maintains that there is no literal resemblance between the truth expressed in a parable and the story expressing it. But, says Crombie, a "faithful" parable will not mislead as to the nature of the underlying reality. We postulate the analogy because we believe the image to be a faithful image. The sense the words bear within the image or parable is drawn from the thoughtful experience of human life. Since the theist believes in God as a transcendent being, what he says about him is intended to refer directly to God and not obliquely to this world. The theist genuinely believes God to be transcendent and therefore beyond our comprehension. God is, on the one hand, a mystery; on the other hand, he is One about whom men attempt to talk intelligibly. Men therefore talk of God only in images.[4] To put the matter negatively, it seems that Lewis and Crombie would agree that biblical anthropomorphic language is the *least misleading* imagery available to men for profound conversation about God.

Lewis noted in *Malcolm* that one is always fighting on two fronts to express the full meaning of God. Among the Pantheists one must stress God's distinctness, his relative independence from his creatures. Among Deists, however—"or perhaps in Woolwich, if the laity there really think God is to be sought in the sky—one must emphasise the divine presence in my neighbour, my dog, my cabbage-patch." Lewis doubted whether

---

[3] (Torchbook ed; New York: Harper & Row, 1958), p. 50-51.

[4] *Faith and Logic: Oxford Essays in Philosophical Theology*, ed. Basil Mitchell (Boston: Beacon Press, 1957), pp. 71-73.

laymen are as theologically naïve as J. A. T. Robinson, the Bishop of Woolwich, seems to suggest in his *Honest to God.*

We should not fail to note that Christianity concerns certain historic events as well as statements about super-natural, unconditioned reality. Lewis thought that anyone sophisticated enough to understand what "taking it literally" means would be unlikely to consider material images as literal statements about spiritual reality. But events on the historic level should continue to be considered literally. It would be improper to apply a metaphorical interpretation to a historic exodus or crucifixion.

Robert J. Reilly noted in his dissertation that Christ was a fact, but that Christ is not Christianity. He asked whether the various views of Christ cannot be considered mythological or metaphorical, culturally conditioned and (to a degree) exchanged in other times and cultures as the Incarnation fact is interpreted afresh? [5] This is certainly the view of Paul Hessert, who wrote in his *Introduction to Christianity* that theologians have often cheapened the theme of Christ's atonement by "trying to absolutize concepts originally meant metaphorically." This was also Lewis' point of view. He noted in *Mere Christianity* that no interpretation of the atonement will ever be quite adequate to explain its reality. Christ's death, he said, has made a difference between men and God somehow. This fact is beneficial to man even without a theory of how it works—just as vitamins and proteins are beneficial to men whether or not they have an adequate theory of nourishment. The idea of the atonement can be expressed in many different ways. If none of these formulas appeals to the reader, Lewis said, he should leave them alone and work with a formula that does.

Scientists like Jeans and Eddington, Lewis continued, may explain the atom by offering a descriptive mental picture. But they also warn that these pictures are not what scientists actually believe. The pictures are intended only as an aid for understanding the formula. Although some readers will not find Lewis' discussion of the atonement fully satisfying, he consistently refused to engage in debate over the relative merits of the several theories. I think he might have agreed with Hessert that each theory contributes something valuable toward the total understanding of Christ's work, even though it is impossible to describe exactly how Christ redeems men.

Lewis made a distinction between thinking and imagining which ap-

[5] "Romantic Religion in the Work of Owen Barfield, C. S. Lewis, Charles Williams and J. R. R. Tolkien," (Ph.D. diss., Michigan State University, 1960) , p. 101.

plies to religious thinking as well as to other kinds of thought. Thinking is carried on with images and in spite of images. But it is not in these physical pictures that men are chiefly interested. One may think of "London," for example, and imagine a scene in Euston Station. A child may think of "poison" and imagine "horrid red things." Not only is there a difference between what is thought and what is pictured, but *"what we mean may be true when the mental images that accompany it are entirely false."* For example,

If a visitor to that house had been warned by the child, "Don't drink that. Mother says it is poison," he would have been ill advised to neglect the warning on the ground that "This child has a primitive idea of poison as Horrid Red Things, which my adult scientific knowledge has long since refuted." (*Miracles*, p. 73)

Applied to religious language, this discussion might suggest that the literalist who believes in a heaven of pearly gates and golden pavements is more nearly correct (though his images be woefully inadequate) than the Marxist who argues that heaven has no meaning whatsoever. Might the fundamentalist who believes in the devil "hoofs, horns, and all" be closer to ultimate truth than the sophisticate who wholly denies the dimension of sin and evil in life? This appears to be Lewis' view, even though his idea is easily subject to misunderstanding when removed from this context of qualification. "Thinking may be sound in certain respects," he wrote in *Miracles,* "where it is accompanied not only by false images but by false images mistaken for true ones." Such thought remains valid in *certain* respects only, we should note. Since metaphors are required, it is best to use these inadequate images consciously and deliberately. But thought does not become totally invalid if the images are occasionally taken to be more literal than they could possibly be by sophisticated literary and theological standards.

"What you think is one thing: what you imagine while you are thinking is another," Lewis maintained. Before going to Oxford University, he said, he had a mental image of what it would be like. In reality, the physical details were quite different. But it would be unfair to conclude that his general conception of a college was thereby a delusion. Relating this notion to religious thought, Lewis concluded,

The earliest Christians were not so much like a man who mistakes the shell for the kernel as like a man carrying a nut which he hasn't yet cracked. The moment it is cracked, he knows which part to throw away. Till then he holds on to the nut: not because he is a fool but because he isn't. (*A Toast,* p. 53)

46

The student unfamiliar with contemporary theology might wonder whether Lewis' emphasis upon religious language as essentially mythical and metaphorical in nature is a private view, conditioned by his experience in the discipline of literary criticism, or whether this viewpoint is somewhat representative of current theology. That the general public has not been aware of developments in the understanding of religious language was probably demonstrated by the intense interest *Honest to God* provoked when it appeared in paperback in 1963. It seems that either laymen were startled to consider that religious language might be nonliteral in intention, or they were surprised to hear that some famous theologians considered that to be the case. Actually, Lewis is firmly in the mainstream of theological thinking, both ancient and modern, in regard to his basic concept of religious language. I will support this claim by brief reference to a number of prominent theologians in the pages which follow.

Theologians did not wait for the publication of Alfred J. Ayer's *Language, Truth and Logic* in 1935 to learn that "the sentences which the theist uses to express [transcendent] 'truths' are not literally significant." Lewis was aware of an ancient tradition in the church when he claimed that he need not hold every sentence of the Old Testament to be scientifically, historically true. In *Psalms* and elsewhere he noted that Jerome (in the fourth century) referred to Moses as a poet, and John Calvin (in the sixteenth century) wondered whether Job should be considered a character of fiction. Lewis might have added that Origen sparked a third-century debate over whether the Genesis creation-story should be interpreted literally, or that Augustine endorsed a nonliteral interpretation of creation in the fifth century. Lewis admitted that naïveté, error, and contradiction—the human qualities of the Bible's raw materials—remain in the Scriptures. The result is not a Word of God which offers impeccable science and history. Rather, the Bible carries the word of God, and modern men may receive that word by attending to wise interpreters and by steeping themselves in its overall tone and message. Educated people in the Middle Ages, Lewis claimed, were aware that the winged men of painting and sculpture were not intended as anything but symbols. Lewis mentions more than once in his writings *Celestial Hierarchies,* a highly influential medieval text by Pseudo-Dionysius, which states that angels were unembodied, pure minds.

Contemporary theologians often hold theological systems, including their own intellectual constructions, under suspicion. They approach their discipline with more humility and with less inclination toward absolutistic pretensions than scholars in other disciplines sometimes sup-

47

pose. They customarily insist that Christians direct their respect and devotion, not toward doctrinal formulations, but toward the living God whose meaning can never quite be represented adequately in language. Sensitive to the dangers of intellectualization in religion, they may even ask, with Kierkegaard, "Can a theologian be saved?" Words and doctrines may "point to" God; they do not fully describe him. We turn now to the thought of some leading twentieth-century theologians who illustrate a sensitivity to the limitations of religious language.

Reinhold Niebuhr pointed out that many great thinkers in the past, including Descartes, Hegel, Kant, and Comte, imagined themselves to deliver a final truth. But "all human knowledge," Niebuhr stressed, "is finite knowledge, gained from a particular perspective." This warning applies to theology as well as to philosophy. When men labor with sufficient earnestness to explicate gospel truth by human wisdom (the very task of theology), they should recognize their work is "subject to historical contingencies, influenced by egotistic passions, corrupted by sinful pretensions and is, in short, under the same judgment as philosophy." [6]

Paul Tillich may be better known for his reservations about religious language than several other leading theologians. He has written, for example,

That which is the true ultimate transcends the realm of finite reality infinitely. Therefore, no finite reality can express it directly and properly. Religiously speaking, God transcends his own name. . . . Whatever we say about that which concerns us ultimately, whether or not we call it God, has a symbolic meaning. It points beyond itself while participating in that to which it points. In no other way can faith express itself adequately. The language of faith is the language of symbols.[7]

Tillich proceeds from this point to discuss his concept of the "broken myth," which we have already mentioned. "One can replace one myth by another," says Tillich, "but one cannot remove the myth from man's spiritual life."[8] This statement is reminiscent of Lewis' observation about religious language that "we can make our speech duller; we cannot make it more literal."

In a somewhat different theological tradition, Karl Barth recognized that no statement about God can ever be regarded as a final statement.

---

[6] *The Nature and Destiny of Man: A Christian Interpretation* (New York: Charles Scribner's Sons, 1951), I, 194-95; II, 230.

[7] *Dynamics of Faith*, p. 45.

[8] *Ibid.*, p. 50.

In his 1956 essay "The Humanity of God," Barth confessed that he once

viewed this 'wholly other' isolation, abstracted and absolutized, and set it over against man, this miserable wretch—not to say boxed his ears with it—in such fashion that it continually showed greater similarity to the deity of the God of the philosophers than to the deity of the God of Abraham, Isaac, and Jacob.[9]

But in announcing his revised viewpoint, Barth was hesitant to conclude that he now held the final, absolute theological truth. He gladly admitted that even his final position, the product of a lifetime of theological reflection and experience, could not be "the last word."

Jewish thought, as well as Christian, has been sensitive to the nature of religious language in this century. Martin Buber has suggested that God is never to be totally identified with the images "through" which men look at the divine "Thou." These symbols of God are "necessarily untrue images." The images are, for Buber, "signs" and "pointers" to God.

Even the current discussion over the possibility of myth in the story of Jesus did not begin with the present century. There was considerable theological controversy when David Friedrich Strauss published in 1835 his first *Life of Jesus,* an interpretation which relied heavily on mythical categories.

Whatever the merits of his major argument in "New Testament and Mythology," Rudolf Bultmann has contributed to a renewed awareness of the extensive use of picture-language in the Bible.[10] In the debate which followed this essay many of Bultmann's sharpest critics accepted the presence of mythical elements in Scripture, while posing such additional questions as these: Is not time-space picture-language inescapable whenever we speak of the invisible becoming visible? Is not science also compelled to speak in myths, as Karl Heim has maintained since the beginning of the century? Was not Augustine aware of the importance of distinguishing between the literal and the symbolic, and did not the medieval Schoolmen theorize this problem almost ad nauseam?

Many modern Christians will disagree with Bultmann on several important points. In a 1959 Cambridge paper entitled "Modern Theology and Biblical Criticism," for example, Lewis charged that Bultmann's scholarly conclusions are sometimes warped by a lack of sound literary judgment. He further thought it preposterous that Bultmann, twenty

[9] *The Humanity of God,* trans. Thomas Weiser and J. N. Thomas (Richmond, Va.: John Knox Press, 1960) , p. 45.

[10] *Kergyma and Myth,* ed. Hans Werner Bartsch (Torchbook ed; New York: Harper & Row, 1952) , pp. 1-44.

centuries later, should claim to understand Jesus' teachings better than did first-century contemporaries. Lewis criticized Bultmann for assuming that the miraculous does not occur, without even bothering to discuss the question on philosophic grounds. As a literary critic himself, Lewis noted that the attempts of critics to reconstruct the genesis of texts—in biblical as well as in other kinds of literature—are often based upon imaginary histories. He concluded the paper by predicting that the Bultmannian school will be temporary in influence and that the future will experience a growth of skepticism about Bultmann's skepticism. While not all will subscribe to the entire demythologization program advocated by Bultmann, few will disagree with Austin Farrer that biblical images which draw on fields of experience unfamiliar to modern man should be replaced by familiar images. Substitution of familiar images for unfamiliar, said Farrer, is not so much demythicization as "remythicization."

A further step for the contemporary communication of the gospel includes not only the replacing of unfamiliar images with the familiar but also the creation of fresh, untarnished images to supplement those that have grown dull and stale across the years. C. S. Lewis, as artist, sensed very early the need for new Christian images which might grasp the imagination and compel the intellect. He then spent his life producing them.

Protesting the widespread confusion over the meaning of the word *God*, Tillich wrote that "you must forget everything traditional that you have learned about God, perhaps even that word itself." [11] Harvey Cox furthers the objection, announcing that "it may well be that our English word *God* will have to die." [12] I myself happen to agree with John A. T. Robinson's statement that the name *God* is "necessary," since our being has depths which naturalism fails to recognize. My reason for introducing this topic at the present, however, is not to argue for a particular solution to a complex problem, but to recognize a related area of difficulty. If traditional God-concepts are unsatisfactory, can anything less be said about traditional representations of evil? Surely devil-concepts or Satan-images are more associated in the minds of most persons with comedies, cartoons, and Halloween costumes than they are with serious theological insight. Lewis knew that the question is not one of whether such concepts as the Fall and Satan have been well represented and intelligently understood in modern culture. They have not been, of course. But a deeper question concerns how some dimensions of human

[11] Tillich, Paul, *The Shaking of the Foundations* (New York: Charles Scribner's Sons, 1948), p. 64.
[12] *The Secular City* (New York: The Macmillan Co., 1965), p. 265.

experience are to be understood and represented at all if traditional terminology is utterly abandoned.

In *Mere Christianity,* Lewis responded to the question "Do you really mean, at this time of day, to re-introduce our old friend the devil— hoofs and horns and all?" He replied, "I am not particular about the hoofs and horns. But in other respects my answer is 'Yes, I do.'" I think Lewis overestimated his audience' ability to appreciate symbolic religious language when he made this remark. Had he told a group of Oxford colleagues that he was "not particular" about supporting belief in a devil complete with hoofs and horns, his remark would surely have been recognized as a bit of wry British humor. But before the mass audience of the BBC, the dramatic imagery survived, and the subtlety was lost. Both fundamentalists and antifundamentalists understood Lewis to be endorsing a more literalistic conception of Satan than (in my opinion) he had any intention of doing. When *Time* magazine featured Lewis on a 1947 cover, the picture there did contain a devil, complete with hoofs, horns, tail, pitchfork, "and all." My impression is that this popular misconception of his thought did nothing to enhance Lewis' stature as a theologian, and it did a great injustice to his understanding of religious language and the spiritual realities represented by such language.

Some theologians advocate that such words as "God" or "God beyond God" be used always in such a way as to distinguish clearly between popular notions of deity and refined theological concepts. Were such a practice followed with regard to Lewis' thought, it would be appropriate to distinguish between "the Devil" and "Satan behind Satan." For what Lewis means by the traditional language differs considerably from what the common reader might suppose upon first seeing the words in print. Lewis regards the devil as a being with consciousness, intelligence, and will (whatever these terms may mean with reference to a spiritual "being"). But in the last analysis, I think he might agree with this statement about evil spirits in Philip S. Watson's *The Concept of Grace:*

When the Bible and the Christian faith speak of spirits, whether holy or unholy, they are speaking of quite concrete realities of human experience. . . . Whether demons and the devil "exist" or not, there are undoubtedly spiritual forces that are real enough in this world, and human nature is by no means insulated against them. There are ideas, doctrines, ideologies, philosophies of life, in which "spirits," good, bad, and indifferent, find expression, and through which they influence men. What such spirits may be ontologically, is perhaps an unanswerable question, and in any case we are not concerned with it here; for we have no need to deny their reality merely because we cannot solve the ultimate problem of their nature and origin. Presumably no one would dispute that when we use pharases like "the spirit of Nazism," "the spirit of Communism," and many more, we are speaking of quite real factors and forces in human life. Nor can it be denied that what we have described as "the spirit of self-will, self-assertion, self-seeking, and would-be self-sufficiency" manifests itself in innumerable disastrous ways, in individuals and groups of men and in the human race as a whole.[13]

In addition to the more lengthy discussions already cited Lewis made a number of allusions to his theory of religious language throughout his writings. It is my judgment that he will be seen to be thoroughly consistent on this matter once his basic position has been recognized. The following references will further illustrate this point.

After writing *Screwtape*, Lewis was often asked whether he "really" believed in the devil. In his preface to the new edition he pointed out that the purpose of this literary work "was not to speculate about diabolical life but to throw light from a new angle on the life of men."
The "devils" of *Screwtape*, he said, may be taken either as symbols of concrete reality or as personifications of abstractions. The author's personal opinion about devils is not of major importance to the reader for an appreciation of this imaginative work.

Lewis went on to admit, however, that he did happen to believe in devils in the sense that certain angels have abused their free will to become God's enemies. There is no independent power opposite to God from all eternity, he said. And perfect badness could not even have the positive quality of existence, much less the good qualities of intelligence, will, memory, and energy. The leader of the fallen angels is known as Satan. Lewis pointed out that his belief in devils is only an opinion. It is not a central doctrine in his faith, and his religion would not be shattered by the loss of that idea.

To affirm a general belief in angels or devils does not commit one to any particular artistic or literary representation of them, Lewis contended. Of course, such creatures must be represented symbolically or not at all. "These forms are not only symbolical but were always known to be symbolical by reflective people. . . . It is only the ignorant, said Dionysius in the fifth century, who dream that spirits are really winged men." Lewis thought that Dante was the master of this symbolical art. Milton's devils, he said, have done much harm, and Goethe's image of Mephistopheles is positively pernicious. A humorous, civilized, sensible devil strengthens the illusion that evil is liberating. In his own symbols

---

[13] (Philadelphia: Muhlenberg Press) , 1959, pp. 48-49.

of hell, Lewis noted, he attempts to portray the passions of self-importance, envy, and resentment.

Lewis noted in *The Problem of Pain* that Von Hügel warned against confusing the doctrine of hell with the imagery used to speak of that doctrine. Jesus spoke of hell under symbols of punishment, destruction, and privation. Perhaps all of these images refer to the fact, said Lewis, that heaven is a place prepared for men while hell was never made for men at all. "To enter heaven is to become more human than you ever succeed in being in earth; to enter hell, is to be banished from humanity." It may be, he suggested, that hell is not at all parallel to heaven, but is rather a darkness in which being fades away into nonentity. The "horrible freedom" which men possess is the power to rebel against God to the very end. Unwilling to abandon self-centeredness, some demand that God leave them alone. He does—and that is hell. These reflections, Lewis reminded his readers, are not about Nero or Judas; they are about "you and me."

Guide George Macdonald in *The Great Divorce* tells a visitor to the precincts of heaven,

All Hell is smaller than one pebble of your earthly world: but it is smaller than one atom of *this* world, the Real World. Look at yon butterfly. If it swallowed all Hell, Hell would not be big enough to do it any harm or to have any taste. (P. 122)

This example well illustrates Lewis' own conception of hell. He does not for a moment deny its reality. But one must admit that a hell so insubstantial that it could be swallowed almost unnoticed by a butterfly is a different kind of reality from that which Bultmann caricatures in his description of a "three-story universe."

Wormwood is informed in *Screwtape* that current diabolical policy is to keep a patient ignorant of the existence of devils. "If any faint suspicion of your existence begins to arise in his mind, suggest to him a picture of something in red tights, and persuade him that since he cannot believe in that, he therefore cannot believe in you." The situation is considered equally desperate for hell if a patient recognizes and flings aside all his images of God or if he retains the images in "full recognition of their merely subjective nature." Hell is not served, Lewis seemed to say, if either a man becomes a silent mystic or if he deliberately continues to use the "broken myths" which he admits are quite insufficient for the reality they represent.

Lewis noted in *Allegory* that he, like others, has been irritated by "the fatuity of most poetical attempts to describe heaven—the dull catalogues of jewellery and mass-singing." Again in *Mere Christianity* he stated that scriptural imagery for heaven—harps, crowns, gold, and the like—is, of course, symbolical. Such language attempts to express in words and images what is really inexpressible. Perhaps Lewis' position on religious language is nowhere summarized more bluntly than in these words: "People who take these symbols literally might as well think that when Christ told us to be like doves, He meant that we were to lay eggs."

Lewis observed in a letter that heaven is presented to man in Scripture under the symbols of a dinner party, a wedding, a city, and a concert. He rhapsodized thus over heaven at the conclusion of *Malcolm:*

Then the new earth and sky, the same yet not the same as these, will rise in us as we have risen in Christ. And once again, after who knows what aeons of the silence and the dark, the birds will sing and the waters flow, and lights and shadows move across the hills, and the faces of our friends laugh upon us with amazed recognition. (P. 124)

He adds, in caution, "Guesses, of course, only guesses. If they are not true, something better will be."

Not only did Lewis recognize the mythical or metaphorical element of traditional religious language, but he deliberately forged new metaphors and myths which would speak more directly to the present age. According to a *College English* essay entitled "Space Ship and Grail," by Charles W. Moorman, Lewis described and defined theological tenets in a way which avoided the normal vocabulary of the church. He appeared to work on the principle that the usual approach to Christianity is no longer effective, and that new and different terms must be created to express the old (and still valid) doctrines.[14] Lewis himself noted in a letter that following his conversion to Christianity, he was led to embody his religious belief "in symbolical or mythopeic forms, ranging from *Screwtape* to a kind of theologised science-fiction."

Perhaps the dominant myth in Lewis is based upon Plato's famous allegory of the Cave. Nowhere is this reflected more dramatically than in *Divorce,* where the visiting "ghosts" encounter the Solid People of heaven. The earth is viewed here either as the Valley of the Shadow of Life or the Valley of the Shadow of Death, depending upon human choices. This shadow theme receives additional treatment in the Narnia stories, especially in the children's conversation with "The Queen of Underland" (in *The Silver Chair*) and at the end of *The Last Battle.* The final chapter of this seven-book Narnia series is entitled "Farewell

[14] P. 403.

to Shadowlands," and its characters are introduced to a new level of life in another world. Walter Hooper appears to have had this theme in mind also when he organized Lewis' poems for publication. He called the first chapter of *Poems* "The Hidden Country" and the last chapter "A Farewell to Shadowlands."

Corbin S. Carnell points out that the so-called Platonic view of ideas is not restricted to Plato and his followers. Whether the greater and unseen reality is spoken of as "above" or "deep within" empirical reality, there are others who affirm an enduring order beyond the obvious empirical world. Paul Tillich and the phenomenologists, says Carnell, are concerned with the old contrast between appearance and reality; and they equally affirm the existence of realities that cannot be empirically verified.[15] Lewis would undoubtedly regard the myth of the Cave as one of those great myths which is continually breaking into history in various forms. But so often does he acknowledge his indebtedness to Plato that there is no reason to suppose that his contrast between shadow and substance derives from any other source.

Lewis also turned easily to the natural world and to the world of mythology for symbols of spiritual reality. His high places tend to be holy places. He noted in *Psalms* that since nature has been emptied of divinity, her sun and mountains can now become magnificent symbols of divinity. On this, as on so many other topics, Lewis emphatically agrees with George Macdonald. Macdonald once asked what idea of God men could have without the sensory experience of the sky: "Think for a moment what would be our idea of greatness, of God, of infinitude, of aspiration, if, instead of a blue, far withdrawn, light-spangled firmament, we were born and reared under a flat white ceiling!"[16]

In his *Preface to Paradise Lost* Lewis states that an author should not introduce novel ingredients in mythical poetry, but he may use the traditional ingredients in novel ways. "Giants, dragons, paradises, gods, and the like are themselves the expression of certain basic elements in man's spiritual experience," he maintains. They are "the words of a language which speaks the else unspeakable."

Whether drawing material from Platonic philosophy, ancient mythology, or from the world of nature, Lewis fashioned a fresh mythology to carry his convictions about God and man. That these fragile constructs but dimly represent divine reality, Lewis was keenly aware. Yet perhaps his myths will enable twentieth-century men to see certain old ideas

---

[15] "Dialectic of Desire," p. 174.
[16] *Macdonald*, p. 70.

anew. Lewis would expect of them nothing more. Certainly he would not want his imaginary creations about God and Satan, heaven and hell, to be taken more literally than they deserve to be taken. He would want no Swedenborgs or Vale Owens among his spiritual descendents. The final words of George Macdonald in *Divorce* appear to echo Lewis' own warning:

Make it plain that it was but a dream. See ye make it very plain. Give no poor fool the pretext to think ye are claiming knowledge of what no mortal knows. (P. 127)

III

Poiema, Logos, and Literary Fantasy

An enlargement of being:

We want to see with other eyes, to imagine with other imaginations, to feel with other hearts, as well as with our own, . . . to go out of the self, to correct its provincialism and heal its loneliness. . . . In the reception of the arts, we are doing this. . . . My own eyes are not enough for me, I will see through those of others. Reality, even seen through the eyes of many, is not enough. I will see what others have invented. . . . In reading great literature I become a thousand men and yet remain myself. . . . I see with myriad eyes, but it is still I who see. . . . I transcend myself; and am never more myself than when I do.

—*Criticism,* pp. 137-41

Every work of literature can be viewed in two ways, Lewis noted in *An Experiment in Criticism.* A literary work is *poiema*—something made. It is also *logos*—something said. As *poiema,* the work is an *objet d'art.* As *logos,* "it tells a story, or expresses an emotion, or exhorts or pleads or describes or rebukes or excites laughter." It is not necessary to believe or to approve the *logos* for a genuine literary appreciation of a work, Lewis said.

Why should men occupy their hearts with events that never happened and enter vicariously into feelings which they would hope to avoid in their own lives? Such experiences provide an enlargement of being as men attempt to see life through the eyes, hearts, and imaginations of others. The individual transcends his provincialism and loneliness as he enters indirectly into a world of experience not his own. That is the great value of literature as *logos.* "It is irrelevant whether the mood expressed in a poem was truly and historically the poet's own or one that he also had imagined. What matters is his power to make us live it."

Literature, for Lewis, should embody some reflection of eternal beauty and wisdom. The artist should be less concerned with the question, "Is it mine?" (reflecting interest in self-expression) than with the question, "Is it good?" Lewis recorded in *Surprised* that Christianity offended his youthful aesthetic sense. It appeared to him that Christianity was associated largely with "ugly architecture, ugly music, and bad poetry." Though Lewis would never excuse shoddy workmanship in artistic creation, he came to believe that Christians have reason to take literature a bit less seriously than cultured pagans who view it as a self-existent thing to be valued for its own sake.

Lewis once expressed in a letter his view that literature and art should either be innocent recreation, or they should be devoted to the service of religious or moral truth. Serious irreligious art ("art for art's sake") never exists when art is flourishing, he said. The literary life was much more than a vocation for Lewis; he was distressed with his colleagues who refused to discuss literature outside of their working hours. He, further, lacked sympathy for artists who appeared more eager to gain public recognition than to devote their artistic skills to genuine public service. The public has no duty to appreciate literary ambition, said Lewis. Too many modern novels, poems, and pictures represent poor workmanship. Haughty indifference to the raw materials of existing audience taste, interest, and capacity "is not genius nor integrity; it is laziness and incompetence."

Lewis' literary theory is reflected occasionally even in his noncritical books. In *Psalms* he calls poetry "a little incarnation" which gives body to what was formerly invisible and inaudible. In *Silent Planet* one of the poetic *hrossa* informs Ransom that "a pleasure is full grown only when it is remembered." And in *Perelandra* the Green Lady learns from Weston that earthly poetry uses beautiful words, well put together, to describe things that never happen and places that never were. This is wisdom, says Weston—uttering for once a view that Lewis endorsed. "The world is made up not only of what is but of what might be," says Weston.

Though both *poiema* and *logos* are present in every literary work, the "something made" takes precedence over the elements of "something said" in genuine literary experience. While ideas may be present in literature in a subsidiary role, Lewis stated in *Allegory* that a man working as a propagandist is inspired by motives which are irrelevant to poetry. "An impurity in intention" is involved in labor at poetry for "some purely unpoetic purpose." Lewis' view of the relationship which should exist between literary form and content appears consistent with prevailing critical views in the field of literature. René Wellek and Austin Warren point out in their *Theory of Literature,* for example, that literature is something other than "ideas wrapped in form." To reduce a work of art to a doctrinal statement "is disastrous to understanding the uniqueness of a work: it disintegrates its structure and imposes alien criteria of value." Literature is more than philosophical knowledge stated in imagery and verse. The view that poetry is primarily an instrument of edification has frequently been called "the didactic heresy," following Poe. On the other hand, one need not deny all philosophical relevance to literature. Often an author hopes to influence the attitudes of his readers, persuade them, or change them. "Literature is not defiled by the presence of ideas literarily used, used as integral parts of the literary work—as materials—like the characters and the settings," said Wellek and Warren. While "philosophical truth" as such has no artistic value, ideological content may actually enhance the artistic values of complexity and coherence. The didactic problem, then, seems to be not so much *whether* ideas are used in literature, but *how* they are used. To be employed successfully in a work of art, ideas must be incorporated into the very texture of the work, must become "constitutive" in its symbols and myths. Too much unassimilated ideology destroys a work of art. "Poetry is not substitute-philosophy; it has its own justification and aim," according to Wellek and Warren.

In theory, at least, Lewis is in full agreement with these basic principles set forth in *Theory of Literature.* He stated in *An Experiment in Criticism* that it is a confusion over the nature of art which leads some critics to esteem books "good" when they present "truths about life," and to praise artists as teachers. For example, the "tragic view of life" is widely appreciated in our day. This philosophy assumes (1) that great miseries come from character flaws; and (2) that extreme miseries reveal human splendor. As a philosophy of life, the tragic view "is the most obstinate and best camouflaged of all wish-fulfilments," charged Lewis. It assumes that, despite the worst, sorrows always have some sublimity and significance. As a matter of fact, tragedy is no truer to life, he said, than comedy or farce. Each art-form selects, isolates, and patterns the raw materials which it requires to make a play. "None of the three kinds is making a statement about life in general," noted Lewis. "They are all constructions: things made *out* of the stuff of real life; additions to life rather than comments on it." Of course, the literary artist ought not be shallow in his thoughts and feelings. He brings to his art all the wisdom, knowledge, and experience that he has. But to construe a work of art as a philosophy "even if it were a rational philosophy, and regard the actual play as primarily a vehicle for that philosophy, is an outrage to the thing the poet has made for us."

A literary work is primarily "something made." As *poiema,* it is neither realistic reporting nor biographical information about the author. After Lewis had received several letters asking whether *Silent Planet* were a true story, he complained to a correspondent, "Some people just don't understand what fiction is." The major reason for the unusually high number of inquiries, he might have admitted, was his quasi-factual material at the conclusion of this story, used to "bestow verisimilitude" upon his fiction. But Lewis found it necessary to insist even that his talking lion Aslan was a fictitious creation. "No, no, I'm not committed to a real belief in Aslan," he wrote in response to another query. "All that comes in a *story.*" Lewis was surprised also at the persistence of the notion that literature is chiefly autobiographical. "A man who lacks invention himself does not easily attribute it to others," he concluded in *Discarded Image.* Even his own work *Pilgrim's Regress,* which draws heavily upon autobiographical elements, is not solely autobiographical.

Commenting upon his own imaginative writing, Lewis explained that "images always come first." The process was something like bird watching. A story always began by his "seeing" vivid pictures, and the gaps had to be filled in later. According to Lewis, an author should not attempt to decide upon a suitable "moral" for his story. He wrote,

Let the pictures tell you their own moral. . . . But if they don't show you any moral, don't put one in. For the moral you put in is likely to be a platitude, or even a falsehood, skimmed from the surface of your consciousness. . . . The only moral that is of any value is that which arises inevitably from the whole cast of the author's mind.[1]

Lewis' "whole cast of mind," however, forced him to include moral and doctrinal elements quite often in his imaginative books. Nearly everyone, he admits, supposes that *Perelandra* was constructed for a didactic purpose. "They are quite wrong," he says. That particular book began with a mental picture of floating islands, and the story about an averted fall developed later on. "I've never," he insists, "started from a message or a moral." [2]

Likewise, according to Lewis himself, the Narnia fairy tales did not begin with any didactic or apologetic impulse. There was nothing Christian about them at all in the beginning. The lion Aslan did not even

[1] *Of Other Worlds: Essays and Stories,* ed. Walter Hooper (New York: Harcourt, Brace & World, 1967), p. 33.
[2] *Ibid.,* pp. 87-88.

appear in the earliest sketch of Narnia, done in 1938. When he wrote *The Lion, the Witch and the Wardrobe*, Lewis had not yet planned for a Narnia series. The Christian element, he says, eventually "pushed itself in of its own accord. It was part of the bubbling."

Lewis certainly had no objection to the presence of ideas in literature as a "subsidiary" consideration. He objected to H. G. Wells's novels-with-a-purpose because they were bad novels, he said. He objected to the preaching passages of Thackeray "not because I dislike sermons but because I dislike bad sermons." Jane Austen, on the other hand, he found a sound moralist—not platitudinous, but firm and subtle. He noted also that when the old poets made a theme of some virtue they were often adoring rather than teaching, and what we may take as didactic they considered simply enchanted.

The didactic content of Lewis' imaginative works has been variously evaluated by critics. The remarks of Corbin S. Carnell and Leonard Bacon are representative of one major point of view. They note a dominant moral quality in his writing, but do not find it overly didactic or objectionable. In his dissertation (which, incidentally, is a model of careful scholarship and balanced judgment) Carnell writes,

In all of his work Lewis is, like Dr. Johnson, always the moralist. He is of course too accomplished an artist ever to engage in pedestrian moralizing, yet his stories, poems, and essays have deeply moral implications which the reader can hardly avoid.[3]

Bacon pays tribute to Lewis' skill as an author in spite of his several reservations about Lewis' particular ideas.

Mr. Lewis is beyond question one of the most exciting and satisfactory writers who has come to the surface out of the maelstrom of these turbulent times. ... He has a powerful, discriminating and, in the proper sense of the word, poetic mind, great learning, startling wit, an overwhelming imagination, a charming and disarming naïveté and the capacity to express himself.[4]

While noting that he does not share all of Lewis' beliefs, Bacon nevertheless confesses that Lewis' vigorous, courteous style often causes one to be most interested when he is least in agreement.

Some persons, it must be reported, have read Lewis without noticing the didactic content that others usually discover there. Lewis once observed in a letter that of sixty reviews of *Silent Planet* only two men-

---

[3] "Dialectic of Desire," p. 108.

[4] "The Imaginative Power of C. S. Lewis," *Saturday Review of Literature*, XXVII (April 8, 1944), 1, 9.

tioned the idea of "the Bent One" as anything other than the author's own invention. He concluded, "Any amount of theology can now be smuggled into people's minds under cover of romance without their knowing it." Clyde Kilby noted that one critic even considered some of the Narnia stories "without Christian implications." And Robert J. Reilly speaks of a striking absence of theology in the science-fiction trilogy. Apparently, Reilly does not recognize as "theology" anything other than discussions about the nature of God or conspicuously elaborated dogmas. If, however, we allow that theology is implicit in an understanding of human nature, then these novels are packed with theological implications.

John D. Haigh, in his perceptive dissertation entitled "The Fiction of C. S. Lewis," concluded that the didactic content of Lewis' imaginative work is excessive. Said Haigh,

Though the best scenes in Lewis's fiction owe their imaginative power to the intensity of his religious vision, the sustained engagement in Christian apologetics is sometimes responsible for limitations and faults. The apologist has to assemble evidence, expound arguments, and give his faith a logical and systematic expression. What was implicit has to be made explicit. Intuitions become theories; personal convictions are publicly asserted; sentiments are more sharply defined. The area of legitimate doubt contracts. This leads to coherence and power, but threatens an accompanying loss of richness and spontaneity.

The novelist works in a different way. He entertains a variety of opinions, and works out the situations he has chosen, or that have imposed themselves on him, with a passionate but detached curiosity. He has an insatiable thirst for what exists, and a comparative unconcern for what ought to exist. He is often impelled to pose a problem, but rarely constrained to provide a solution. Like Keats's "chameleon poet" he has the gift of 'negative capability'—'that is, when a man is capable of being in uncertainties, mysteries, doubts, without any irritable reaching after fact and reason.' [5]

There are, then, different evaluations of the *logos* in Lewis. A few readers are oblivious to the ideological content. Many others are aware of Lewis' ideas but do not find that they overshadow the *poiema*, the dominant interest of a work of art. Still others, like Haigh, feel that the *logos* in Lewis tends to interfere with his success as a creator of *poiema*. The critics are not agreed on the matter. Perhaps each reader must form his own judgment on whether the *logos* in Lewis enriches the *poiema* by introducing valuable elements of complexity and coherence, or damages the *poiema* by introducing distracting and alien material into art.

[5] P. 375.

Lewis was particularly interested in the literary forms of allegory and myth. His first major literary study was *The Allegory of Love: A Study in Medieval Tradition*. Many of his imaginative works contain allegorical elements, although such works as the science-fiction trilogy, the Narnia chronicles, and *Faces* are best understood as myths rather than as allegories. Familiarity with the distinction which Lewis maintains between allegory and myth is helpful for an understanding of his imaginative work.

An allegory, for Lewis, was a composition "in which immaterial realities are represented by feigned physical objects," as Cupid represents erotic love or as Bunyan's giant represents Despair. Allegory generally provides a one-to-one relationship between a particular fictional character and a particular abstract entity. Lewis noted in *Allegory* that allegory is more than a mere device, a figure of rhetoric, or a fashion. As men turned their gaze inward at a certain stage in history, they found "contending forces" which could not be described apart from allegory. Allegorical form does not mean that the author is talking about nonentities. He is talking, rather, about the inner world—about those very realities he knows best. Men can hardly speak or think of inner conflict without resorting to metaphors; and "every metaphor is an allegory in little." An allegory should be read as a continued simile. Allegory should never be a chilling, irrelevant addition to a story. Its function is not to hide but to reveal, and "it is properly used only for that which cannot be said, or so well said, in literal speech."

There are two ways, continued Lewis, in which the mind can develop a fundamental equivalence between the material and the immaterial. When one begins with immaterial fact—experienced passions, for example—and invents *visibilia* to express them, he is making use of *allegory*. It is possible to reverse this process, however, and to view the material world as itself a copy of an invisible world. When one attempts to read something else through the sensible—to discover archetype in the copy—he is engaged in *symbolism* or *sacramentalism*. The allegorist leaves behind the given (his passions) to talk about the less real. The symbolist leaves behind the given to find what is more real. Medieval allegorists were aware that they were inventing fictions. But Greek symbolism, as it is found in Plato's dialogues, is different. "Symbolism," said Lewis, "is a mode of thought, but allegory is a mode of expression."

It is the nature of language to represent what is immaterial in pictures. That which is good or happy has always been pictured as "high like the heavens" or "bright like the sun." Since ancient times, evil and misery have been considered "deep" or "dark." Certain "married pairs of sensibles and insensibles" have been linked for many centuries in human thought, Lewis wrote in *Allegory*.

In a fascinating discussion in the same book, Lewis described the gradual allegorization of the Greek pantheon for literary purposes. With the ever-deepening twilight of the gods, allegory arose from the ruins of former mythology. The gods were "disinfected of belief," and the world of "the marvellous" came to light in human imagination. A "third world" slipped into European consciousness under the pretext of allegory. It was not a world of religion, but of imagination—"the land of longing, the Earthly Paradise, the garden east of the sun and west of the moon." This stage in literature represented a change of religious belief. The gods were not for European literature what they had once been for the pagans. Lewis noted,

We are apt to take it for granted that a poet has at his command, besides the actual world and the world of his own religion, a third world of myth and fancy. The probable, the marvellous-taken-as-fact, the marvellous-known-to-be-fiction—such is the triple equipment of the post-Renaissance poet. (P. 82)

When we turn to the imagery of myth we find it to be more complex than the imagery of allegory. While a single meaning is placed in allegorical representation, myth is a higher genre. Mythical symbols take on new life and represent principles (not otherwise accessible) uniting whole classes of concepts. A myth is a story from which ever-varying meanings grow for different readers and different generations. Myth is invaded by meanings of which the author himself may not be aware. When allegory is at its best it approaches the genre of myth. But myth is grasped, not with the intellect, but with the imagination.

Lewis elaborated in *Criticism* upon the special sense in which he used *myth*. He did not include under that term all the stories which anthropologists might lump there. A great myth, he maintained, is essentially an "extra-literary" story, even though it has been embodied in several particular literary expressions. The pleasure which myth gives depends little upon suspense or surprise. It is felt to be inevitable from the beginning. Sympathy for individual mythical characters is minimal; we sense, rather, the relevance of the story for ourselves and for all men. Myth is "fantastic" in that it deals with impossibles and preternaturals. It is always grave and awe-inspiring—an experience of the numinous.

Lewis made it clear in *Criticism* that his discussion concerns those myths of which men are conscious—"myths contemplated but not believed, dissociated from ritual, held up before the fully waking imagination of a logical mind." Since he defined myths in terms of their effect, he recognized that a given story may be a myth for one person and not for another. Those who have the capacity to appreciate myth, he believed, belong to a subcategory of those who appreciate literature in general. He thought, at least, he had never met an unliterary person who had any taste for myth.

In terms of Lewis' understanding of allegory and myth, he made some scattered comments that apply to his own imaginative works. He repeated often his conviction that the wit of man cannot devise a story in which the wit of someone else cannot find an allegory. But he insisted that "the fact that you *can* allegorize the work before you is of itself no proof that it is an allegory."

Lewis did not consider his great lion of Narnia an allegorical figure. Aslan, rather, is "an invention giving an imaginary answer to the question, 'What might Christ become like, if there were a world like Narnia and He chose to be incarnate and die and rise again in *that* world as He actually has done in ours?'" Nor is Ransom in the science-fiction trilogy simply an allegorical representation of Christ. He plays the role of Christ to some extent because "in reality every Christian is really called upon in some measure to *enact* Christ." Lewis did acknowledge, however, that Ransom follows the pattern of Christ more spectacularly than do most people.

An author may not understand the meaning of his own story any better than anyone else, admitted Lewis. This is especially true regarding the genre of myth. Lewis once offered his own interpretation of *Till We Have Faces* "simply for what it is worth," writing about those levels of which he himself was conscious. Since a book's meaning involves the emotions, reflections, and attitudes which it produces in the reader, its meaning differs with different readers. The author is not necessarily the best judge of a book's meaning. Even if he intended it to have a particular meaning, he cannot be certain that it does have, or that other meanings are not also possible. An author but rearranges the elements of language which God has provided, Lewis said. As an author recombines elements made by God and containing His meanings, it is impossible for him to know the full meaning of his own work. A meaning which he did not intend may indeed be the best and truest meaning.

The type of imaginative literature which especially appealed to Lewis was what is generally called *fantasy*. His own novels might well be described in words he once applied to George Macdonald's works—"fantasy that hovers between the allegorical and the mythopoetic." Rudolf

B. Schmerl, in a dissertation which contains a section on Lewis' fiction, defines *fantasy* as follows:

Fantasy is the deliberate presentation of improbabilities through any one of four methods—the use of unverifiable time, place, characters, or devices—to a typical reader within a culture whose level of sophistication will enable that reader to recognize the improbabilities.[6]

Some persons are attracted to literature which has a strong emphasis upon improbability, impossibility, or supernatural creatures; but other readers in this rather realistic age definitely are not. John Haigh feels that this preoccupation of Lewis limited his popularity and effectiveness. Haigh wrote,

The susceptibilities of readers sharing the liberal humanistic ideals exemplified in the fiction of E. M. Forster and Virginia Woolf are as violently offended by the unabashed supernaturalism of Lewis's fiction as were Tennyson's readers by Swift's picture of human bestiality in the Yahoos.[7]

Edmund Fuller, on the other hand, is quite appreciative of this direction in Lewis. The poets and mythmakers have always known, Fuller said, that fantasy and symbol are the closest approaches to elusive reality that man can make. Lewis presents what is essentially the reality structure proclaimed by Christianity. To the Christian, it is viewed as truth; to the non-Christian, it can be seen as a tale. In any case, the overall reality of life transcends the immediate impressions which the five senses present as "real"; on this much both the modern physicist and the mystic agree. Speaking of fantasy in general, Fuller wrote,

Fantasy has high entertainment value and has been much practiced for that legitimate end alone. Yet across the range of time and type of story, the so-called fantastic has also served to illuminate our understanding of the so-called real. . . . The integrity and courage of an imaginary being in his world may sustain us to integrity and courage in the face of a mundane and pressing dilemma in our own living.[8]

No one ever sees reality as such, said Fuller, but only a small segment of total reality. Fantasy explores the mysteries, the intangibles, and the enigmas of man's deepest questions, and thus in its own way fantasy reveals certain dimensions and truths about human nature.

---

[6] "Reason's Dream: Anti-Totalitarian Themes and Techniques of Fantasy" (Ph.D. diss., University of Michigan, 1960), p. 2.

[7] "Fiction of Lewis," p. 381.

[8] *Books with Men Behind Them* (New York: Random House, 1962), p. 136.

In his chapters on fantasy and realism in *Criticism*, Lewis stressed that literary fantasy should not be confused with psychological fantasy. The former represents neither delusion (imaginative constructions mistaken for reality) nor morbid castle-building (incapacitating daydreams). It should even be distinguished from the kind of normal castle-building motivated by egoistic considerations. Fantastic castle-building leads to fiction in which literary invention exists for its own sake; the dreamer may not even be present in his own daydream. But the egoistic castle-building, said Lewis, demands superficial realism and does not like genuine fantasy. "Disinterested castle-building may dream of nectar and ambrosia, of fairy bread and honey dew; the egoistic sort dreams of bacon and eggs or steak."

There is a sense in which all reading involves "escape," said Lewis, as attention is transferred from actual surroundings to things imagined. Even fiction about "the present crisis" carries the reader away from the unpaid bills and unanswered letters stacked before him on the desk. Escape does not appear to be harmful, said Lewis, unless it becomes a substitute for more appropriate action. Most of the great literature which the world has thus far produced, he noted, has not been "realistic" in its content.

In reviewing *Criticism*, David Daiches felt that Lewis' defense of non-realistic fiction was exaggerated. "The fact is," wrote Daiches, "that never more than now have serious critics of fiction relished certain kinds of fantasy, symbolic landscapes and other non-realistic aspects of the novel." But John Haigh registers a contrary point of view. He concludes that Lewis' eagerness to use forms of fantasy and mythology in an anti-metaphysical age has not enhanced his reputation among critics.

Even in the early *Spirits in Bondage*, written while he was still an atheist, Lewis promised to sing of the Hidden Country that none had seen. In *Sixteenth Century* he reported that writers influenced by Neo-Platonism have not felt that it was escapist to create fiction about what might be or what ought to be. In considering such topics these authors were but asserting man's divine origin. Lewis once made the following comment about realistic literature in a letter:

One can hardly say anything either bad enough or good enough about life. The one picture that is utterly false is the supposed realistic fiction of the XIX century where all the real horrors and heavens are excluded. The reality is a queer mixture of idyll, tragedy, farce, melodrama: and the characters (even the same character) far better *and* worse than are ever imagined. (*Letters*, p. 267)

An important key for understanding Lewis' concept of imaginative literature is found in his essay "On Stories." One of the functions of literature, he maintains here, is "to present what the narrow and desperately practical perspectives of real life exclude." [9] A story, of course, may be a means to something else—an opportunity for delineating character or for making social criticism. But there is also a kind of story in which everything else is present for the sake of the imagined events. Books like *Jack the Giant-Killer* or H. G. Wells's *First Men in the Moon* present some permanent aspect of human experience as an intuition.

The plot of a story may be essentially "a net whereby to catch something else," perhaps a quality of giantness, otherness, or desolation in space. In both art and life we try "to catch in our net of successive moments something that is not successive," said Lewis—some sense of the eternal surprise and mystery of our human condition. It appears that Lewis was concerned primarily to evoke just such an "idea of otherness" or "dimension of the spirit" in his science-fiction trilogy and his Narnia tales. David Lindsay, he said, was the first writer to discover the real value of distant planets for fiction.

No merely physical strangeness or merely spatial distance will realize that idea of otherness which is what we are always trying to grasp in a story about voyaging through space: you must go into another dimension. To construct plausible and moving "other worlds" you must draw on the only real "other world" we know, that of the spirit. (*Other Worlds*, p. 12)

When men travel to the moon, the actual journey will fail to satisfy the impulse men now attempt to gratify in space stories, Lewis believed. "The real Moon, if you could reach it and survive, would in a deep and deadly sense be just like anywhere else."

It is not so much that Lewis attempted novelistic character development and failed, as that he lacked the usual modern interest in character delineation. His interest in fiction concentrated elsewhere. He was more concerned to evoke a sense of the numinous than he was to delineate character. He was more concerned with Everyman than he was with any particular man. Some types of fiction, he maintained, ought *not* to display deep and sensitive characterization. He wrote concerning science-fiction, for example,

Every good writer knows that the more unusual the scenes and events of his story are, the slighter, the more ordinary, the more typical his persons should be. Hence Gulliver is a commonplace little man and Alice a commonplace little

<hr>

[9] *Other Worlds*, p. 10.

girl. If they had been more remarkable they would have wrecked their books. The Ancient Mariner himself is a very ordinary man. To tell how odd things struck odd people is to have an oddity too much: he who is to see strange sights must not himself be strange. He ought to be as nearly as possible Everyman or Anyman. (*Other Worlds*, pp. 64-65)

Lewis found even *Hamlet* less a play about the motives of a prince than a drama about the mystery of life itself. The true hero of *Hamlet*, he said, is "haunted man"—

man with his mind on the frontier of two worlds . . . unable either quite to reject or quite to admit the supernatural . . . struggling to get something done . . . yet incapable of achievement because of his inability to understand either himself or his fellows or the real quality of the universe which has produced him. (*They Asked for a Paper*, pp. 68-69)

The great mystery in *Hamlet*, according to Lewis, is that same darkness which enwraps all human beings. The play succeeds because it evokes the sense of surprise and mystery which is a permanent aspect of human life.

Edmund Fuller speaks of Lewis' science fiction as "Christian theology projected beyond Earth and man, a theology of the universe in the dawn of the space age." While there is a measure of truth in this, the statement may also be slightly misleading. Lewis would not deny the possibility that other inhabited worlds somewhere in the universe may be as important to the Creator as is the planet earth. But that possibility was by no means the main concern of his imaginary journeys in space. Lewis' chief interest was not in Mars and Venus but in the present inhabitants of Earth. He introduced the interplanetary framework not as scientific speculation but as imaginative mythology. Martin J. Heinecken, in his *God in the Space Age*, takes space-age theology more seriously than did Lewis. For Lewis, as for Paul Tillich, space-age theology was a theoretical possibility, but actually a rather remote concern. When the World Student Christian Federation published in 1966 a selected bibliography of a dozen books relating theology and space, *Student World* demonstrated a more practical interest in space-age theology than ever Lewis did.[10]

For Lewis, the physical "heavens" had little to do with that heaven which is the object of man's spiritual quest. Travel in space may shift the locale of man's activity without bringing him a step nearer his true

---

[10] "Faith in the Space Age," special issue, LIX (Fourth Quarter, 1966), 345-440.

destiny. As Lewis said in a poem about science fiction, "Heaven has given us the slip."

> Stars and sky, sky and stars
> Make us feel the prison bars. . . .
>   Where we are
> Never can be sky or star.
> From prison, in a prison, we fly;
> There's no way into the sky.

In another poem Lewis registers a protest against science-fiction writers who lure readers through the abyss of light years with talk of crooks and spies and "the same old stuff we left behind." A more appropriate theme for science fiction is the unearthly, with all its suggestions of strange beauty and wonder. Lewis mentions two books which first stimulated his interest in writing science fiction—*Last and First Men* by Olaf Stapledon and *Possible Worlds* by J. B. S. Haldane. Both of these writers, Lewis thought, took the idea of space travel seriously but offered no moral perspective upon the enterprise. He noted in "On Science Fiction" that he is not concerned with "the fiction of engineers." His special kind of story requires only the most superficial appearance of plausibility in pseudoscientific apparatus. Lewis admitted that his literary purpose demands just enough popular astronomy to create a "willing suspension of disbelief" in the ordinary reader. He acknowledged a considerable amount of scientific falsehood in his stories—some of it, he said, "known to be false even by me when I wrote the books."

In his Swiftian voyages to distant places Lewis managed to provide settings against which human conditions assume sharper perspective. Mythical counterparts of Christian theology are found scattered throughout the science-fiction trilogy. Fuller called these fantastic novels Lewis' "finest apologetics" and said that they disclose as rich a gift for sheer imaginative writing as our literalistic age can boast. "Once again," added Fuller, "the artist and the spinner of tales proves the best persuader." John Lawlor noted that these other planets were sufficiently distant from actuality to provide Lewis with ample room for his sustained imagination. Lewis himself claimed that his special kind of "scientifiction" represents man's ancient imaginative impulse laboring under the special conditions of the twentieth century. With the spread of geographical knowledge the dark forests and distant isles of earth have lost whatever haunting quality they formerly possessed. It becomes necessary to travel farther to explore imaginary regions of strange beauty and awe.

Mythological beings such as dragons and gods, giants and paradises, are for Lewis symbols for qualities present in our own world. From his early poetry to his late novel *Faces*, Lewis used the Pagan deities as spiritual symbols. These beings and creatures were for him "words of a language which speaks the else unspeakable." He said, "Nature has that in her which compels us to invent giants: and only giants will do." In his poem "Impenitence," Lewis observed that the beasts "all cry out to be used as symbols / Masks for Man, cartoons, parodies by Nature / Formed to reveal us" to each other in gentle laughter.

In his imaginary land of Narnia, as well as on distant planets, Lewis discovered another world of adventure and invention against which ordinary human life can be seen in sharper perspective. Clyde Kilby suggested that two purposes guided Lewis in writing of the Narnia tales. He wanted, first of all, to tell a good story. But he also wanted to suggest analogies (not allegories) of Christian theology. Lewis said that he wrote these "children's stories" or fantasies because this particular art form commended itself to him as the best for something he wanted to say. Although he had a young audience in mind as he wrote, Lewis emphasized (as Tolkien demonstrates in his essay "On Fairy-Stories") that "in most places and times, the fairy tale has not been specially made for, nor exclusively enjoyed by, children." Giants, dwarfs, and talking beasts were for Lewis "an admirable hieroglyphic" to convey psychology and character types to a wider audience than lengthy novels will reach. "I am almost inclined to set it up as a canon," he said, "that a children's story which is enjoyed only by children is a bad children's story. The good ones last." The reader of the Narnia tales—whether child or adult—will enjoy enchanting adventure, and indirectly he will receive insight on the Christian understanding of the nature and destiny of man.

Near the end of the nineteenth century, Andrew Lang wrote about the relationship between fairy tales and reality. C. S. Lewis would undoubtedly agree with these words of Lang:

In the old stories, despite the impossibility of the incidents, the interest is always real and human. . . . The hero and heroine are persecuted or separated by cruel stepmothers or enchanters; they have adventures to achieve and difficulties to overcome. They must display courage, loyalty and address, courtesy, gentleness and gratitude. Thus they are living in a real human world, though it wears a mythical face, though there are giants and lions in the way. The old fairy-tales . . . unobtrusively teach the true lessons of our wayfaring in a world of perplexities and obstructions.[11]

[11] "Modern Fairy Stories," quoted in Green, *C. S. Lewis* (London: The Bodley Head, 1963), p. 52.

Do dramatic stories of giants and witches frighten the young? Lewis stated that he certainly did not want to contribute to any haunting, pathological fears or phobias in children. But, he continued, it would give children a false impression and it would be ill-conceived escapism to keep from them the fact that they are "born into a world of death, violence, wounds, adventure, heroism and cowardice, good and evil."

> Since it is so likely that they will meet cruel enemies, let them at least have heard of brave knights and heroic courage. . . . Let there be wicked kings and beheadings, battles and dungeons, giants and dragons, and let villains be soundly killed at the end of the book. Nothing will persuade me that this causes an ordinary child any kind or degree of fear beyond what it wants, and needs, to feel.[12]

Edmund Fuller notes (correctly, I believe) that nothing in the Narnia chronicles "matches for audacity of conception and boldness of invention the analogue of the crucifixion and resurrection." Aslan, the great golden lion, surrenders himself to a cruel death, then rises again to life. Lewis wrote concerning this chapter in *Lion*, "The reason why the Passion of Aslan sometimes moves people more than the real story in the Gospels is, I think, that it takes them off their guard. In reading the real story the fatal knowledge that one *ought* to feel a certain way often inhibits the feeling."

Stella Gibbons mentioned the considerable shock that came to her while she was reading *The Last Battle* and began to realize that the pronouns which referred to Aslan were all capitalized. Most modern Christians, she ventured, tend to see Christ as pictured—static and in the past. Lewis attempts to overthrow this static conception. At the close of *The Voyage of the Dawn Treader*, Aslan informs Lucy and Edmund that they are growing too old for Narnia and can never return to that land. In the future, Aslan promises, they will meet him in their own world. "Are you there too, Sir?" Edmund inquires. "I am," says Aslan. "But there I have another name. You must learn to know me by that name. This was the very reason why you were brought to Narnia, that by knowing me here for a little, you may know me better there."

Since Lewis virtually ignored the kind of character development which is a dominant interest of modern literature, a number of critics have found his work perplexing. For example, Stella Gibbons confesses that she finds *Faces* a puzzling book. She thinks that Lewis must have had clear in his own mind what his allegories and symbols meant, even

[12] *Ibid.*, p. 54.

though they are not clear to the reader. An understanding of Lewis' theory of literature is a real asset for interpreting such work as this. For one thing, the work is not an allegory at all, but a myth—as the subtitle itself proclaims. The *New York Times Book Review* captured the essence of this work in reporting that *Faces* "exerts far beyond most novels that combination of awefulness, wonder and attraction which is what the word 'fascination' in its Latin form, really means." Even the word *fascination* used in this review recalls Rudolf Otto's discussion of the numinous and the idea of holiness. One of the most adequate interpretations available on *Faces* is to be found in Robert Reilly's dissertation, although I myself question whether Lewis is as much concerned with the psychology of primitive man as Reilly seems to think[18] In this myth *retold,* I find dominant twentieth-century implications in the universal themes of love and hate, faith and doubt.

Charles Moorman finds Ransom of *Perelandra* a warm and sympathetic figure and thinks that the characterization demonstrates Lewis' increasing knowledge of the technique of fiction. This is a dubious conclusion. As has been indicated earlier in this chapter, Lewis was not especially interested in character development in fantastic literature and would even have considered such characterization a structural flaw. Furthermore, in the third novel of the trilogy, Ransom becomes a less personal figure than he was even in the first novel of the series. If Lewis' knowledge of fiction technique developed during the writing of the trilogy, it might be argued that he learned how to avoid sharp characterizations.

Many modern critics are certain to object to Lewis' treatment of character in fiction. So sensitive and informed a critic as John Haigh said that Lewis' practice of viewing character from the outside, from the position of a near-omniscient arbitrator, "often precludes the fullest kind of engagement with human weakness and sin." Haigh also protested Lewis' treatment of the infernal on the grounds that "what is absent from the Apostles' Creed and peripheral in the New Testament is made central. A dimly apprehended mystery, figuratively expressed, becomes literal and concrete." If this objection is valid, it must be extended to apply not only to the representations of hell in *Screwtape* and *Divorce* but also to paradise pictured in the science-fiction novels and in the Narnia chronicles. Haigh concluded that these theological images prove disturbing and misleading to the pious nonintellectual, and that *Screwtape* is for the sophisticated believer, not for the simple-minded seeker.

It is true, as Lewis himself declared, that "some people just don't

<hr>

[18] See "Romantic Religion," pp. 103-22.

understand what fiction is!" It is an aid to understanding his work to have a knowledge of both Lewis' theory of religious mythology and his theory of fantastic literature. His meaning is not obscure. Nor do his interpretations of theology and literature differ greatly from the views generally held in the scholarly world. The meaning of Lewis' work is quite clear when sufficient attention has been given to his prefaces and his critical works as well as to his theological and imaginative works. It is helpful to consider Lewis' works as a whole since the various types of literature so closely supplement each other. A knowledge of the interrelationships between the books enriches the reader's understanding of Lewis' views.

Chad Walsh summarized Lewis' dominant literary interest in a 1967 article in *Good Work,* a quarterly of the Catholic Art Association. Walsh wrote,

God's universe is a more interesting object of study and field of action than the individual's psyche. . . . Quite possibly, at some time that no one can predict, the Ego-probing and Id-probing of our times will lose its fascination, and men will suddenly see an interesting world outside themselves, a world with which they can enter into significant relations. . . . If this happens, Lewis may serve as a spiritual mentor for many of them. He is the specialized guide through a world that he did not create, the world that is simply *there* because God put it there.[14]

[14] "The Elusively Solid C. S. Lewis," XXX (Winter 1967), 24.

IV

A Critique of Some Lewis Critics

Concerning careful reading and literary criticism:

A great many people start by thinking they know what you will say, and honestly believe they have read what they expected to read. But for whatever reason, it is certainly the case that if you are often reviewed you will find yourself repeatedly blamed and praised for saying what you never said and for not saying what you have said.

—"On Criticism," *Other Worlds,* p. 47.

In his essay "On Criticism" Lewis expressed amazement over the portion of book reviews based upon hasty and careless reading. Quite aside from the matter of evaluation, he said, it is not unusual for reviews to contain direct falsehoods about what a given book does or does not contain. Like other popular authors, Lewis received a large amount of inept criticism. Some of the more perceptive criticism is discussed elsewhere in these pages. But it will be helpful here to single out for special attention some of the patterns of misinterpretation which have plagued Lewis. Certain unsound ideas about his work have been quoted repeatedly, believed, and passed on in literary tradition without having been sufficiently criticized.

It is my purpose in this chapter to examine briefly some of the most persistent misunderstandings of Lewis' work. Occasionally it will be obvious that a critic's conclusion is based upon a very cursory acquaintance with the Lewis corpus. At other times the root of the problem lies in a failure to understand the nature of theological language. Or the problem may be traced to a lack of appreciation for the nature of imaginative literature. Particular critics are cited here only by way of illustration. It is not my intention to depreciate the whole work of these critics, or even to suggest that they represent the most flagrant examples of misinterpretation. If, however, views such as those presented in this chapter are found in the published work of thoughtful critics, it can be assumed that similar problems and questions arise for the general reader who attempts to understand Lewis' work.

When I first learned of a book published in England under the title of *C. S. Lewis and Some Modern Theologians*, I wondered whether the area proposed for my research had already been treated in print. I came to discover, however, that only seven pages of this rather pretentious-sounding volume are devoted to Lewis. The whole discussion on Lewis, in fact, centers upon three quotations from a single book (*Problem of Pain*). The author Ernest George Lee claims that Lewis attempts to convince his readers through shock tactics rather than through reason. "Mr. Lewis is ready to throw over reason altogether, and thus deny one of the basic realities of modern experience," Lee concludes. This generalization is based upon an inadequate exposure to the writings of C. S. Lewis; the more common objection against Lewis is that he is overly rationalistic.

Mr Lee, writing as a Unitarian, is particularly troubled by Lewis' claim that Jesus is the "Son of God." "Whatever else Jesus was," Lee writes,

he was a good man, and if he claimed to be the Son of God, there are plenty of other explanations for the claim, without turning him into a bad or diseased man, and without damaging in the least his supreme goodness.[1]

It is not my desire at this point to enter into the complex theological issues involved in Christology. The view held by Lewis, however, is not an unusual interpretation of Jesus, even in contemporary Christendom; and the case for Jesus' divinity is stronger than Mr. Lee admits. For a more thorough discussion of the issues raised by Lee, the interested reader may turn to such books as Donald Baillie's *God Was in Christ*, Archibald Hunter's *The Unity of the New Testament,* or the brief and popular *The Meaning of Christ* by Robert Clyde Johnson. Although Lee's book has probably given some readers a negative impression of Lewis' work, it is unlikely that any scholar will defend this brief discussion as an adequate survey of Lewis' thought.

Two other critics who thoroughly misrepresent Lewis are Alistair

[1] Ernest George Lee, *C. S. Lewis and Some Modern Theologians* (London: Lindsey Press, 1944), p. 13.

Cooke and Kathleen Nott. In a lengthy *New Republic* review that bristles with hostility Mr. Cooke speaks of the alarming vogue of Lewis and concludes, "in doubting times completely unremarkable minor prophets are pressed into making a career of reassurance." Lewis' works are so far removed from encouraging peace of mind that, to my knowledge, this charge has never been made by any other critic. Lewis states frankly in *Pain* that not much snug, settled happiness is to be found anywhere on earth. Furthermore, when Cooke speaks of Ransom's relationship with the naked Green Lady as a Puritan exaltation of sexlessness, he demonstrates again how thoroughly he has missed the point of the novel *Perelandra*. Lewis' attitude toward sex is discussed in many places, and it is not at all what Cooke assumes it to be. It is regrettable that Cooke could not have read, for example, "Psycho-Analysis and Literary Criticism" [2] before drawing his conclusions. Edgar Boss is right when he states that is it doubtful that Cooke understands Lewis at all.[3]

Kathleen Nott's book *The Emperor's Clothes* is an attack on the theology of T. S. Eliot, Graham Greene, Dorothy Sayers, C. S. Lewis, and others. She castigates Lewis for being preoccupied with hell and for failing to stress the joys of salvation. I must concur with the judgment of Clyde Kilby that "such a preposterous claim leaves open no possibility but that Miss Nott has failed to read Lewis." Perhaps Lewis had in mind this kind of person when he spoke of the "theophobia" of contemporary men. Some scholars appreciated Lewis' contributions to literary criticism, but felt that he should not have ventured from his professional field. One suspects that there is considerable truth in the statement about Lewis made by Sydney J. Harris that "while real criticism can be made of his position, what inspires the wrath of most of his critics is very simple, if very rare: he is a convinced Christian who knows how to write."

One of the common misunderstandings of Lewis is based upon the assumption that his imaginative works are primarily allegorical. In Chapter 3 we examined Lewis' distinctions between allegory and myth and found that the category of allegory is inadequate to explain most of his work. With few exceptions Lewis does not provide the kind of one-to-one relationship between fictional figures and abstract entities which is characteristic of allegory. Lewis mused in *Psalms* that some of the allegories imposed on his books were so ingenious and interesting that he was sorry not to have thought of them himself. Some interpreta-

---

[2] *Paper*, pp. 120-38.
[3] "The Theology of C. S. Lewis," (Th.D. diss., Northern Baptist Theological Seminary, 1948).

tions were less fortunate. Stella Gibbons thinks that Mrs. Beaver in *Lion* "stands for" the practical, sensible woman that Lewis himself approved. It is doubtful that Lewis was representing anything so specific in this kindly, fussy little creature who insisted on taking her sewing machine with her as she fled through the forest from the witch's wolves. The attempt to discover allegorical meanings often ends in strained interpretations quite distant from the mind of the author. Dorothy L. Sayers once found it necessary to point out to a *Spectator* reviewer that the lion Aslan did not, for Lewis, represent an archangel. Nor is Aslan simply Lewis' allegorical image of Christ, as Martha Hook indicated in her thesis "Christian Meaning in the Novels of C. S. Lewis." Lewis considered Aslan an imaginary invention of what an incarnation might be like in that particular imaginary world.

Martha Hook called the Narnia tales "mediums for an allegorical study of the world in relation to biblical principles." She documented a large number of parallels between biblical events and Narnia adventures. It is certain that biblical images suffused the thought of Lewis as he wrote of this imaginary land, its creation and destiny, its struggles and battles. However, there is so very much more to these stories than biblical parallels. Even if there is some resemblance between the high cliff in *Silver Chair* and Mount Sinai, between Jill's signs and the signs of Deuteronomy 6, how are the *major* characters and events to find meaningful allegorical interpretation? Some scriptural parallels undeniably exist. But it is a heavy-handed misuse of biblical categories if the reader is led to neglect the delightful character of Puddleglum, the marsh-wiggle, or to slight the major adventure—the search for a lost prince. To hold that these stories are essentially allegorical represents a flat rejection of Lewis' own insistence that the material is not allegorical. If it is maintained that the Narnia tales are allegorical in spite of the author's claim, then what do the figures of the Parvensie children "stand for" literally? Can material be allegorical if the leading characters have no allegorical significance? It appears that Miss Hook has not adequately considered myth, or "supposal" as Lewis sometimes called it, as an alternate category for interpreting the Narnia stories.

Miss Hook also considered *Faces* an "allegorical explanation of Christian conversion." The work may be interpreted, she said, as "an allegorical account of a rational man's search for God." The great difficulty of this particular allegory, she said, is due to the fact that "Lewis is more of a true novelist in this work than in his previous fiction." But Lewis maintained that the purpose of allegory is to clarify, not to obscure. Miss Hook likewise applied allegorical interpretation to the science-fiction trilogy. She saw Weston simply as "the personification of evil," despite the fact that the Oyarsa of Malacandra noted Weston's loyalty to humanity and declared him more "bent" than broken. For Miss Hook, it seems, any person or event which suggests an extended meaning is "allegorical." She mentioned no other category of literary interpretation. The reader's appreciation of Lewis' work will likely be increased, however, if he allows for a rich variety of genre, with methods of interpretation that are appropriate to each.

Another common misunderstanding of Lewis is based upon an exaggeration of his apologetic motives. Clyde Kilby and Richard Cunningham have both written significant books on C. S. Lewis. But both of these scholars quote Lewis as saying, quite meaningfully, "Most of my books are evangelistic." Taken out of context, however, this remark by Lewis can be misleading. Specifically, it arose in a dispute between Norman W. Pittenger and Lewis over the depth and merit of three or four of Lewis' theological works.[4] It was Lewis' intention, I think, to indicate that the books under consideration were addressed to ordinary laymen and nonchurchmen, not professional theologians. In light of what he says elsewhere, I cannot believe that Lewis would want this casual remark taken as a comprehensive statement applying to all his published work, including his fiction and his literary criticism. To insist upon anything more, it would be necessary to conclude that Lewis' literary practice was inconsistent with his own literary theory (discussed in Chapter 2).

Cunningham suggests that in a broad view of the nature and purpose of apologetics, even Lewis' scholarly writings have apologetic value, though they have no direct apologetic purpose. In my opinion, several of Lewis' books have so little to do with a defense of the Christian faith that it is a disservice to both the author and to his scholarly publications to suggest that such a motive always figures prominently in his writing. I think Lewis would be quite uncomfortable with Cunningham's remark that "the best hope of reaching many modern unbelievers is not in the obvious knock of the Christian salesman at the front door, but in the subtle, covert knock at the rear."[5] This statement borders on accusing Lewis of deception and duplicity. It is wholly out of character with

[4] Pittenger, "Apologist versus Apologist: A Critique of C. S. Lewis as 'Defender of the Faith,'" *Christian Century*, LXXV (October 1, 1958), 1104-7; Lewis, "Rejoinder to Dr. Pittenger," *Christian Century*, LXXV (November 26, 1958), 1359-61.

[5] *C. S. Lewis: Defender of the Faith* (Philadelphia: Westminster Press, 1967), p. 204.

the open, honest, courageous approach for which Lewis is noted. The charge, I think, stems from an exaggerated notion of Lewis' didactic or apologetic intent.

Edgar Boss gave a similar interpretation of Lewis in his ambitious, though flawed, 1948 dissertation on Lewis' theology. Boss saw Lewis' imaginative works as "indirect apologies" for Christianity. He neglected to draw any distinction between fiction and nonfiction sources as he documented Lewis' beliefs. Without elaboration he assumed that Ransom's statements always represented Lewis' convictions. Unfortunately, this indiscriminate use of sources mars the attempt to outline Lewis' theology.

Despite Lewis' warning against undue interest in angels, Boss devoted a ten-page chapter to a discussion of Lewis' "angelology." This is highly unsatisfactory. Lewis said little about angels in his prose works. Nearly all of Boss's references in his third chapter are to Lewis' imaginative works, especially to the science fiction. It may or may not be that Lewis thought of angels as something like his *eldils* of Malacandra. But a direct parallel cannot be established between this imaginative world and the real world. Lewis populated his world of Narnia with fauns and fairies, nymphs and satyrs. But it would be inappropriate to document the author's actual beliefs about *longaevi* (long-livers) according to what these creatures do and say in his imaginative literature.

Boss is at his weakest when he claims that Lewis teaches about God's power "by indirection." Since Lewis had the devil do certain things in *Perelandra*—and since God is a greater supernatural being than the devil— (said Boss) we may therefore draw certain conclusions about Lewis' doctrine of God. Not only does this kind of reasoning ignore the fact that *Perelandra* is an imaginative story, but it even ignores the fact that the character Ransom was enraged by the manipulation which the devil practiced (and of which—Boss assured us—God also is capable). This illustration should stand as a warning against any attempt to construct Lewis' "teachings" from his imaginative material. Boss should be credited as one of the first students to recognize Lewis' books as worthy of scholarly attention. But his work is limited in value because he lacked an understanding of the nature of literature.

Lewis was not the active, aggressive evangelist that some critics border upon suggesting. This is by no means to deny that his imaginative writings often echo and amplify ideas found in his religious prose writings. But there are also other leading motives involved. Furthermore, Lewis had some important reservations about apologetic, evangelistic activity. We noted earlier that he refused to permit his own religious

convictions to obtrude upon his tutorial duties or his social relationships. He once noted in a letter that "an importunate bit of evangelisa-
tion from a comparative stranger would *not* have done me any good
when I was an unbeliever." He wrote in another letter that with rare
exceptions, what we practice, rather than what we preach, is our contribution to the conversion of others. He mused in a letter to Dorothy
Sayers, "Apologetic work is so dangerous to one's own faith. A doctrine
never seems dimmer to me than when I have just successfully defended
it." A pastiche of John Donne expresses a similar reserve about the
significance of formal apologetics. Lewis writes in "The Apologist's Evening Prayer,"

> From all my lame defeats and oh! much more
> From all the victories that I seemed to score;
> From cleverness shot forth on Thy behalf
> At which, while angels weep, the audience laugh;
> From all my proofs of Thy divinity,
> Thou, who wouldst give no sign, deliver me.

Patricia Spacks said that Lewis' attempt to make science fiction an
instrument of theology and social comment ends in failure. She thought
that his religion was escapist, and that his didactic intent diminished
the power of his mythmaking. Other critics appear to appreciate Lewis
primarily because of his assumed apologetic nature. But if Lewis is correct
in his literary theory, creative literature should neither be rejected nor
endorsed upon the basis of the ideas it contains. Ideological content
has a subsidiary relationship to the work as a whole. Lewis' novels should
be evaluated primarily as works of art.

We turn now to another recurrent misunderstanding of Lewis' work.
Some readers will be surprised to hear that Lewis is considered by several
critics to be "antiscientific." Kathleen Nott, for example, charged that
Lewis discredits scientific thinking. Philip Deasy referred to Lewis' "total
and unrelenting attack on science." Rudolf Schmerl wrote concerning
Lewis' science fiction, "Although science is never explicitly attacked as
an instrument of the devil in any of the three books, it is linked with
the new phase of Satan's rebellion in such a way as to make inescapable
the conclusion that it is indeed the devil's tool."
Even within the works of science fiction themselves, there is ample
evidence to suggest that these critics are not wholly correct in their
judgment of Lewis' attitude. Schmerl referred to the character Ransom
in support of his argument, but we also read in *That Hideous Strength*

that the physical sciences are "good and innocent in themselves." Chad Walsh noted that while the fanciful agency N.I.C.E. operates under the prestige of science, remarkably little scientific research appears to be carried on there. In *Silent Planet,* Ransom has nothing but admiration for the brilliant scientific accomplishments of the sēroni. These creatures know how to use their advanced knowledge and skill, and they neither apply their science to immoral purposes nor construct a cult around it. Even Devine comes to respect the scientific achievement of Malacandra when he discovers that the creatures there can "split the atom or something pretty like it."

There is no more reason to assume that Lewis is against science when he develops Weston as a monomaniac physicist than to assume that he is opposed to law and order when he develops Fairy Hardcastle as a brutal, perverted policewoman. Every area of life is susceptible to corruption—including the religious area, as Lewis was particularly fond of pointing out. When Lewis criticized particular clergymen, he did not thereby become anti-Christian. Since it is highly unlikely at this stage in history that a celebrated university professor would oppose science *per se,* it would appear that this charge should have been well-documented when it was advanced. It has not been supported by evidence, nor can it be.

These particular critics have failed to recognize the ordinary scholarly distinction between science and scientism. They have mistaken a criticism of the potential misuse of science for an attack upon science itself. In these days following Dachau and Hiroshima, one might expect that every educated person would be familiar with the difference between pure scientific knowledge and the adulation of science and technology as part of a system which allows no criticism and which is subject to no moral direction. The distinction between science and scientism is widely recognized in the intellectual world. It is no invention of Lewis. Not only is it found in scores of philosophy textbooks, like D. Elton Trueblood's *Philosophy of Religion,* but it is also a major theme in popular books like *Science is a Sacred Cow* by physicist Anthony Standen and *The Organization Man* by William H. Whyte, Jr. In their confused reaction to a critique of scientism these particular critics have inadvertently illustrated the very danger against which Lewis sought to warn modern man.

It is true that Lewis refused to believe that new ideas are always better than old ideas. He felt that the modern "archetypal image" of the machine should not be applied indiscriminately to the realm of ideas. Every idea should be evaluated for its own merit, not accepted because of its newness. But such philosophical reservations about "progress" are not contrary to genuine scientific achievement. Lewis made this quite clear in a number of his books. He noted in *Abolition* that "nothing I can say will prevent some people from describing this lecture as an attack on science. I deny the charge, of course." He wrote in a letter that many who follow "scientific humanism" know little science, just as many who go to church know little theology. His appreciation of genuine science is reflected as well at several spots in the imaginative literature. Screwtape warns his subordinate not to attempt to use "the real sciences" as a defence against Christianity. Genuine science, he fears, will positively encourage men to think about unseen realities. Lewis was not as antiscientific as a few critics have concluded from a hasty reading of one or two of his books.

Another misunderstanding of Lewis' work centers around the idea that he is a theological fundamentalist. T. V. Smith placed Lewis in this category when he reviewed *Miracles* in the *Saturday Review of Literature.* Kathleen Nott repeatedly referred to Lewis as a fundamentalist in her book *The Emperor's Clothes,* although she failed to support her interpretation with any evidence. It appears that Miss Nott was not only ill informed about the Christian doctrine of the Fall (as she admits), but she lacked understanding of contemporary theology in general. This deficiency vitiates her understanding of Lewis and disqualifies her as an important interpreter of his work.

Edgar Boss, a theological conservative, acclaimed Lewis as a champion of fundamentalists, even though he charged that Lewis was overly receptive to evolutionism and to liberal trends in biblical criticism. Nevertheless, said Boss, Lewis has presented supernaturalism to a wide audience, and he deserves the praise of fundamentalists for this accomplishment.

It appears that both friends and foes who consider Lewis a fundamentalist have failed to understand his sophisticated use of religious language. Both groups have assumed a more literalistic meaning behind his theological terminology than Lewis himself would have allowed. In some cases, literalistic assumptions have been read into Lewis' thought in such a way that his own meaning is distorted. For example, Boss attributed to Lewis generalizations which he did not document and which, I think, are not found anywhere in Lewis' writing. He thought that Lewis said "if something is said in the Bible it ought be accepted." He attributed to Lewis the statement, "The New Testament is genuine history." Statements of this kind sound very unlike Lewis, and to my knowledge Lewis never made such pronouncements. Boss observed that Lewis believed in a literal heaven and hell, the existence of angels, a personal devil, and the fact of miracles. Without elaborate qualifications and reservations, however, this simplified statement is bound to be widely misleading and to misrepresent Lewis' theological thought. A similar instance of hasty theological summary is found in Clyde Kilby's book:

Lewis defends the proposition that the devil is alive and active, and he goes further than most of us in his belief concerning the reality and work of angels. He believes one enters heaven immediately at death. He thinks the Bible teaches clearly the Second Coming of Christ, and he thinks this may be the next great event in history.[6]

This statement is not wholly false. But as these ideas are popularly understood, this paragraph does not adequately represent the substance of Lewis' theology. These details—some of which Lewis acknowledges as "speculative opinion"—are not at all the essential features of the Christian faith which Lewis expounded in book after book. They may be central in the doctrines of theological conservatives, but they are not central in the teaching of C. S. Lewis. Professor Kilby occasionally slips into a religious vocabulary which seems to me not fully representative of Lewis. I do not think Lewis used such phrases as "real contact with Christ" or "after a man is saved." Salvation for Lewis was a continuing, dynamic process.

Lewis' theological thought has been variously criticized for fundamentalist, liberal, and even for neo-orthodox tendencies. He has been called an evolutionist by some and antiscientific by others. He has been charged with being an extreme rationalist as well as an antirationalist. It might be well to acknowledge that Lewis' theology resists location in simple categories. Lewis was opposed to neat theological classifications, in theory and practice. In surveying Macdonald's religious thought, Lewis once remarked, "I am no great friend to such pigeon-holing." Late in his life he noted, "A great deal of my utility has depended on my having kept out of dog-fights between professing schools of 'Christian' thought."

Chad Walsh speculated that Lewis took more jabs at the liberal extreme in theology than at the fundamentalist extreme for the simple reason that he had less contact with fundamentalists in his Oxford environs. Walsh, himself an Episcopalian priest, located the theological Lewis as "squarely in the middle of the Christian tradition: an uncom-

[6] *The Christian World of C. S. Lewis* (Grand Rapids: Eerdmans Publishing Co., 1964), p. 160.

promising defender of the doctrines telescoped into the Creeds." It is my belief that this judgment by Walsh is correct.

We turn now to the criticism that Lewis' work lacks compassion. It is not as easy to call this a simple misunderstanding of Lewis as it is to so label the interpretations which exaggerate his allegorical, apologetic, antiscientific, or fundamentalist attitudes and intentions. This criticism persists even among those who are quite familiar with Lewis' work, in a way that the other criticisms often do not. C. E. M. Joad said of *Screwtape* that "Mr. Lewis possesses the rare gift of being able to make righteousness readable," but he considered the work infected with Pharisaism and censoriousness. Joad wondered how Lewis could so confidently rail against the shortcomings of others. A. C. Deane discovered in *Divorce* a metallic hardness of tone, an air of disdain, untouched by sympathy. Monica Furlong found in *Screwtape Proposes a Toast* a Swiftian distaste for humanity; the new letter, she said, focuses upon "a lumpish Them" rather than upon individuals. This latter criticism, incidentally, represents another pole from the usual complaint about *Screwtape* that Lewis' individualistic religion ignores social problems.

The interpretation of Lewis as a dogmatist was summarized by Alec Vidler, a theologian and author who was in general an admirer of Lewis' work:

For all its resourcefulness, Lewis' mind was hard and unreceptive to what was not congenial to it. Men who disagreed with him felt that he was more eager to refute them than to listen to what they had to say for themselves and to do justice to this truth. He was temperamentally dogmatic in the bad as well as in the good sense of the word.[7]

Many reputable Lewis critics agree with Vidler's conclusion. Surely there is that in Lewis' work which lends itself to this interpretation. But it seems to me that these critics may have overlooked another strain which permeates his work as well—the mood of confession and humility, of doubt and uncertainty. This will be illustrated in greater detail in a following chapter, but the quality should be noted here. Regarding his attack on "other people's shortcomings," Lewis plainly admits in *Surprised*, "The key to my books is Donne's maxim, 'The heresies that men leave are hated most.' The things I assert most vigorously are those that I resisted long and accepted late."

[7] "Unapologetic Apologist," *Book Week*, I (July 26, 1964), 3.

In the preface to *Mere Christianity*, Lewis admitted that he was reluctant to write much about temptations to which he himself had not been exposed. In the preface to *Screwtape* he wrote that he did not require years of study in moral theology to learn how temptation works: " 'My heart'—I need no other's—'showeth me the wickedness of the ungodly.' " In the preface to *Pain* he noted that he had originally requested permission of his publisher to write this book anonymously, since the subject would require him to make statements of such fortitude that they would appear ridiculous to anyone who knew him personally. What weight should be given to such prefatory remarks as these when it comes to evaluating the works themselves? Should the entire work be read in light of them, or should they be ignored as material hidden away in a distant corner? If they are seen as the underlying assumptions upon which the book is built, Lewis appears a more compassionate author than he does otherwise. If these statements are forgotten, he often appears blunt and brusk. It is true that he does not often repeat these reservations in the course of his main discussions.

There are, I think, other reasons why Lewis sometimes appears to settle for simple answers rather than to explore the complexities and depths of issues. He occasionally warned his readers that he was over-simplifying an idea in the interests of clarity and brevity. While it may not satisfy professional theologians, this approach may be necessary to some extent when books are written for a large popular audience. *Screwtape* and *Mere Christianity*, it will be remembered, were prepared originally in very brief units—the former as serial articles in *The Manchester Guardian* and the latter as short BBC broadcasts. To be perfectly fair about it, an author can hardly be expected to hedge about his chief ideas with elaborate qualifications when they are being prepared for quick delivery to a mass audience. If such an assignment in theology is to be undertaken at all, it is necessary to resort to some sort of summary statements, either from the creeds or of one's own composition.

In an earlier chapter we commented upon Lewis' use of dramatic assertation as a teaching tachnique. He found this method intensely stimulating when he studied under Kirkpatrick, and he assumed that others would benefit from the method as well. To some extent, at least, Lewis delighted in controversy and welcomed rational opposition. His passion for debate and dialectic sometimes drove him to represent his position as practically unassailable even when he knew full well that it was not.

Finally, when Lewis wrote about religious faith, he was interested in presenting classical Christianity, not his own intellectual difficulties and personal anxieties. The reader will generally be aware that the author was for eighteen years an atheist and that he wrote as a twentieth-century man who was not unacquainted with the intellectual struggles and anxieties of our time. What Lewis wanted to offer his readers, however, was not spiritual autobiography but a cogent case for the Christian faith. Individual believers may be disturbed over all sorts of intellectual and emotional problems. Nevertheless, traditional Christianity has made some rather definite, affirmative statements about God and man. It was Lewis' intention to set forth these central beliefs as clearly and as forcefully as he could.

It may not be a misunderstanding to think of Lewis as a dogmatic writer. When allowance is made, however, for (1) the abbreviated interpretation required by his popular audience and situation, for (2) the reservations which were set forth in several of his prefaces, for (3) the use of dramatic assertation as a teaching technique, and for (4) the fact that he was presenting traditional Christianity rather than spiritual autobiography, Lewis appears somewhat less dogmatic and self-righteous than would otherwise be the case. It is easier to demonstrate that critics sometimes misrepresent Lewis by assigning to him unwarranted allegorical, apologetic, antiscientific, and fundamentalist motives. Lewis did not, however, adequately protect himself against the charge of dogmatism. Whether or not his is to be judged as a serious flaw in his work will depend upon the weight the reader assigns to Lewis' scattered admissions that he often failed to reach in practice the ideals which he felt obliged to recommend.

V

Man as He Was Intended: Creation, with Fresh Images of Composite Creatures

The double nature of Man:

We were made to be neither cerebral men nor visceral men, but Men. Not beasts nor angels but Men—things at once rational and animal.

—*Regress*, p. 13

According to C. S. Lewis, man is a composite creature. He is an *animal rationale,* akin to both angels and tomcats. Although closely related to nature, man cannot be understood solely in natural terms. He is a thinking/feeling being. He is related to his Creator both through reason and through longing desire. It is our purpose to examine now in some detail Lewis' ideas on the created nature of man, and to note how this concept is reflected in his imaginative work. Particular attention will be given in the final pages of this chapter to Lewis' concept of *Joy*—a dominant theme in his life and work.

Like so many poets and philosophers before him, Lewis is sensitive to both the aspiring and the fragile natures of man. He mused, "We live for a day. What are we? What are we not? A man is a dream about a shadow." These lines remind one of Pascal's reflections on "the grandeur and the misery" of man. They are reminiscent of Yeats's cry that the poet's heart, "sick with desire and fastened to a dying animal," knows not what it is. Lewis felt, with Milton, that the key for understanding the nature of man lies in the knowledge of "how the world began, and how man fell."

Lewis noted in *Miracles* that the naturalist believes the vast process in time-space to exist on its own and that nothing else exists. While naturalism can admit a certain kind of "God," there is no God who made nature and who stands outside it. *Nature,* for the naturalist, means "the whole show." The consistent naturalist cannot believe in free will. There is no independent power for originating events beyond the total series already in process. The supernaturalist, on the other hand, believes that the time-space process is derivative, and that something else does exist in its own right. This "Self-existent" is what supernaturalists call "God" (or "gods"). That which exists on its own has produced the time-space framework with its procession of interrelated events. *Nature,* for the supernaturalist, means the derivative framework. Belief in supernaturalism does not necessarily include belief in miracles; God may never, in fact, interfere with the natural system.

If any single thing can be demonstrated to exist which *in principle* cannot be accounted for within the natural process, naturalism is exposed as an inadequate philosophy. For naturalism to remain true, every finite thing and event must fit somewhere within the total system. The key question then becomes this: is there anything in the universe which does not admit a naturalistic explanation? Lewis maintained that there are at least two dimensions within human experience itself which permit no such explanation. In these two ways man reflects his supernatural origin.

For one thing, the reasoning process itself cannot be explained solely in terms of natural causes. Without the validity of reasoning, there would be no knowledge. No scientific information could be considered "true." There would be no means for discriminating between truth and error if all thought were simply the product of the total system and nothing more. Naturalism can be maintained in argument, but in actual practice the validity of reason is to some extent always *assumed,* said Lewis. Men do not treat all their ideas as mere feelings in their own minds. They believe that some of their thoughts, at least, represent genuine insight into a reality beyond their minds. In contradiction to his basic theory, a naturalist may even offer reasons why he believes naturalism to be true. But no view—his own included—can be superior to any other if all views equally are caused by the movement of molecules and are absolutely nothing else.

Lewis stated succinctly in *Miracles,* "*No thought is valid if it can be fully explained as the result of irrational causes.* . . . [For the consistent naturalist] the finest piece of scientific reasoning is caused in just the same irrational way as the thoughts a man has because a bit of bone is pressing on his brain." When the naturalist assigns irrational causes to the thoughts of others, he should recognize that his own philosophy is not exempt from similar interpretation. The fact is that men *do* assume the validity of reasoning—at least their own reasoning. Once this fact is acknowledged, it is evident that "rational thought or Reason is not interlocked with the great interlocking system of irrational events which we call Nature." This one thing in the universe, at least, is discovered to transcend the realm of nature. "It is a matter of daily experience that Rational thoughts induce and enable us to alter the course of Nature—of physical nature when we use mathematics to build bridges, or of psychological nature when we apply arguments to alter our own emotion." Within each normal human being there is an area of activity which exists independent of nature. The human mind, then, is in this one sense a "supernatural" entity.

Lewis admitted that rationality functions in each mind only imperfectly and intermittently. No one mind can actually *be* eternal, self-existent Reason. It appears, therefore, that human minds are not the only supernatural entities that exist: they themselves must be derived from a self-existent, rational Being—in other words, from God. Men are creatures to whom God has given reason, but who yet remain distinct from God. Human thought is not God's thought, but it is "God-kindled." Each mind is "an offshoot, or spearhead, or incursion of that Supernatural reality into Nature." Human rationality is "the little telltale rift in Nature" which indicates something else behind or beyond it. "That spearhead of the Supernatural which I call my reason links up with all my natural contents—my sensations, emotions, and the like—so completely that I call the mixture by the single word 'me.' "

Of course, rational thought is conditioned by nature—for example, by the state of the brain. The reception of a radio broadcast depends partly on the state of the receiving set; but the apparatus which conditions the program does not originate it. The supernatural works its way into nature, using at each point the conditions that nature offers. Where conditions are unfavorable, supernature is repulsed. "A man's Rational thinking is *just so much* of his share in eternal Reason as the state of his brain allows to become operative." Rational thought always involves the condition of the brain, but "Reason is something more than cerebral bio-chemistry." In thinking about nature, naturalists have given insufficient attention to the fact that they do, as men, actually *think*. Since one's own thinking cannot be merely a natural event, something besides nature does exist. Denial of this depends upon "a certain absent-mindedness."

There is a second way in which, according to Lewis, man exhibits a supernatural dimension, thus providing additional difficulty for naturalistic interpretation. Human beings make moral judgments. They employ concepts of "ought" and "ought not," of "right" and "wrong." But men will not heed judgments which they themselves realize spring from nonrational, nonmoral causes. If the whole moral dimension could be explained fully in terms of irrational and nonmoral categories, "morality" would be an illusion and would no longer be binding upon anyone. To say "I ought" would resemble "I itch." It would cease to be a true moral judgment about a proposed action. For consistent naturalists, moral judgments are about the speaker's feelings and not about a real moral quality existing independently of the speaker.

Again the ordinary practice of naturalists refutes their theory, said Lewis. After admitting that good and evil are illusions, they exhort their fellows "to work for posterity, to educate, revolutionise, liquidate, live and die for the good of the human race." Even naturalists like H. G. Wells and Karl Marx write with passionate indignation, as men proclaiming what is really good and denouncing what is really evil. If one is persuaded, however, that his impulse to serve posterity is on the level with his fondness for cheese—"now that its transcendental pretensions have been exposed for a sham"—why should he pay any further attention to it? Evidence indicates that the human animal does continue to make moral judgments and—in practice—does not treat his conscience as a mere product of blind natural forces. This moral dimension of human experience leads Lewis to acknowledge a supernatural source for the concept of good and evil. Nature, being nonmoral and nonrational, cannot be the cause of the human moral sense. The conscience must be grounded in an absolute Moral Being. Though they do not necessarily prove the existence of "God," both human reason and morality, according to Lewis, may be taken as proofs of "the Supernatural."

Lewis' concern over what it means to be *human* is reflected often in his works of fiction. For example, on the planet Malacandra, Ransom finds most of the creatures rational and friendly, but he concludes that *human* refers to something more than bodily form and rational mind. It includes also that community of blood and experience which unites the people of the earth. The creatures of Malacandra are not the stock science-fiction figures of bug-eyed monsters, but neither are they specifically human. In the children's stories, both talking animals and wild animals live in Narnia, and human children sometimes find it difficult to tell them apart. Peter observes, "Wouldn't it be dreadful if some day, in our own world, at home, men started going wild inside, like the animals here, and still looked like men, so that you'd never know which were which?" Aslan warns the talking-ones of Narnia not to return to the ways of the dumb beasts lest they lose their distinction. "For of them you were taken and into them you can return. Do not so."

What are the characteristics which separate man from the other forms of animal life, and how is man to maintain his distinctiveness? The answer to these questions was for Lewis grounded in the doctrine of Creation. As Aslan said to Prince Caspian when the latter expressed sorrow upon discovering that he was a descendent of pirates, "You come of Lord Adam and the Lady Eve. That is both honour enough to erect the head of the poorest beggar, and shame enough to bow the shoulders of the greatest emperor on earth. Be content."

For Lewis, as for contemporary theology in general, the creation myths of Genesis imply these two ideas: (1) that nothing in this world is ultimate, since the universe is finally dependent upon God; and (2) that since the world had its origin in God, the whole of creation is basically good.

In his student days Lewis composed a poem charging "a god" with wanton cruelty for forcing the burden of existence upon creatures without their prior consent. He maintained then that God did not exist, although he admits that he was angry with him both for not existing and for creating the world as well. In more mature years Lewis became convinced that only those who believed in a God of creation could fully appreciate nature. Supernaturalists, he thought, recognize nature as it really is—considering it as God's creation and regarding it neither too much nor too little. In a memorable passage in *Miracles*, Lewis speaks of nature as

this astonishing cataract of bears, babies, and bananas: this immoderate deluge of atoms, orchids, oranges, cancers, canaries, fleas, gases, tornadoes and toads. How could you ever have thought this was the ultimate reality? How could you ever have thought that it was merely a stage-set for the moral drama of men and women? She is herself. Offer her neither worship nor contempt. Meet her and know her. (P. 67)

Lewis' intense love for his natural environment is evident in many of his books. He once recorded his suspicion of any religion based upon a contempt for the natural world. He appreciated the two spiritual maxims which were used often by Charles Williams: "This also is Thou" and "Neither is this Thou." Lewis understood these words to mean that the image of God is found in every created thing, but that one never finds more than God's image there. To isolate any object from its source, to follow that object for its own sake, is to establish an idol whose service leads to destruction. Perhaps Lewis was not aware of it, but it seems likely that Williams' maxims were derived from two Hindu principles: *tat-tvam-asi* ("That thou art") and *neti-neti* ("Not this, not that").

Lewis' views on the derivative and essentially good character of the world are reflected in several imaginative works. Screwtape chuckles over the human inclination to claim ownership of time and bodies. Such claims, he states, sound equally funny in heaven and hell: men persist in thinking that they "own" their bodies in spite of the fact that bodies are given to them and are taken from them without their consent! Prince Caspian of Narnia is amazed to learn that the Pevensie children come from a round world, a world shaped like a ball. The young prince has always loved fairy tales about round worlds, but he has never believed in any real ones. Now he desperately longs to visit a round world. "It isn't like that," Edmund observes. "There's nothing particularly exciting about a round world when you're there." One is persuaded while reading Lewis that the world is always an exciting and enchanting place for those who have eyes to perceive. In *Silent Planet* a contrast is drawn between "space" as the modern, dead, cold, black vacuity and that living, empyrean ocean of radiance which the ancients had called "the heavens." It is suggested that a changeover from a conception of space to a conception of heaven is desperately needed.

The relationship between man and nature entails a temporal particularity which evokes Lewis' praise despite the pain which this arrangement inevitably involves. As John sings his dying song in *Regress,* he is sure that "it is not for nothing that the Landlord has knit our hearts so closely to time and place—to one friend rather than another and one shire more than all the land."

> But Thou, Lord, surely knewest Thine own plan
> When the angelic indifferences with no bar
> Universally loved but Thou gav'st man
> The tether and pang of the particular.

Nature represents the goodness of God's creation, but nature is not divine, as pantheism maintains. Like man, nature is in some ways a fallen creature—a good thing corrupted. Nature retains many of her original beauties, but she is now tainted. Though the Devil could make nothing, said Lewis, he has infected everything. Lewis wrote in a letter,

"I have always gone as near Dualism as Christianity allows—and the New Testament allows one to go very near." The higher a thing is in the natural order, Lewis pointed out in *The Silver Chair*, the more demonic it can become. "It's not out of bad mice or bad fleas you make demons, but out of bad archangels." Screwtape echoes this idea: evil can be produced only by twisting what is originally and naturally good.

It is evident that "reality " for Lewis involved more than an empirical universe, more than the data of logical positivism. He pondered in *A Grief Observed*, "Five senses; an incurably abstract intellect; a haphazardly selective memory; a set of preconceptions and assumptions so numerous that I can never examine more than a minority of them— never become even conscious of them all. How much of total reality can such an apparatus let through?" In *Silver Chair* the Witch-Queen of Underland attempts to place an enchantment on the children, encouraging them to believe that any world other than the one they are immediately experiencing is but a dream. "Put away these childish tricks," she pleads. "I have work for you all in the real world. There is no Narnia, no Overworld, no sky, no sun, no Aslan." What is this *sun* that you all speak of?" she asks. "Do you mean anything by the word? . . . When you try to think out clearly what this *sun* must be, you cannot tell me. You can only tell me it is like the lamp. Your *sun* is a dream; and there is nothing in that dream that was not copied from the lamp."

It is difficult to say what "reality" is involved even when a person sits reading, noted Lewis in *Reflections*. Psychologists and theologians use different symbols to probe the depths behind the façade called *you*. But even when these symbols and the figures of mathematics are true about reality, said Lewis, they should not be mistaken for reality itself. Screwtape warns Wormwood, the apprentice devil, not to encourage his patient's thought about universal issues or "truth." It is now dangerous, he maintains, even to attempt to use science against Christianity: physics may encourage a person to think about realities he cannot touch and see. Since men "find it all but impossible to believe in the unfamiliar while the familiar is before their eyes," a devil's job is to fix his patient's attention on the stream of immediate sense experiences. Humans should be taught that sensory impressions are "real life." They should be encouraged not to ask what is meant by "real."

As we consider the relationship between God and the whole realm of nature, a further question arises: what about the possibility of miracles? Is God's creative activity assigned to the past only, or does it continue in the present? Lewis has been suspected at times of being a fundamentalist because he did not regard as unhistorical every biblical narrative which includes a miraculous element. One reviewer of *Miracles* notes, "The people who may well be assisted in the extension of their credulity are those who have already swallowed the Divine Camel but shrink from a miraculous gnat."

In crude and popular terms, "miracle" means an interference with nature by supernatural power. Lewis contended that human reason and morality point to the reality of something in the universe beyond the natural process. But the existence of the supernatural need not involve miracles. A case could be made against miracles either on the grounds that the character of nature or the character of God excludes their possibility.

It should be noted that *Miracles* is subtitled *A Preliminary Study*. This book is concerned with the philosophic question of the possibility or probability of the miraculous, since what one "sees" in experience depends upon the philosophy he brings to experience. To demonstrate the philosophical possibility, or even the probability, of miracles does not commit one to a belief in any particular miraculous account. "Most stories about miraculous events are probably false," Lewis continued in *Miracles*—just as most stories about natural events are false. The principle of uniformity in nature unquestionably applies to the overwhelming majority of events. But Christians believe there are at least a few exceptions—for example, the great central miracles of the Incarnation and the Resurrection. Lewis admitted that by the standards of David Hume such events are "infinitely improbable. But alternate explanations for the life, sayings, and influence of Jesus appear to the Christian to be even less satisfactory. Most people, Lewis went on, will never in their lives see a miracle. "God does not shake miracles into Nature at random as if from a pepper-caster. They come on great occasions."

It is sometimes supposed that belief in miracles arose when men were ignorant about the regular course of nature. This explanation is inadequate. Lewis noted, "Nothing can seem extraordinary until you have discovered what is ordinary. Belief in miracles, far from depending on an ignorance of the laws of nature, is only possible in so far as those laws are known." Joseph, he observed, "knew just as well as any modern gynaecologist that in the ordinary course of nature women do not have babies unless they have lain with men."

Another objection to the possibility of miracles is that people once believed in them because they thought the earth the largest thing in the universe and man the most important creature in it. Now we know better. But, as Lewis often insisted, the immensity of the universe is not at all a recent discovery. He wrote in *Miracles,*

More than seventeen hundred years ago Ptolemy taught that in relation to the distance of the fixed stars the whole Earth must be regarded as a point with no magnitude. His astronomical system was universally accepted in the Dark and Middle Ages. The insignificance of Earth was as much a common-place to Boethius, King Alfred, Dante, and Chaucer as it is to Mr. H. G. Wells or Professor Haldane. Statements to the contrary in modern books are due to ignorance. (P. 50)

It is from the human mind, however, that the material universe derives its sense of awe. Geological periods and light years are mere arithmetic until the shadow of man falls upon them.

Lewis did not find the character of nature such as to exclude the possibility of "supernatural interference." The laws of nature do not cause events: they state the orderly pattern to which natural events customarily conform. These laws are based upon observed regularity. They cannot, in themselves, claim that no suspension is possible, or that no new factors can be introduced. Yet a miracle, if there is such, is by definition an exception.

It is misleading to suggest that a miracle "breaks" the laws of nature. The moment any event from beyond nature enters the natural realm, it obeys natural laws. "The divine art of miracle is not of suspending the pattern to which events conform but of feeding new events into that pattern." Reality, of course, must be consistent and interrelated. But one part of reality should not be mistaken for the whole. A miracle is not an event without cause or results. Its cause is God. Its results follow natural law.

Miracles reveal the total harmony of all that is. If miracles interrupt the usual course of nature, they assert—even as they do so—"the unity and self-consistency of total reality at some deeper level." D. E. True-blood, in his *Philosophy of Religion,* considers the question of whether nature is better understood as (1) a mechanical order, a "closed" system; or (2) a purposive order, an "open" universe which involves regularity but is flexible enough to include the emergence of novelty. He concludes that the latter view is preferable. It may be that Trueblood's discussion of "Naturalism and Supernaturalism" owes something to the thought of C. S. Lewis. Trueblood is one example of a professional philosopher who is well acquainted with Lewis; the index to this particular text includes ten references to Lewis' works.

Lewis found nothing in the character of a personal and loving God that would prevent the possibility of occasional miracles. Some people think it unworthy of God that he would ever want to break his own laws. But there is no particular reason, said Lewis, to assume that the universe was so designed as not to require further attention from the Creator. If miracles do occur, the real inconsistency with divine purpose would be for God not to perform them.

Lewis noted in *Perelandra* that men gain a certain comfort in distinguishing between natural and supernatural. This practice eases "the burden of intolerable strangeness which this universe imposes on us by dividing it into two halves and encouraging the mind never to think of both in the same context." If divine initiative had anything to do with the original creation of the earth, however, there is no reason to to rule out the possibility of divine activity in the subsequent process. In a poem which serves as the preface to *Miracles*, Lewis emphasized how readily new events are incorporated by the plastic powers of nature:

> All that is Earth has once been sky;
> Down from the Sun of old she came,
> Or from some star that travelled by
> Too close to his entangling flame.
>
> Hence, if belated drops yet fall
> From heaven, on these her plastic power
> Still works as once it worked on all
> The glad rush of the golden shower.

Two contrasting arguments have been used against religion in the name of a scientific worldview, said Lewis. Some claim that life on earth developed by only a millionth chance in a universe which is generally hostile to life. This view is intended to show the absurdity of belief in a God who is interested in living creatures. But others claim that in the vast expanse of the universe there are probably many inhabited globes. This view is intended to show the absurdity of the parochial belief that Man really matters to God. It is sometimes proposed today that the discovery of life on other planets would be a severe blow to the Christian doctrine of Incarnation. If a million races inhabit a million planets, how can Christians defend the belief that God once came to earth for the salvation of men?

Before belief in God's action for human salvation is threatened by a new worldview, Lewis said, several questions need answers. Is it true that animal life actually does exist beyond the earth? If so, do these animals have "rational souls," with abilities to abstract and to calculate, to apprehend values and to appreciate morality? If rational beings do exist elsewhere, are they "fallen" so that they need the kind of redemption required by men? If fallen, then have they been denied an incarnation of Christ for their own world? Or in a different situation, might the means of redemption be quite different from God's plan for the earth? [1]

It is possible, Lewis admitted, that the divine process of redemption is intended to begin with man and to spread throughout the universe. This would put man in a pivotal position, although it would not necessarily imply either superiority in man or favoritism in God. It is far more likely, however, that contact between man and any unknown race would be a calamity. We know already how fallen man customarily treats strangers. The history of civilized man meeting savage man is a tale of plunder and death, slavery and corruption. Considering what crimes humans commit against persons with different features and pigmentation, is there any doubt what man would do if he found rational creatures who did not even appear human?

Should a meeting of planets occur, Christians should resist every attempt at exploitation and theological imperialism. Christians might find themselves closer spiritually to certain sons of God with shells or tusks than to other human beings. If so, primary loyalty would still be due to God and not to the human species. Lewis does not believe that men will make any new discoveries which will overturn the fundamental claims of Christianity. We can thank God, he said, that extensive space travel is still far distant. Astronomical distances may prove a quarantine against human contamination.

Lewis repeatedly chided the ignorance of those who suppose that a religious worldview depends upon a mistaken scientific estimate of the nature of the universe. For medieval thinkers, the cosmic insignificance of the earth was commonplace, he said. The medieval model was anthropoperipheral. Men were considered "creatures of the Margin." Maimonides, in the twelfth century, maintained that every star is larger than the earth. For medieval man, according to Lewis in *Sixteenth Century*, the belief in the cosmic centrality of the earth did not imply preeminence. Though central in location, the earth was considered dynamically marginal—a dark and deadly part of the universe which was the rim of being the farthest away from the hub.

Lewis illustrated a common misunderstanding of the religious worldview with a scene in *Regress*. Mr. Enlightenment assures John that he

---

[1] *Last Night,* pp. 84-88.

can easily explain away religion by several methods. There is no Land-lord at all, for example; that whole idea is merely an invention of the Stewards. Anyone with the benefit of scientific training should know that, he says. John is delighted to learn that there is no Landlord. The news lifts a great weight from him. "I dare say," continues Mr. Enlighten-ment, "it would be news to you to hear that the earth was round—round as an orange, my lad!" "My father always said it was round," replies John. "No, no, my dear boy," says Mr. Enlightenment, "you must have misunderstood him. It is well known that everyone in Puritania thinks the earth flat."

Lewis maintained that medieval man was less naïve about the nature of the universe than modern men often suppose. He felt that this theme was so important, and so misunderstood by scholars today, that he returned to stress the idea in half a dozen of his books. Aristotle had taught that the perceptible world (the realm of growth, decay, and weather) is "a nothing" compared with the whole universe. Ptolemy's compendium had taught that, for astronomical purposes, the earth must be regarded as a point without magnitude. This view was accepted by the Middle Ages, said Lewis.

It was not merely accepted by scholars; it was re-echoed by moralists and poets again and again. To judge from the texts, medieval man thought about the insignificance of Earth more persistently, if anything, than his modern descen-dants. We even find quite popular texts hammering the lesson home by those methods which the scientific popularizer uses today. We are told how long it would take you to get to the sphere of the fixed stars if you travelled so many miles a day. The figure brings the distance out at something near 118 million miles. (*Studies in Literature*, p. 46)

Modern astronomers may indeed know the distance to the stars to be well beyond 118 million miles, but the imaginative and emotional im-pact of this calculation is hardly altered by substituting fresh figures, said Lewis.

Medieval man imagined a universe which was immense; but it was quite definitely finite. When he looked at the stars, he did not feel that he was staring into an abyss—a "dark, cold indifferent desolation." He gazed, rather, upon a patterned, spiritually inhabited, limited cosmos. This is the significant difference between the medieval and the modern point of view. Medieval man looked out upon "heaven" rather than upon "space." While the medieval model of the universe provided our ancestors with a built-in significance, the sensitive man of today often feels himself "confronted with a reality whose significance he cannot

99

know, or a reality that has no significance; or even a reality such that the very question whether it has a meaning is itself a meaningless question."

It is misleading to say that the medievals thought of the universe "like that" while we now know that it is "like this," said Lewis. Part of our discovery is that we do not now know, in the old sense, what the universe is like. We cannot be confident that *any* model we can build will be quite right. Models are useful; they attempt to get in all the known phenomena of a given period. They are to be respected, but not idolized. It is this point that Lewis had in mind when he wrote in *Discarded Image*, "No model is a catalogue of ultimate realities, and none is a mere fantasy." To an important degree the questions asked always help to shape the model; they partly determine "how much of total truth will appear and what pattern it will suggest."

Man is both a derivative creature and a finite being in this vast universe. "On any conceivable view," Lewis said, "he finds himself dwarfed by reality as a whole."

It is a profound mistake to imagine that Christianity ever intended to dissipate the bewilderment and even the terror, the sense of our own nothingness, which comes upon us when we think about the nature of things. It comes to intensify them. Without such sensations there is no religion. (*Miracles,* p. 52)

It may even be a religious experience to abandon a glib religion under the realization of how majestically indifferent most of reality is to man. As Lewis wrote in *Other Worlds*, "Those who brood much on the remote past or future, or stare long at the night sky, are less likely than others to be ardent or orthodox partisans." Contemplation on the dimensions of the universe can help to set ourselves and our own interests in perspective. This mood is reflected in *Silent Planet* as Dr. Ransom looks back at the antics of worldings from the distance of Malacandra. The wise *sorn* has speculated that Ransom came to his planet from Thulcandra, the silent planet. From a mountain chamber Ransom's attention is directed to a coin-sized bright disk on a telescope-like instrument. He recognizes the land masses of northern Europe and North America. "It was all there in that little disk—London, Athens, Jerusalem, Shakespeare. There everyone had lived and everything had happened; . . . 'Yes,' he said dully to the *sorn*. 'That is my world.' It was the bleakest moment in all his travels."

Lewis was open to the possibility of life on other planets in the universe, but he was not committed to a belief in such life. The interplanetary novels are about human nature, even though they might apply as well to other forms of rational life. Actually, theologians Paul Tillich and Karl Barth were probably as open to the possibility of other inhabited worlds as was Lewis. Tillich remarks in his *Systematic Theology* that the Incarnation is unique for the special group in which it occurs. This "leaves the universe open for possible divine manifestations in other areas or periods of being. Such possibilities cannot be denied." Barth, likewise, may have reflected space-age consciousness when he mentioned that the Incarnation was for *man,* whereas "the thought of any insignificant being outside of human cosmos being far more worthy of divine attention than man is deeply edifying and should not be lightly dismissed." [2]

In another approach to the distinctiveness of human nature, in *Studies in Words,* Lewis said that man might be defined as a reflexive animal. "A person cannot help thinking and speaking of himself as, and even feeling himself to be (for certain purposes), two people, one of whom can act upon and observe the other. Thus a man pities, loves, admires, hates, despises, rebukes, comforts, examines, masters or is mastered by, 'himself.'" In his "Poem for Psychoanalysts and/or Theologians," Lewis hinted at the thoughts of innocence which accompany dawning human consciousness (individual or racial, perhaps), and at the endless earthly quest which follows lost innocence.

> Wise was the fangless serpent, drowsy.
> All this, indeed, I do not remember.
> I remember the remembering, when first waking
> I heard the golden gates behind me
> Fall to, shut fast. . . . Forth on journey, . . .
> I went, I wander still. But the world is round.

At a particular stage in evolution, there emerged a self-aware creature who could say "I," who had a sense of ought and guilt, who distinguished self from environment, and who had a sense of past and future. Lewis once said in a letter that he "had pictured Adam as being physically the son of the anthropoids on whom God worked after birth the miracles which made him Man; said in fact, 'Come out, forget thine own people and thy father's house.'" Abraham's call would be a smaller instance of the same type of thing, he noted. Lewis considered man to be participating even yet in the process of evolution. Or better still, he said, man continues "in process of being created."

[2] *Humanity of God,* p. 73.

101

The gradual dawn of consciousness is powerfully and beautifully portrayed in the novel *Perelandra*. Upon meeting the Green Lady, Ransom announces that he has come in peace. With a puzzled expression, the Lady wonders, "What is 'peace'?" Other earthly concepts are equally foreign to her—ideas of time, pain, self-transcendence, relatives, and possessions. "Which is *my* island?" she asks. "What is *home*?" "What is *dead*?" Ransom tells her that self-transcendence is a stepping into the "Alongside" to look at oneself. He attempts to communicate the meaning of freedom and evil in the vocabulary of the Lady's idyllically limited experience. "In our world," Ransom explains, "not all events are pleasing or welcome."

The Green Lady has remained in such close communion with her creator Maleldil that she is astonished to think that it might have been otherwise. "I thought," she said, "that I was carried in the will of Him I love, but now I see that I walk with it." After further reflection, she admits that it is possible to conceive that one might send his soul after the good expected instead of turning it to the good received. Becoming aware that it was out of her own heart that she always turned from the anticipated good to the given good, she understands how one actually might refuse the real good and turn it into something not good. Although she cannot imagine herself ever finding it hard to turn from the thing she desires to the thing Maleldil sends, she begins to sense the delight and the terror of freedom.

The Oyarsa of Malacandra assures Ransom that although he and his earthly guest are somewhat unlike each other, both are "copies of Maleldil" who made the world. The idea that man is created in the image of God with free will is reflected also in *Screwtape*. Wormwood is told that God really does want to fill the universe with persons whose wills freely conform to his. He wants men united to him, but yet distinct. The two weapons which God will never use to win men, says Screwtape, are the irresistible and the indisputable.

In an apt phrase, Richard Cunningham calls Lewis "the Reasoning Romantic." Both intellect and feelings are a part of the human composite-creature, and both play a role in man's relationship to the Creator. A dominant image in the *Regress* allegory concerns avoiding the extremes of both dogmatism and emotionalism. The "North" in this "country of man's soul" is inhabited by men of rigid systems, both skeptical and dogmatic; the purists and the doctrinaires live in this land of barren and aching rocks. The "South" is inhabited by uncritical and slovenly artists who believe that every feeling is justified by the mere fact that it is felt; this is a land of fetid swamps. Lewis' point is that the only safe road on which a man can travel lies between these two extremes. Some obscurity in this book results from the fact that the intellectual and spiritual route which Lewis himself took was not as familiar to his readers as he once supposed. In the preface to the third edition of *Regress*, Lewis lists these four stages in his own intellectual journey toward Christianity:

1. from popular realism to Philosophical Idealism;
2. from Idealism to Pantheism;
3. from Pantheism to Theism; and
4. from Theism to Christianity.

Lewis had an exalted view of the role of reason in life and faith. He urged his readers not to accept Christianity unless it appeared reasonable. Further, all possible knowledge—including scientific knowledge—depends upon the validity of rational thought. When reason is abandoned, as he illustrated in *Hideous Strength*, what follows is a process of dehumanization—the elimination of rational, moral man. Nevertheless, it may be misleading to say, as does Charles R. Courtney, that "Lewis' arguments are based entirely on an appeal to reason." [3]

Lewis noted in *Discarded Image* that prior to the eighteenth century, moralists generally regarded reason as the organ of morality. Reason meant more than the process of deducing one proposition from another, of moving from premises to consequences. It included also *intellectus*, or understanding, by which certain truths were recognized as self-evident. Plato preserved from Socrates the idea that morality was an affair of knowledge. The Stoics thought that all rational men, by virtue of their reason, recognized a natural law binding upon all. The ancients believed that to recognize a duty was to perceive a truth, not because of any particular goodness but because of human intelligence.

While Lewis appreciated the role of reason behind faith, he knew also that rigorous thought can lead one into atheism. Lewis himself turned away from Christianity when he became aware of the problem of pain and alternative worldviews such as spiritualism, theosophy, and Greek and Latin mythology. It seemed probable to him then that the Christian God also was a myth. He was especially impressed for a time with the Argument from Undesign, and his poetry echoed a bitter denunciation of the "red God" who would not lend an ear. "Let us curse God most High," he cried out in "De Profundis." The poems in *Spirits*

---

[3] "The Religious Philosophy of C. S. Lewis" (M.A. thesis, University of Arizona, 1955), p. 4.

in Bondage are filled with praise for the "draughts of cool oblivion," for sleep and death, by which men escape from meaninglessness.

Though his respect for clear, logical thought was high indeed, Lewis did not make rational investigation an end in itself. He pointed out in *Psalms* that to be a great theologian is not the same thing as to be a good Christian. His statement reminds us again of Kierkegaard's famous question, "Can a theologian be saved?" There is more to both life and faith than sheer reason.

Some thinkers, Lewis noted in *Reflections,* would have us believe that reason is nothing more than "the unforeseen and unintended by-product of a mindless process at one stage of its endless and aimless becoming." But this position, he wrote, "is the same as saying: 'I will prove that proofs are irrational,' or more succinctly, 'I will prove that there are no proofs.'" Chemical theories of thought are so irrelevant to what actually takes place in thinking that they can illustrate just as well the sequences of a maniac's thoughts as those of a rational man. Surely some important factor is missing in this kind of explanation. "No model yet devised has made a satisfactory unity between our actual experience of sensation or thought or emotion and any available account of the corporeal processes which they are held to involve," Lewis said in *Discarded Image.* A "scientific cosmology," he maintained, excludes not only Christianity, but it excludes science itself.

If minds are wholly dependent on brains, and brains on bio-chemistry, and bio-chemistry (in the long run) on the meaningless flux of the atoms, I cannot understand how the thought of those minds should have any more significance than the sound of the wind in the trees. (*A Toast,* p. 58)

Lewis admitted that he did not understand theologians who considered human reason and conscience without value. It appears that Lewis did not grasp the distinction that neo-orthodox theologians made between reason and rationalism. According to H. R. Macintosh, theological rationalism eventually developed to the point where reason was placed on the seat of judgment, with the demand that every Christian doctrine undergo trial in its court. The maxim of rationalism became "I will believe nothing I cannot understand," and only that which could pass as rational might be retained by theology. Rationalism included the belief that religious problems could be solved by the same methods as scientific problems. With the confidence that reason could explain everything, mystery was eliminated. The doctrines of Christ's divinity, original sin, the Atonement, the sacraments, and the miracles were set aside: they could not be explained adequately in rational terms.

Developed as a complete metaphysical system, rationalism became a substitute for traditional religion.[4] Neo-orthodoxy revolted against this gigantic movement which would have established reason as a self-sufficient authority for determining matters of religious truth. The protest was more against the self-sufficiency of human reason than it was against the value of rationality *per se.*

Lewis' respect for reason is reflected in many of his imaginative works. Screwtape warns Wormwood: "It is jargon, not reason, you must rely on." In *Regress,* Philosophy and Theology are the two younger sisters of Reason. And it is finally Reason who drives John to Mother Kirk at sword point. The scene echoes Lewis' theme in *Surprised* that he himself was a "reluctant convert" who was at last persuaded by the "facts." In *Silent Planet,* Ransom is startled to discover that three distinct species have reached rationality on Malacandra without exterminating one another. He had always assumed that inhabitants of any alien world would be some "monstrous union of superhuman intelligence and insatiable cruelty." Now Ransom is embarrassed to be questioned about humanity. He attempts to avoid discussion of wars and economics. Later, he is taken to a great scientist *sorn* and decides to be frank about human history. The *sorns* are astonished at what he tells them about human war, slavery, and prostitution. The Malacandrans conclude, benevolently, that men cannot help themselves. Creatures need always to be ruled by *eldila.* But men now know no *eldila,* and each wants to be a little *Oyarsa* (deity) himself. In a delightfully ironic scene the physicist Weston attempts to intimidate the "natives" of Malacandra and to impress them with bright beads. They respond to his silliness with uproarious laughter. He concludes that these creatures are far less intelligent than he had supposed.

There is a further scene in *Regress* in which Reason provides a needed corrective. John meets a giant named "Spirit of the Age" whose eyes allow everything they look on to become transparent. A woman is near, but John does not know that it is a woman because "through the face, he saw the skull and through that the brains and the passages of the nose, and the larynx, and the saliva moving in the glands and the blood in the veins: and lower down the lungs panting like sponges, and the liver and the intestines like a coil of snakes." It is Reason who explains to John that the giant has shown him something that is not really visible, to make him believe that life is ugly. "Is it surprising that things

[4] *Types of Modern Theology* (New York: Charles Scribner's Sons, 1937), pp. 13-19.

should look strange if you see them as they are not?" Yet, adds Reason, "It will do you no harm to remember from time to time the ugly sights inside. You come of a race that cannot afford to be proud."

While Lewis stressed the rational approach to religion, he recognized also that emotions may play an important role. He observed in *Malcolm* that men cannot think clearly unless they are unemotional. But neither can they think deeply if they remain unemotional. The ancient Persians, he noted, debated everything twice—once when drunk and once when sober.

It is clear that Lewis placed emotion in a subservient role to reason and will. He thought George Macdonald relegated feeling to its proper place when he said, "Heed not thy feelings: Do thy work." In themselves, Lewis taught, feelings have no importance. God chose to be incarnate in a man who wept at the grave of a friend and sweated blood in Gethsemane. The lesson for us here is this: it is by a man's will that he is good or bad.

Many of Lewis' letters concern the fluctuation of feelings. He advised a godchild at confirmation time not to expect all the feelings he would like to have. They may or may not appear. If they do, one should be glad. If they do not, one should be patient. God will give us the proper feelings as He wishes. Lewis warned a lady not to depend upon a continuing religious excitement. This present condition will certainly pass, he said, as a response of the nervous system. The change will not mean that genuine religious experience has gone; it may be most operative when one feels it the least. Lewis asked another correspondent whether God seemed real to him. The feeling varies, he noted. Many of the things we firmly believe in feel more or less real at different times, including, for example, even the certainty of our own death. In another letter Lewis charged, "Don't bother much about your feelings. . . . What matters is your intentions and your behaviour." Feelings are not really you; they are only a thing that happens to you. To an inquirer about devotional life he replied, "Never, never try to generate an emotion by will power."

Lewis returned to the theme of fickle emotions in *Malcolm*, one of his final books. Prayer, he noted here, is an irksome burden for most people. But it should be undertaken by an act of will, from a level deeper than feeling. Feelings may be affected by the weather, one's general health, or various fleeting incidents. So much in feeling is not really our own. Therefore, the prayers worth the most to God may actually be those least supported by devotional feelings and accompanied even by the greatest disinclination. Lewis commented in *Mere Chris-*

tianity that these general principles regarding emotions apply also to marriage. There is no value in trying to keep an old thrill alive. It should be given up. In the period of quieter interest and happiness which follows, one will discover new thrills occurring all the time. "But if you decide to make thrills your regular diet and try to prolong them artificially, they will all get weaker and weaker, and fewer and fewer, and you will be a bored, disillusioned old man."

Lewis' attitude toward religious feelings is brilliantly reflected in some passages of his fantasies. Humans, writes Screwtape, are amphibians—a revolting hybrid of half spirit and half animal. Devils must understand this aspect of human nature in order to exploit the dry periods produced by the "law of Undulation." Spirit can be directed to an eternal object, but human bodies, passions, and imaginations are subject to time and continual change. Man's life, therefore, is a series of troughs and peaks. Undulation affects every area of a man's life—including his interest in work, his affection for friends, and his physical appetites. If a person can be kept from suspecting this law, he may assume that any phase in his life is a permanent condition and hence open himself for many temptations. Faith is primarily an effect of the will. "Our cause is never more in danger," warns Screwtape, "than when a human, no longer desiring, but still intending, to do our Enemy's will, looks round upon a universe from which every trace of Him seems to have vanished, and asks why he has been forsaken, and still obeys."

At another time Screwtape advises Wormwood to prepare to work hard on the disappointment or anticlimax which will be coming soon in the religious experience of his patient. If a man gets through the initial dryness successfully, and thus becomes less dependent upon emotion, he confesses, he is much harder to tempt. Perhaps it is something of this "law of Undulation" that Lewis has in mind when in *Silver Chair*, Aslan instructs Jill to remember, remember, remember the signs for the children's quest—to repeat them upon waking in the morning and upon lying down at night. "Here on the mountain," says the great Lion, "I have spoken to you clearly: I will not often do so down in Narnia." For Lewis, obedience comes first in the religious life. Feelings may follow. If they do, one can rejoice in their coming. But one becomes a Christian primarily through self-examination, repentance, and restitution—not through emotional excitement. A Christian should simply make his Communion and continue as well as he can in prayer and daily duties.

In a highly provocative essay entitled "Transposition," Lewis observed that emotions as various as falling in love, enjoying fine music, or feeling ill may stimulate the very same sensation in the nervous system. Why is it that a flutter in the diaphragm in one instant is associated with pleasure and in another context is related to misery? What is the relation between human emotions and physical sensations?

Said Lewis, while the nervous system responds to emotions, its resources are far more limited than are human emotional resources. Since possible variations in the nervous system are few, the senses compensate by using one sensation to express many emotions—even opposite emotions. "Transposition" must occur constantly in the relation between the mind and body as experience is adapted from a richer medium to a poorer medium. A similar kind of transposition is seen when a language with an extensive vocabulary is translated into one with a small vocabulary, or when an orchestra score is adapted for a single instrument.

The principle of transposition suggests a related religious problem. Human "spiritual life" may appear to be nothing more than ordinary elements from the natural life. But does this mean logically that it is simply derived from nature? If we are willing to grant that the emotional life is more diverse than a nervous system can register, and that a two-dimensional painting can represent a three-dimensional world not actually seen within the frame, why not allow also that imagery and emotions borrowed from the rest of nature may reflect a rich reality of spiritual life? In fact, how could spiritual reality express itself in humanity in any other way?

Spiritual reality may be expressed in the natural world even though the former is not entirely derived from the latter. The religious man attempts, perhaps in a dim and confused way, to use natural acts and images and language with an entirely new value. He approaches the reality he experiences "from above," as does the man who knows his emotional reactions more subtle and complex than any laboratory apparatus can indicate. If one approaches an experience only "from below," he can, perhaps, reduce it to a case of "merely" or "nothing but," taking account of all the facts while neglecting all the meaning.[5]

Robert Reilly called Lewis a "congenital romantic." [6] Unless Lewis' fascination with what he calls *Joy* is related to his rigorous demands for reason, however, Lewis will be misinterpreted. At one level, he makes a personal report on certain intense moments of his own life experience. At another level, he undertakes the theologizing of the experience of

[5] "Transposition," *Transposition and Other Addresses*, pp. 9-20.
[6] "Romantic Religion," p. 81; see espec. chap. 3, "C. S. Lewis and the Baptism of the Imagination."

romantic longing which has attracted the attention of many poets and novelists. Reilly saw Lewis as an advocate of "romantic religion," by which he meant "an attempt to reach religious truths by means and techniques traditionally called romantic, and an attempt to defend and justify these techniques and attitudes of romanticism by holding that they have religious sanction."

Lewis' *Joy* is related to Goethe's "blissful longing" and to W. M. W. Tillyard's "Primal Joy-Melancholy." According to Corbin Carnell, Lewis illuminates a state of mind which has been a recurrent theme in literature—a theme reflected not only in Blake, Wordsworth, Arnold, and Thomas Wolfe, but also in Dreiser and O'Neill. He is concerned with the compulsive quest "which brings with it both fleeting joy and the sad realization that one is yet separated from what is desired." [7] *Joy,* for Lewis, is a key both to the nature of man and to the nature of man's Creator.

Sometimes Lewis referred to these "fits of strange desire" simply as *Joy.* At other times he spoke of them as Desire, romantic longing, or *Sehnsucht. Sehnsucht,* said Carnell, is not to be identified with "nostalgia." It is not just the "wistful, soft, tearful longing" noticed by Matthew Arnold. Lewis gave a special sense to the word, causing it to include also turbulent, passionate aspiration. *Sehnsucht* always involves an underlying sense of displacement or alienation from the object of its desire. While *Sehnsucht* has been reflected in the literature of every age, Carnell thinks that the theme is unusually conspicuous in our time. Developments in this century, he says, appear especially to encourage a preoccupation with the dimension of experience which gives rise to longing. Lewis' concept of *Sehnsucht* provides a useful and illuminating approach to a great many modern authors—both to new romantics, such as Thomas Wolfe and Dylan Thomas, and to others whose interest in the theme is less intense.

In *Surprised by Joy,* the spiritual autobiography of his early years, Lewis reported some of his most "idiosyncratic sensations" in the belief that others would recognize similar experiences of their own. The Castlereagh Hills, seen in the distance from his nursery window, he said, taught him longing and made him for good or ill a votary of the "Blue Flower" before he was six years old. (The Blue Flower is a symbol of longing in German literature and Scandinavian ballads, dating back to the Middle Ages.)

Lewis' first remembered moment of intense longing or desire came as

---

[7] "Dialectic of Desire," p. 14.

109

he stood one summer day near a flowering currant bush. Suddenly there arose in him, like Milton's "enormous bliss" of Eden, the memory of an earlier morning, "as from a depth not of years but of centuries." Of this sudden moment, Lewis wrote in *Surprised,*

> Before I knew what I desired, the desire itself was gone, the whole glimpse withdrawn, the world turned commonplace again, or only stirred by a longing for the longing that had just ceased. It had taken only a moment of time; and in a certain sense everything else that had ever happened to me was insignificant in comparison. (P. 19)

In time there came other such moments of sharp longing. Lewis encountered the "Idea of Autumn" in a story book, and sensed with surprise something of "incalculable importance," something "in another dimension." A brief line from Longfellow filled him for a fleeting moment with an indescribable desire of almost sickening intensity. This unsatisfied desire seemed itself more desirable than any other satisfaction. Lewis used the technical term *Joy* to apply to all such experiences. One who has experienced it will want it again, he asserted. "I doubt whether anyone who has tasted it would ever, if both were in his power, exchange it for all the pleasures in the world." And yet it is not quite like happiness; it bears a touch of unhappiness or grief. And a person can never control it through his own power, in the way that he can pleasure. *Joy* differs both from pleasure in general and from aesthetic pleasure. "It must have the stab, the pang, the inconsolable longing," wrote Lewis.

For many years *Joy* was absent and forgotten in Lewis' life. Then one day he happened across these words (without knowing their meaning): *Siegfried and the Twilight of the Gods.* Immediately he found himself engulfed in "Pure Northernness." Plunged back into his own past, he recalled with heartbreak the *Joy* he had once known and had lacked now for years. But this "unendurable sense of desire and loss," coming to him as to one recovering from unconsciousness, vanished in the very moment of recognition. In succeeding days he experienced something like a religious adoration—a disinterested self-abandonment—for Wagner and Northernness. It was, in fact, a quality of feeling which as a believer he had never known toward God. Yet it was no new religion; for it contained no belief, and it imposed no duties.

Joy always reminds, said Lewis. It does not become a possession. It remains the desire for something long ago or far away or soon to be. Lewis discovered that both nature and books were repeated sources for these peculiar stabs of *Joy*. Books about Norse mythology were found especially fruitful. Eventually the inner life of quest for these experiences became so important that it was quite distinct from his ordinary outer life. Lewis began to feel that he was living two lives which had nothing to do with each other.

When he cultivated a scholar's interest in Valhalla and the Valkyries, it became evident to Lewis that this was different from the original thrill. The glory was gone. Even the memories of these sharp experiences were themselves a kind of *Joy*. All things in their own way reflect heavenly truth, claimed Lewis—especially the imagination. But pangs of *Joy* do not necessarily lead to any higher spiritual life. Lewis discovered the frustration of deliberately seeking thrills of *Joy*, in poetry, music, or nature. As long as he sought a particular state of mind, *Joy* was absent; the thrill would come only as a by-product when his attention was fixed upon something else. "Startled into self-forgetfulness," he wrote, "I again tasted *Joy*. But far more often I frightened it away by my greedy impatience to snare it, and, even when it came, instantly destroyed it by introspection, and at all times vulgarized it by my false assumption about its nature."

Through his own experience as a young man, Lewis discovered that *Joy* was not disguised sexual desire. Sex might be a substitute for *Joy*, but *Joy* was no substitute for sex. "I sometimes wonder," mused Lewis, "whether all pleasures are not substitutes for *Joy*."

The poet William Butler Yeats was instrumental in leading Lewis to question his own early materialistic viewpoint. "Had he been a Christian," admitted Lewis, "I should have discounted his testimony." But Lewis discovered in Yeats an authority who was neither orthodox nor materialistic. Yeats believed in a world of "ever living ones" and thought contact between that world and ours possible. A "drop of disturbing doubt" fell upon Lewis' previous materialism.

Lewis was ripe to try something else, perhaps even Occultism or Satanism, when he happened upon a copy of George Macdonald's *Phantastes*. In its work his imagination was "baptized" by a new "bright shadow" —a quality which made "erotic and magical perversions of *Joy* look like sordid trumpery." Unlike other visitations of *Joy*, this new experience did not turn the ordinary world briefly into a desert. The bright shadow, rather, came out of the book and rested upon the real world, transforming common things. The quality appeared without his asking, even without his consent.

It was as though the voice which had called to me from the world's end were now speaking at my side. It was with me in the room, or in my own body, or behind me. If it had once eluded me by its distance, it now eluded me by

111

proximity—something too near to see, too plain to be understood, on this side of knowledge. It seemed to have been always with me; if I could ever have turned my head quick enough I should have seized it. Now for the first time I felt that it was out of reach not because of something I could not do but because of something I could not stop doing. If I could only leave off, let go, unmake myself, it would be there. (*Surprised,* p. 145)

For awhile, Lewis reported, he thought of this longing as a kind of aesthetic experience. Eventually he was able to identify the voice more accurately: the bright shadow was Holiness.

Lewis began to note that the great literary figures who portrayed the depth, roughness, and density, of life were usually religious men, while writers who did not suffer from religion generally seemed a bit thin or "tinny." He came eventually to believe that all the images and sensations of *Joy* pointed to something else. It was not just the experience of longing which was desired but some object of which the longing was only a reminder. Lewis gained a sense of holding something at bay, of shutting something out. Finally, he was compelled to surrender to "the steady, unrelenting approach of Him whom I so earnestly desired not to meet." He reports, "In the Trinity Term of 1929 I gave in, and admitted that God was God, and knelt and prayed: perhaps, that night, the most dejected and reluctant convert in all England." The prodigal who had so long resisted interference was "brought in kicking, struggling, resentful, and darting his eyes in every direction for a chance of escape."

The God who had trapped Lewis was not yet recognized as the God of the Christian faith. That step, too, came in time. What happened to the experiences of *Joy?* The old bittersweet stabs continued to come. But after his conversion to Christianity, Lewis nearly lost interest in them. They were recognized as pointers to something other and outer, not as important states of mind. Why, Lewis asked, should one stop and stare at signposts when he is enroute to the Holy City?

The dialectic of desire may serve as a kind of ontological proof for God, according to Lewis. He announced his intent in *Regress* as "not to propound, but to live through a sort of ontological proof." If pure and spontaneous pleasures in sensuous and aesthetic life are "patches of Godlight" in experience, as Lewis suggested in *Malcolm,* then it is well to recognize the real source. Experience, he said, is an honest thing.

You may take any number of wrong turnings; but keep your eyes open and you will not be allowed to go very far before the warning signs appear. You may have deceived yourself, but experience is not trying to deceive you. The universe rings true wherever you fairly test it. (*Surprised*, p. 143)

Romanticism, or romantic desire, is for Lewis an intense urge which begins in uncertainty about its object. The human mind devises for it many mistaken identifications—nostalgic, erotic, aesthetic, occult, or intellectual. *Surprised by Joy*, claimed its author, was written by one who had proved each of these possibilities wrong through his own ontological search for God. Experience leads us to overcome the initial mystery as it compels us to reject false objects and finally to rest in God.

Corbin Carnell agrees with Lewis that romantic longings cannot long be cherished and maintained in isolation from an ontology which provides a satisfactory frame for them. But he is not persuaded that Lewis' "ontological argument" is the only possible explanation. "I cannot share his faith in rational argument as something which will virtually compel a man, if he is honest, toward God," wrote Carnell. Whether Lewis was correct in his understanding of the origin of this human phenomenon, there are those who would hold a different set of convictions about reality and hence would arrive at different explanations. I think it likely that Lewis intended his ontological argument as strong "evidence" for the reality of God, and not as a "proof for God" in the sense of classical philosophy. In his poem "The Apologist's Evening Prayer," for example, he showed that he knew better than to attempt the latter.

In his discussion of *Joy*, Lewis testifies to an experience of God's grace and pursuit that is reminiscent of the experiences of Paul and Augustine. The literary reader cannot help but recall Francis Thompson's "Hound of Heaven" as he reads *Surprised by Joy*. Speaking of Macdonald's *Phantastes* in *The Great Divorce*, the narrator admits, "I had tried not to see that the true name of the quality which first met me in his books is Holiness." Lewis headed a final chapter of *Regress* with this "police maxim": "You may as well come quiet."

The elusive, reluctant convert was trapped at last. Robert Reilly said that the leading figure behind Lewis' doctrine of *Joy* is Coleridge. This is an overhasty conclusion. Coleridge was neither the first nor the most important figure to urge that theology should go behind dogma to experience. More influential on Lewis' concepts in this area, I think, was Rudolph Otto's *The Idea of the Holy*, a book mentioned often in Lewis' works. And behind this was the great Augustinian theme that "unless God wanted you, you would not be wanting Him."

The concept of *Joy* is treated often in both Lewis' fiction and his nonfiction. *Joy* always emphasizes the pilgrim status of man. It reminds, it beckons, it awakens desire. But it remains unsatisfied with everything in this world. Lewis claimed in *Pain* that there is no Christian solution to the problem of evil which does not take heaven into account. It is not very stylish to discuss heaven, Lewis admitted, and sometimes he thought people do not even desire heaven. "But more often I find myself wondering whether, in our heart of hearts, we ever desired anything else." Surely this is the goal of man's incommunicable and unappeasable want, he concluded. Man is born with desire, tantalized by immortal longings, and dies recognizing that his promises are not yet fulfilled. In heaven individuals shall come to know, to love, and to praise God.

Interestingly, there was a period in Lewis' life when he was in revolt against the romantic longing that had played such an important role for him since childhood. As he explained in the preface to the 1950 edition of *Dymer,* he was under the influence of Oxford's "new psychology" when he composed this poem in 1926. Wishful thinking and fantasy were problems which greatly vexed his academic circle in those days. Lewis himself reacted in angry revolt against the spell of *Sehnsucht,* and was determined to unmask and defeat this enemy. Except for a vigilant rejection of Christianity, he reflected, his mind had no fixed principles when he wrote this poem. He had been attracted by the western garden system, represented in Milton, Morris, and the early Yeats. Now he regarded this as exactly the type of illusion that it was necessary for an honest man to overcome.

In his long poem, Dymer is a young man attempting to escape from illusion. At first he supposes that the universe will be friendly, allowing him to repeat his moment of youthful rapture. But as he is rebuffed by experience, Dymer sinks into despair and turns to pessimism. He is disillusioned over the world of the imagination, the world of natural beauty, and over himself and his freedom. Finally he accepts "reality," wards off further temptations to wish-fulfillment and illusion, and faces his dark destiny. M. Milne said that the process of the monster becoming a god in this poem means that the poet's "old romantic longings pass through the grave and gate of death and new and vital poetic powers are released." [8] Chad Walsh said that the work symbolizes spiritual rebirth, as Dymer is finally slain, and returns to life.[9] I cannot so understand this work, and I wonder whether these interpretations are not more optimistic than Lewis intended. I find Dymer dying a double death—first of the body, then of the soul—to rise no more.

[8] "Dymer: Myth or Poem?" *The Month,* N.S.VIII (September 1952), 173.
[9] *C. S. Lewis, Apostle to the Skeptics* p. 59.

Dymer is a poem about disillusionment and realism. Its meaning might be summarized in these words:

> 'I'll babble now
> No longer,' Dymer said. 'I'm broken in.
> Pack up the dreams and let the life begin.' (P.59)

Dymer has come reluctantly to this decision about the meaning of life:

> Can it be possible
> That joy flows through and, when the course is run,
> It leaves no change, no mark on us to tell
> Its passing? . . .
> Joy flickers on
> The razor-edge of the present and is gone. (P. 51)

Dymer is irritated that life is so empty even as he concludes that this is the truth:

> Is it not wrong
> That men's delusions should be made so strong? (P. 79)

Although Dymer renounces experiences of *Joy,* there are occasional glimpses which indicate the difficulty he finds in resisting the power of this temptation:

> He knew that no desire could keep
> These hours for always, and that men do die
> —But oh, the present glory of lungs and eye! (P.25)

Lewis' imaginative work which displays the most concern over *Joy* is the semiautobiographical allegory *The Pilgrim's Regress.* As he admitted in the preface to the third edition, Lewis unintentionally used the word *romanticism* in a private sense in this work. He intended the term to refer here to the recurrent experience of intense longing which dominated his early life. As the characters of *Regress* journey through "the country of man's soul," we learn that the "pictures" which trouble John are symbols for the objects of the imagination.

One day John catches a vision of an Island like nothing else he has ever seen—a vision of such indescribable beauty and calm that he is haunted with sweetness and pang and forgets everything else. With "sad excitement" he is certain that he knows now what he wants in life. Years pass, however, and the sight of the yearned-for Island fails to return. At times John is determined to see it again—or at least to produce

115

the feeling which it originally evoked. But the Island does not come, and the feeling will not begin.

Finally John discovers a naked and laughing brown girl who declares, "I am better than your silly Islands; it was me you wanted." The deception does not last for long. Before John manages to acknowledge his mistake, however, a whole mob of little brown girls have been born of his misdirected desire. He runs away as fast as he can. But for a long time thereafter, little brown girls keep popping up to haunt him whenever he sits down to rest. Later on his journey, John becomes acquainted with Media Halfways. As they kiss and talk of sad and beautiful things, John exclaims, "This is what I have been looking for all my life. The brown girls were too gross and the Island was too fine. This is the real thing." "Love," Media declares, "is the way to the *real* Island." But her brother charges in and exposes Media as just another of the brown girls.

When John wonders whether his belief in the Island may not indeed be a creation of his own desire, the virgin Reason warns him that disbelief in the Landlord may be the actual wish-fulfillment dream. Since John was so relieved to be free of the Landlord earlier, Reason cautions, "I do not say that any theory should be accepted because it is disagreeable, but if any should, then belief in the Landlord should be accepted first."

Mr. Sensible encourages John and his companion Vertue to moderate their passions and enjoy a life of pleasure and ease. After all, contentment is the best of riches, their new host maintains. Men should not engage in useless speculation. When John protests, "I am trying to find the Island in the West," Mr. Sensible responds, "We have all been fools once. . . . That wild impulse must be tasted, not obeyed." John asks his host, "Do *you* believe in the Landlord?" "No part of our nature is to be suppressed," Sensible replies. "Least of all a part that has enshrined itself in beautiful traditions. The Landlord has his function like everything else as one element in the good life." John concludes that these "sensible" men are parasitic and that their culture is precarious. Mr. Sensible's philosophy, observes Vertue, "seems to teach men that the best way of being happy is to enjoy unbroken good fortune in every respect." Not everyone, he adds, will find this advice extremely helpful.

At the end of his journey West, John finally sees again his Island in the distance. He discovers it to be the same shape as the summit of the Eastern Mountain which his neighbors back home had always called "The Landlord's Castle." In fact, John has now encircled the world and has come up on the other side of that same familiar mountain. The

116

only route to the Mountain-Island is in retracing his steps to the East until he can at last "cross the brook." When John rediscovers the Landlord, it occurs to him that he has lost interest in finding the Island for which he has searched so long. Even if there is such a place, he concludes, he is no longer free to spend himself in seeking it. He must follow the Landlord's designs instead. It now seems to him that his final goal is more like a person than like a place.

Discussing his experiences with History, John wonders whether the Island-idea is always needed. History informs him that the Landlord sends many different kinds of pictures to men. "What is universal is not the particular picture, but the arrival of some message, not perfectly intelligible, which wakes this desire and sets men longing for something East or West of the world." The Island (or *Joy*) is

something possessed, if at all, only in the act of desiring it, and lost so quickly that the craving itself becomes craved; something that tends inevitably to be confused with common or even with vile satisfactions lying close to hand, yet which is able, if any man faithfully live through the dialectic of its successive births and deaths, to lead him at last where true joys are to be found. (*Regress*, p. 157)

These pictures of something beyond, these patches of Godlight, lead surely to their true source if one is able and willing to enter into the dialectical process and to live out the proof.

Though Lewis elaborated his thinking about *Joy* in *Regress*, he returned often to the theme in his other books—in poetry and letters, in science fiction and children's tales. In *Dawn Treader*, Lucy finds a book in the magician's house and comes upon the description of a spell "for the refreshment of the spirit." She is enthralled by the story and is convinced that this is the loveliest thing she has ever read or ever will read. She decides at once to read the account again. But the pages of the magic book cannot be turned back. She can only go ahead. And to her distress, the intense experience begins quickly even to fade from her memory. Lewis said in *Malcolm* that men may neglect new facts of God's glory if they insist upon harking back to former experiences. These experiences were never intended to last. The prayer which God is least likely to answer is the prayer for an encore. "How should the Infinite repeat Himself?"

Even Screwtape reflects a knowledge of *Joy* in his instructions to his infernal inferior. He writes, "The truth is that the Enemy, having oddly destined these mere animals to life in His own eternal world, has guarded them pretty effectively from the danger of feeling at home

117

anywhere else." It is the business of hell to build up in humans a firm attachment to earth, to persuade men that earth, through planning, can become a heaven at some future date, and to keep them from thinking of anything beyond their immediate existence on this planet.

Probably Lewis' best fictional account of *Joy* is found at the end of *The Last Battle,* the final Narnia story. The children have now come to Narnia to stay: they have been killed in a railway accident "in the Shadowlands." Now begins the Great Story which no one on earth has read, the story which continues forever, with each new chapter better than the previous one. The reader feels certain that the children, and Lewis, share the Unicorn's ecstasy upon arrival at their destination:

I have come home at last! This is my real country! I belong here. This is the land I have been looking for all my life, though I never knew it till now. The reason why we loved the old Narnia is that it sometimes looked a little like this. (P. 172)

When he was still the atheist-poet writing *Spirits in Bondage,* Lewis could not resist singing of "lands unknown" and dreaming of the "Hidden Country." Nearly half a century later, he was convinced that he understood more clearly man's nature and destiny. Lewis' doctrine of Creation and his concept of *Joy* are represented well in those famous opening words of Augustine's *Confessions:* "Thou hast made us for Thyself, and our heart is restless till it finds rest in Thee."

VI

Man as He Has Become: The Fall, with Fresh Images of "Bent" Men

The reality of evil:

To him evil is a spiritual reality: it is not caused by a dislocation of genes or hormones or a set of psychopathic fixations. It is a gigantic negative force aimed at the reduction of the cosmos ordained by the Divine Will, and it operates through the degradation of fallible human beings.

—Nathan Starr[1]

In reading Lewis criticism it becomes evident that some authors are quite unfamiliar with a contemporary theological understanding of the "Fall" of man. Robert Reilly presents a tangled discussion on this theme and wonders whether Lewis means by the Fall "that man lost *all* consciousness, so became no longer man, and then was (so to say) re-created over aeons as consciousness returned slowly by stages of evolution." [2] No, this is not what Lewis meant by the Fall. Rudolf Schmerl puzzled over what Lewis' account of the temptation of Perelandra's Eve could possibly have to do with Earth's fallen humanity. "For us," he said, "the question is how to resist evil here and now." [3] This is precisely the relevance of the Perelandrian temptation account, just as it is the primary relevance of the Genesis temptation account. Modern

---

[1] Nathan Starr, *King Arthur Today* (Gainesville: University of Florida Press, 1954), p. 165. These words by Starr refer to Lewis' close friend and fellow Inkling Charles Williams, but Corbin Carnell notes in his dissertation that they fit Lewis as well.

[2] "Romantic Religion," p. 120.

[3] "Reason's Dream," p. 127.

theologians regard the Adam myth more as a story of Everyman than as a bit of ancient history. Perhaps it is not as irrelevant as Schmerl believes to suggest that one should "trust in God and live accordingly" —provided, of course, that these concepts are interpreted and applied in depth. Some fundamentalists, like Edgar Boss, are distressed that Lewis acknowledged the presence of myth in the Bible, even in an elevated sense. Boss prefers to think of the Genesis creation stories as "history." So eager is he for a literal interpretation that he misapplies to the Genesis stories themselves a comment which Lewis makes about the apple in *Paradise Lost*. Perhaps many of Lewis' readers have a purely historical understanding of the nature of the Fall. But Lewis' own views on this doctrine appear close to the interpretations of the major theologians of this century.

In the biblical view man was created good. But he is found at present open to the influence of evil, corrupting powers. He is estranged from his Creator. As Philip S. Watson wrote, "When, how, or why this originally happened, we do not know. That lies outside the realm of our experience, since we are born as members of a humanity already in subjection. We can therefore speak of it only in mythological terms like those of the story of the Fall of Adam." [4] This picture of man is not scientifically conclusive. Nevertheless, it does present a truthful account of the human existential plight. Man is not, as things now stand, fully human. He is not what he is intended in the purposes of God to be.

Contemporary theologians understand the Fall to refer to man's refusal to trust God and to obey him. Every man is both born into, and himself participates in, a "fallen" world. One either denies God entirely, or he rebels against divine authority in some measure. The human being is not satisfied with creaturely self-realization; he repeatedly attempts autonomous realization. This is the process of self-deification. Through pride and overweening self-assertion, each man arrogantly usurps the position of God and claims for himself the center of existence and significance. To establish his own security, man would himself be divine and independent, rather than created and contingent.

Dr. Clyde Kilby said of Lewis, "If his view of contemporary man is low, it is because his estimate of man's eternal potential is high." Likewise, Berdyaev noted that the myth of man's Fall is a myth of man's greatness. The doctrine of original sin, he observed, is not nearly so humiliating to man as the belief that he is essentially a nonentity, with

---

[4] *The Concept of Grace*, p. 45.

his origin in the mud. Said Berdyaev, "Man fell from a height and he can rise to it again." According to this orthodox position, man is a sick being. The human soul is divided, with opposing elements engaging in an internal agonized conflict. Unaware of his own essential condition, man frequently misinterprets himself both to himself and to others. "All rebellion against God," wrote Berdyaev, "is a return to non-being."

Lewis appears to have agreed with the major theologians of our time when he wrote in *The Problem of Pain* that the only proper function of the doctrine of the Fall is to declare that "man is now a horror to God and to himself and a creature ill-adapted to the universe not because God made him so but because he has made himself so by the abuse of his free will." The doctrine of the Fall, Lewis maintained, guards against both the theory that God himself created man's evil nature, and the theory that an independent power, equal to God, is responsible for evil. Human choice, one of the good things of God's creation, includes the possibility of evil. Taking advantage of this possibility, man has become evil.

No one, Lewis continued, knows precisely what happened when man first fell. For long centuries God perfected the animal which was to become "human," the creature which was to bear His "image." Lewis had no objection, of course, to thinking of man as physically descended from other animals. Eventually this particular organism received a new kind of consciousness. It could know God and make judgments about truth, beauty, and goodness. It could perceive the flow of time. God was served in obedient love and ecstatic adoration by this early "man," said Lewis. Perhaps these creatures were not designed originally for senility and death. We know neither how many of these creatures God made nor how long they remained in the condition of Paradise. But eventually they were tempted to be gods, on their own, and they fell. "They wanted to be nouns, but they were, and eternally must be, mere adjectives." We do not know, of course, in what particular act, or acts, the self-contradictory, impossible wish found expression. Some act of self-will, utterly false to the true creaturely position of man, was performed. This condition has been transmitted by heredity ever since: a new kind of man, a new species, has "sinned itself into existence." "Our present condition, then, is explained by the fact that we are members of a spoiled species." Man is unable, however, merely to accept his present condition as a fact: he remains aware that his situation is detestable. What is good for man in his fallen state needs to be especially a remedial or a corrective good. It seems, said Lewis, that human pain plays an important role in the remedy.

121

In his *Preface to Paradise Lost*, Lewis summarized the doctrine of the Fall as it has come from Augustine into Western Christendom.[5] According to Augustine, God created everything good, and "bad" denotes privation of good. What we call bad things, therefore, are good things perverted. Such perversion arises through pride—i.e., when a conscious creature becomes more interested in itself than in God. Creatures remain good *in nature* even when they are perverted *in will*. God knows that some will voluntarily make themselves bad, but he also knows the good use to which he will turn this badness. "Those who will not be God's sons become His tools."

The Fall, of course, consisted of disobedience. There was nothing bad or harmful in the fruit of Eden except insofar as it was forbidden. Disobedience involved in the Fall resulted from pride—a revolt against being subject to God. The Fall involves an essentially dependent being which, as Augustine said, "tries to set up on its own, to exist for itself." From the moment one becomes aware of himself as distinct from God, an alternative has arisen—that of choosing God or self as the center of the universe. The Fall, said Lewis, is the basic sin behind all the particular sins. It is experienced in the life of every individual, every day. The temptation to be like God, he said, is the theme that runs through *Paradise Lost* as if it were the subject of a fugue. When we recall the temptations-to-disobedience themes in *Regress, Perelandra,* and *Magician's Nephew,* the same could be said for some of the major works by Lewis.

Lewis wrote in *Mere Christianity* that God created men with free will, the freedom to do right or wrong. This condition makes possible genuine love and goodness and joy, but it also makes possible all human evil. God apparently thought the risk of a state of war in the universe a price worth paying for free will. Without freedom, nothing of real importance could happen in a world; it would be a toy world if men moved as automata whenever God should pull the strings.

The occasion of sin for our remote ancestors was the desire to "be like gods." They hoped that they

could set up on their own as if they had created themselves—be their own masters—invent some sort of happiness for themselves outside God, apart from

---

[5] Actually, he said that the doctrine is that of "the whole Church." This is not quite correct since the Eastern branch of Christendom was never much influenced by Augustine. This view did, however, become dominant in the West. See "The Fall" and "Pride," *A Handbook of Christian Theology,* ed. Martin Halverson and Arthur A. Cohen (Meridian Books ed.; Cleveland: World Publishing Co., 1958), pp. 132-35; 278-81.

God. And out of that hopeless attempt has come nearly all that we call human history—money, poverty, ambition, war, prostitution, classes, empires, slavery —the long terrible story of man trying to find something other than God which will make him happy. (*Mere Christianity,* pp. 53-54)

Men were created for a close relationship with God. It is impossible for them to find happiness and peace in any other way. Elaborate civilizations and excellent institutions have been devised by man, but whenever they attempt to operate as independent of God the fatal flaw brings them crashing down.

In its rebellious and fallen state mankind was left with a sense of right and wrong (conscience), and with "good dreams" (the stories of dying and rising gods). God has undertaken, as well, to repair man's situation through certain historic events. He selected the Jews for a particular role in his revelation, and eventually he came to earth in a special way in Jesus. God "landed on this enemy-occupied world in human form."

The problem of evil, said Lewis, is that man discovers himself in "a universe that contains much that is obviously bad and apparently meaningless, but containing creatures like ourselves who know that it is bad and meaningless." The Christian view is that this is a good world gone wrong, a world which retains the memory of what it should have been. Badness is not a genuinely independent quality. It results only from "spoiled goodness"—from the pursuit of some good (such as pleasure, money, power, or safety) by the wrong method, or in the wrong way, or too much. Dualism, according to Lewis, is an inadequate philosophy since evil must have the qualities of existence, intelligence, and will—things which are in themselves good. Traditional Christianity has therefore spoken of the devil as a fallen angel—i.e., evil is a parasite, not an original independent force.

The New Testament, noted Lewis, speaks much of a Dark Power in the universe—

a mighty evil spirit who was held to be the Power behind death and disease, and sin. . . . Christianity thinks this Dark Power was created by God, and was good when he was created, and went wrong. Christianity agrees with Dualism that this universe is at war. But it does not think this is a war between independent powers. It thinks it is a civil war, a rebellion, and that we are living in a part of the universe occupied by the rebel. (*Mere Christianity,* p. 51)

This world, claimed Lewis, is enemy-occupied territory. An evil power has made himself temporarily the prince of the world. But the rightful king has landed, and all men are called to take part in the great sabotage

123

campaign against the power of evil. While Lewis spoke often of the "Dark Power" or the "Great Rebel," we have noted elsewhere that he intended more by these terms than a popular, literalistic interpretation of Satan.[6] Lewis mentioned in *Pain* the tradition that man was not the first creature to rebel against God since a mighty created power was at work for evil in the world prior to man's Fall. He admitted that this is a "speculative" idea, which has never been included in the creeds, but he affirmed his own belief in the existence and fall of Satan, an evil angelic being. It may be, said Lewis, that some power older and mightier than man, emperor of darkness and lord of darkness and lord of this world, first tempted man to disobedience. Lewis pointed out in *Preface to Paradise Lost* that Milton believed that what is detestable is also ridiculous; therefore, his Satan is involved in absurdity. In the long run, asserted Lewis, Christians believe that "the Devil is an ass."

Lewis' thoughts about the Dark Power are reflected at several points in his imaginative works. Oyarsa explains to Ransom in *Silent Planet* that except in the vicinity of Thulcandra (Earth), the eldila are free to move about the heavens of the entire universe. There was once a great, bright Oyarsa in charge of Thulcandra, but he became "bent." Following a great war in heaven, this evil Oyarsa was bound to the air of his own planet. For many, many years the creatures of Malacandra have received no messages from Earth, and they are therefore especially curious about its subsequent history.

For another example of evil influence, the dwarf Nikabrik (in *Prince Caspian*) becomes impatient with the promised help of Aslan and decides to turn to "other powers." The White Witch once ruled over Narnia for a hundred years—a century of winter. That, thinks Nikabrik, is really power—something practical. Though this witch was killed long ago, "Who ever heard of a witch that really died? You can always get them back." With the assistance of a hag and a werewolf, Nikabrik engages in black sorcery in an attempt to persuade the White Witch to return.

In the original preface to *Screwtape,* Lewis spoke of two opposite errors into which man may fall regarding devils. It is wrong, he wrote, to totally disbelieve in their existence. But it is equally bad to have an excessive, unhealthy interest in them.

Lewis admitted that the Fall has impaired man's moral perception. But, he observed, "there is a difference between imperfect sight and blindness." Scripture suggests that man's knowledge of the right is not

[6] See Chap. 2, espec. pp. 50-53.

so depraved as his ability to do the right. Lewis warned against any theology which would represent man's practical reason as radically unsound. Once we say that what God means by goodness is "sheerly different" from what men judge to be good, there no longer remains any difference between pure religion and devil worship.

According to Walter Hooper, C. S. Lewis was probably the first author of science fiction to write about the possibility of fallen terrestrial invaders discovering unfallen rational beings on other planets. As we have observed already, Lewis felt that men are morally unfit to visit other inhabited worlds. This theme is developed in "The Seeing Eye" (in *Reflections*) and in "Religion and Rocketry" (in *World's Last Night*) as well as in the science-fiction trilogy.

Lewis considered a sense of sin to be essential to Christianity. He noted in *Pain* that Christ and the ancient world took it for granted that men are bad, deserving Divine anger. The Gospel then came as good news. The modern world, however, is so nurtured on illusions about man's basic nature that the reality of sin hardly seems credible. Christianity is now compelled to preach the diagnosis of the human condition (bad news, in fact) before the good news can receive an intelligible hearing.

There are many reasons why sin is not taken seriously by the modern world. For one thing, our century has concentrated upon the feeling of "kindness" as the chief virtue. It is easy to attribute this quality to ourselves on inadequate, subjective grounds. Further, psychoanalysis has produced the public impression that repressions and inhibitions are bad and that a sense of shame should be overcome. In Christianity, however, it is important to protect the capacity for feeling shame. Even pagan society, noted Lewis, usually considered "shamelessness" as the nadir of the soul. It is even better to be a hypocrite, he said—to pretend to be better than you are—than to have no sense of shame.

There are other reasons why an illusion about human nature has grown strong in modern times. We tend to judge actions externally. We are not accustomed to acknowledge—either to others or to ourselves—the degree of deception and sin within the human heart. The idea of corporate guilt, though proper in itself, can also distract attention from plain private sins. Further, there is the notion that the passage of time can somehow cancel sin, so that if errors were made in the distant past they may now be reported with laughter. Or we tend to feel that there is safety in numbers and that if enough people are bad, badness itself must be excusable. Some who protest an excessively moralistic interpretation of Christianity may use their protest as an evasion of the real issues. "God may be more than moral goodness," said Lewis, but "He is not less." Modern man often attempts to shift the responsibility for his behavior to some inherent necessity of life—to human finitude or to his present stage in evolution, for example. This assumes that the responsibility for sin actually belongs to the Creator, not with man.

Lewis held no optimistic view of the essential goodness of human nature. He was well aware of the capacity for evil in the best of our species. Under the proper circumstances, he said, the ordinary cruelty within anyone might blossom into something terrible. At bottom none is especially different from a Hitler or a Stalin. Lewis found the cursings and the maledictions of certain psalms well worth Christian consideration. We may be far more subtle than the old poets in disguising our ill will, he maintained, but "we are, after all, blood-brothers to these ferocious, self-pitying, barbaric men." In an incidental passage in *Sixteenth Century,* Lewis discussed the harshness and cruelty of the period when Servetus was burned at the stake. He concluded his remarks with this telling little sentence: "It was an age very like our own."

Lewis further noted in *Psalms* that these Hebrew songs should help men to become sensitive to the psychology of oppression. One natural result of cheating, oppressing, or neglecting other human beings is to arouse their resentment. Sins of omission are as serious as sins committed. In Jesus' parable of the sheep and the goats, Lewis noted, the "goats" are condemned solely for their sins of omission. Perhaps the greatest charge against each person hangs not upon what he has done but upon those things which he has not done—"perhaps never dreamed of doing."

Screwtape Letters has been criticized recently upon the grounds that Lewis aimed at rather small targets in the age which produced Auschwitz. It is well to remember, however, that *Screwtape* would lack universal literary appeal if its chief patient were a prominent official of the Nazi S.S. Lewis' point here is that "the safest road to Hell is the gradual one," and this theme is appropriate to every generation and situation. Lewis said, further, that the temptations of which he wrote are mainly those which he himself had "met in battle."

Lewis observed in *Rehabilitations* that Shelley felt conviction of sin to be an extremely dangerous condition—a condition which leads first to self-contempt and later to misanthropy and cruelty. For the Christian, however, conviction of sin is good since it is the necessary preliminary to repentance. But Lewis agreed with Shelley that "if a man will not become a Christian, it is very undesirable that he should become aware of the reptilian inhabitants in his own mind." Perhaps Lewis had something of this idea in mind when he wrote a poem about animal books and spoke of catching a glimpse of the "shadowy zoo" within the human heart.

Lewis' ideas about fallen human nature are clearly reflected in his imaginative works in many places—especially in the Narnia tales, in *Regress,* and in the science fiction. In *Magician's Nephew* the newly created talking-animals of Narnia are mystified upon first hearing that "an evil" has entered their world: *"What* did he say had entered the world?—a Neevil—What's a Neevil?—No, he didn't say a Neevil, he said a weevil—Well, what's that?" Even in delightful Narnia the age of innocence draws quickly to a close.

A test of obedience is arranged in *Magician's Nephew* as Aslan sends Digory to get an apple from a distant walled garden with gates of gold. Despite instructions that the fruit can be safely picked only for others, Digory is driven by hunger and thirst to consider indulging himself. Have the instructions, perhaps, been only advice—not really orders? Can it really be wrong to taste *after* providing for others? The Witch lurks nearby to press the case further. This is the very "apple of life," she tells Digory; he ought to eat it himself instead of carrying it back to that greedy Lion. Or, if he will not use the fruit himself, why not take it back to his long-ill and deeply beloved mother? A single bite might heal her. Digory is tormented by doubt over whether he is doing the right thing. But he remains determined to keep his promise to Aslan. The crisis and turmoil over, he returns to the waiting Lion with a greeting that is moving for its bare simplicity: "I've brought you the apple you wanted, sir." Having successfully passed the test of obedience, Digory is awarded an apple which can restore temporarily his mother's health.

Some of the creatures in *Last Battle* are not so successful in resisting temptation. Shift, a clever Ape, finds an old lion skin and persuades Puzzle, his dull donkey friend, to wear it to impersonate Aslan. Think of the good we can do, Shift exclaims, if everyone will do whatever we tell them! The ruse works temporarily. But Shift soon drops his pretense about doing good and instead has the other animals occupied in furnishing him with large supplies of fine nuts.

An "old wives' tale" in *Regress* similarly illustrates the misuse of God's good creation. In response to the travelers' inquiry about whether some catastrophe has left the main road running up to the edge of the precipice, Mother Kirk tells her story. Once upon a time the Landlord farmed this area himself, but he decided the whole thing was too good to keep to himself. His first tenant was a young married man. Now it happened that there was a variety of mountain-apple on the farm that the Landlord had planted there just for himself. It was such a strong fruit that only those who were mountain bred could digest it properly. So the Landlord warned the new tenant on no account to eat these apples. Sometime later, the farmer's wife made a new acquaintance— one of the Landlord's children who had quarreled with his father and had set up on his own. Somehow this woman was persuaded that what she needed the most was a nice mountain-apple. And she, in turn, passed the fruit along to her husband. Just then there was a great earthquake and a gorge appeared where the farm had been. The country people call the gorge the *Grand Canyon,* but it has also been known as *Peccatum Adae* (the Sin of Adam). The first taste of mountain-apple created such a craving in the farm couple that they thought they could never get enough wild apples. They planted more and more of them. They grafted mountain-apple into every other kind of tree so that all their fruit would have a dash of that special taste in it. All foods are now so infected, says Mother Kirk, that no one today has tasted anything quite free from it. Where all the food is more or less poisoned, she concludes, one needs complicated rules to keep healthy at all.

Edmund Fuller said that Lewis' science-fiction trilogy represented a fresh telling of the Christian myth of the Fall of man. So used, *myth* does not mean fiction, of course, but truth through symbolism. Said Fuller, Lewis

dramatizes and clarifies for our age the Christian teaching about man's peculiar dilemma in the order of Creation. The tragic fact of man's condition is that he is other than he was intended to be; the deep springs of his will have been subverted—he cannot do consistently the good that he would do, but does instead the evil that he would not do.[7]

Schmerl spoke of these novels as "an imaginative extension of Christian mythology, centering around a new battle between God and his angels and Satan and his devils, fought on three planets."[8] *Perelandra* in particular is significant in this regard. It might be considered an analogue of the Garden-of-Eden story. According to Fuller, "The tempting of the first woman of Perelandra entails an extraordinarily intricate, far-reaching debate at the deepest level of moral theology."

At the beginning of *Perelandra,* Ransom has come to regard the earth as enemy-occupied territory, ruled over by maleficent eldils who are at war both with men and with the eldils of Deep Heaven. The present ruler is variously known as "The Dark Lord," "the bent Oyarsa,"

[7] *Books with Men Behind Them,* p. 155.
[8] "Reason's Dream," p. 60.

"the depraved Oyarsa of Tellus," and "the black archon." Ransom's former companion Weston has now given himself over to the powers of evil so completely that a diabolical spirit takes possession of his body. He becomes, in fact, an "Un-man."

Perelandra is an idyllic planet made up primarily of floating islands. Maleldil the Creator has left but a single rule for this planet: no one is to sleep on the Fixed Land. One may visit the Fixed Land during the daytime, but he is not to remain there overnight. The Un-man, as might be expected, challenges Tinidril the Queen to disobey this one rule. His arguments are varied and ingenious. Certainly, he begins, there is no harm in *thinking* about staying on the Land; people on earth make stories about "might be" and consider this wisdom. Perhaps, further, Maleldil wishes his creatures to become more independent, to become their own, through some minor disobedience. Could it be that he only *seemed* to forbid so that one might *seem* to disobey? Surely this is a petty rule, not a universal command. In fact, reason suggests that it is forbidding merely for the sake of forbidding.

According to the Un-man, Maleldil "longs—oh, how greatly He longs —to see His creature become fully itself, to stand up in its own reason and its own courage even against Him." Tinidril might become wise by following this stranger's advice. Would not the King love her more if she were wiser than he? On earth, reports Un-man, women's minds always run ahead of Maleldil's commands. They recognize what is good even before Maleldil does. They are themselves little Maleldils.

This temptation ordeal lasts several days—the Queen wondering, yet resisting, and Ransom occasionally arguing against Un-man's designs. The Un-man attempts to appeal to the Lady's vanity, without conspicuous success. He elaborates upon stories of women who have stood forth alone to brave terrible risks for their children, their lovers, or their people. Each heroine has been temporarily misunderstood and reviled, but is later magnificently vindicated for her sacrifice. The King should be compelled to be free, says the Un-man. The thought of becoming a risk-bearer or tragic pioneer exploits the Lady's love for the King and for her future children. The matter is cruelly complicated, observes Ransom; what the Un-man says is always so very close to the truth. It becomes evident to Ransom finally that this battle cannot be won by the "spiritual" means of reasonable argument. He must himself risk pain and death in physical combat with this enemy. The ensuing battle and (to me) tedious subterranean journey occupies several chapters.

Weston argues in *Perelandra* that "the world leaps forward through great men and greatness always transcends mere moralism." Ordinary people may consider certain things which the Life-Force commands to be diabolical, but a great commitment "utterly overrides all our petty ethical pigeonholes." Weston has now become a convinced believer in emergent evolution. His mission is no longer to spread the human race (as in *Silent Planet*), but to spread "spirituality." In a response that Bonhoeffer or Barth might appreciate, Ransom replies that he does not know much about the "religious view of life" since he happens to be a Christian. Weston, however, is sure that only a few theological technicalities stand between them. His God, he admits, is in no way personal; it would be better, in fact, to call it a Force. "Anthropomorphism is one of the childish diseases of popular religion." The sheer brutality of this new Weston, or the Un-man which he soon becomes, is illustrated by the trail of injured and dying frogs which, in one scene, he leaves behind him. Without hatred, without interest, perhaps without thought, the Un-man rips up the bodies of frog after frog and hurls their remains along his path. Such purposeless destruction is a jarring event in the paradise of Perelandra. We are here given a glimpse of evil in its near purity.

After beginning to learn the language of Malacandra in *Silent Planet*, Ransom is compelled to tell the inhabitants that he has been brought to their world by two "bent" men. This is the nearest term he can discover for translating "bad" into something the *hrossa* will understand. The mere instincts of the *hrossa*, he has learned, resemble the unattained ideals of humanity. In an adventurous and successful *hnakra*-hunt, Ransom's *hross*-companion Hyoi earns the title of *hnakrapunti*, an accomplishment that he has dreamed of all of his life. But in the very moment of his joyous triumph, a rifle shot rings out, and Hyoi is felled by the "bent" earthlings. Ransom sobs, "We are all a bent race. . . . We are only half *hnau*—Hyoi. . . ." Ransom knows no Malacandrian words for *forgive* or *sorry*, but his dying *hross* friend seems to understand. With his last breath, Hyoi extends to Ransom the honor which he himself cherishes most highly. It is a strangely moving scene in which Ransom is called *hnakrapunti* by his dying *hross* companion.

Near the conclusion of *Silent Planet*, Oyarsa concludes upon interviewing Weston that "a bent *hnau* can do more evil than a broken one." Weston has taken a lesser moral law, that of loyalty to kin, and has elevated it as the supreme law. Loyalty to one's own kind is recognized by all *hnau* as an important principle, but it should not drive one to disobey other laws which are even more important. Weston is prepared to sacrifice all other forms of rational life in the universe to his "loyalty to humanity."

Lewis, it seems to me, has chosen a very fortunate and provocative image for translating *sin* on Malacandra. "Bent" suggests distortion, since things are not usually *made* bent. But it also suggests the possibility of correction, since that which is merely bent is not completely broken. Perhaps Lewis got this term from Augustine, who spoke of man as "curvatus." Or he may have gained it from Anders Nygren's *Agape and Eros,* with which he was familiar.

Edmund Fuller says that the third novel in Lewis' science-fiction trilogy, *Hideous Strength,* "pictures an attempt at the dehumanization of man fully as deadly as those imagined by Huxley and Orwell, with the added value that Lewis' vision of the actual nature of man which is being violated is much more profoundly grounded than that of the other two." This book concerns the activities of the "National Institute of Co-ordinated Experiments" (generally known simply as "N.I.C.E.") in its efforts to fuse state and laboratory "to get science applied to social problems." It is a response to the philosophy that existence is its own justification—an idea represented, for example, by C. H. Waddington, the eminent Cambridge embryologist. Waddington is mentioned by name both in *Abolition of Man,* Lewis' lectures on this theme, and in *Hideous Strength,* the novelistic interpretation of the problem. Both books deal with what Lewis called in *Reflections* "the few conditioners and the many conditioned."

N.I.C.E. aims at "Man Immortal and Man Ubiquitous . . . Man on the throne of the universe." The Institute, backed by the whole force of the state, has its own legal staff and police force, freed from the customary restraints. Forty interlocking committees meet at N.I.C.E. daily. A half-million-dollar "Pragmatometer" prints committee findings, and coordinates all relevant parts, every half hour. An official at N.I.C.E. explains the general arrangement to sociology professor Mark Studdock who is considering joining the staff there. Lord Feverstone (the former Dick Devine) admits that he is somewhat vague regarding "any distinct knowledge of its official programme." But the basic idea is that humanity has now reached a crossroads at which man can take control of his own destiny. "If Science is really given a free hand it can now take over the human race and re-condition it: make man a really efficient animal." Certain obscurantists fail to appreciate the vision of N.I.C.E. But Studdock agrees that the preservation of the human race is certainly a "pretty rock-bottom obligation."

"Man has got to take charge of Man," declares Feverstone. "That means, remember, that some men have got to take charge of the rest. . . .

131

You and I want to be the people who do the taking charge, not the ones who are taken charge of." The procedure at N.I.C.E. will involve

simple and obvious things, at first—sterilization of the unfit, liquidation of backward races . . . selective breeding. Then real education, including pre-natal education. . . . A real education makes the patient what it wants infallibly: whatever he or his parents try to do about it. Of course, it'll have to be mainly psychological at first. But we'll get on to biochemical conditioning in the end and direct manipulation of the brain. (*That Hideous Strength,* p. 42)

There are internal disagreements over some details of the N.I.C.E. program. Filostrato dreams of a day when all forests can be removed and natural trees can be replaced by "art" trees of lightweight aluminium. "We will clean the planet," he asserts. "No leaves to fall, no twigs, no birds building nests, no muck and mess." The birds themselves will be replaced by art birds. "Consider again the improvement. No feathers dropped about, no nests, no eggs, no dirt." There will probably come a time when man can sustain himself with chemicals; he will no longer have to stuff himself with dead brutes and weeds, no longer need to reproduce himself with copulation. Man's goal is the conquest of organic life—i.e., the conquest of death.

As the story unfolds, it is revealed that top officials at N.I.C.E. have already succeeded in experiments to produce a new species—the next step in evolution. They have actually preserved the head of François Alcasan, a guillotined murderer-scientist. An ingenious apparatus allows the head to regain consciousness and to speak whenever the air and artificial saliva taps are properly adjusted. Stimulants are introduced to increase the brain's capacity for superhuman consciousness. All of this demonstrates that man can survive death. He can exist nearly independent of nature. It is perfectly proper, N.I.C.E. leaders maintain, to think of this "new type of man" as the "God" of the future. Other heads are to be selected for preservation from among the persons now living at N.I.C.E. These chosen heads will then reign as gods forever.

It becomes clear rather early in *Hideous Strength* that a conflict is shaping up between "Belbury" (the headquarters of N.I.C.E.) and "St. Anne's-on-the-Hill." At St. Anne's a small company is gathered about Mr. Fisher-King (the former Ransom), awaiting orders from the eldils. This company believes that criminal eldils have established their headquarters on the planet earth, and that N.I.C.E. is not concerned basically with materialistic power at all. They suspect that eldilic energy and knowledge lie behind the N.I.C.E. facade. At N.I.C.E. apparently Frost alone is aware (until he informs Studdock) that the Institute is no longer in contact with Alcasan's mind when the Head speaks: the vocal organs and brain are instead relaying communications from the *macrobes*—intelligent organisms above the level of animal life. The orderly society of St. Anne's is in sharp contrast with the chaos which reigns at N.I.C.E. headquarters. A further contrast is seen in the treatment of animals at the two centers. At Belbury, caged creatures await vivisection; at St. Anne's they are jesters, servants, and playfellows.

Lewis gives this third science-fiction novel the subtitle *A Modern Fairy-Tale for Grown-Ups*. A Lyndsay quotation on the title page, concerning the Tower of Babel, indicates the book's theme. Man's effort to reach heaven through his own power—his attempt to play God— is destined to end in chaos and destruction. By denying objective value and by affirming independence from the natural world and from the divine source of his being, man constructs towers toward heaven which can lead only to confusion and misery. Biblical scholars have noted often that the Tower of Babel myth (Genesis 11) enjoys symbolic reversal in the Pentecost experience of the early church (Acts 2). Whereas confusion of tongues is the result in the former account, communication which transcends language barriers is the characteristic of the latter. Lewis appears to be working with this dual theme in *Hideous Strength*. In Chapter 15 ("The Descent of the Gods"), the company gathered at St. Anne's enjoys "toppling structures of double meaning" and "skyrockets of metaphor and allusion." As at Pentecost, "A stranger coming into the kitchen would have thought they were drunk." The group participates in intense sensory experiences, and Ransom finds himself "sitting within the very heart of language, in the white-hot furnace of essential speech." At the Belbury banquet, on the other hand, Lewis paints a scene—hilarious at first, but later tragic—in which the participants' ability to communicate wholly disintegrates. In crystal clear articulation, the main speaker of the evening proclaims: "The madrigore of verjuice must be talthibianised." Further, "The surrogates essemplanted in a continual of porous variations." A startled Deputy Director assumes the platform to quiet the crowd. "Tidies and fugleman," he begins. "I sheel foor. . . ." The gibberish accelerates. It is the beginning of the end for Belbury.

Unlike the other volumes in the triology, *Hideous Strength* is basically an "earth" story. Lewis deemphasized the science-fiction element in behalf of another framework—the Arthurian legend. A reader unacquainted with Arthurian tradition will find much in this book that is puzzling. According to the myth used by Lewis, King Arthur stands perpetual guard over England. Following Malory's *Morte d'Arthur*, it is said that Merlin, the king's magician, was cast into a deep sleep in Nimue, to awaken centuries later. Ransom has become in this story "Mr. Fisher-King" (of the Grail myth), and he is also the "Pendragon" (a successor to Arthur). Ransom's gathered household is the remnant of "Logres," that idealized Britain which, according to Charles Williams, remains ever in conflict with the secular reality. The Arthurian material offers an internal and parallel myth to the cosmic myth of this novel.[9]

Because of its several mythical systems, some of which are likely to be unfamiliar to many readers, *Hideous Strength* is a complex and difficult work. Lewis maintains a relationship with the characters and events of his earlier science-fiction stories. But to this he adds a particular stream of Arthurian tradition, a biblical contrast between Babel and Pentecost, planetary "intelligences" of Medieval tradition, a theological interpretation of the source of evil, and an imaginative account of futuristic society in England. Rudolf Schmerl thinks that Lewis' trilogy distorts too much for full effectiveness; using too many improbabilities, it fails to give the "new and sharper insight into reality" which readers have a right to expect of fantasy. In the case of *Hideous Strength*, I would have to agree. The complexities and improbabilities of the material detract from the impact of the work.

Lewis also uses the genre of fantasy to point in the direction of a remedy for man's fallen condition. One of his most striking theological interpretations is his popular *The Lion, the Witch and the Wardrobe*. The story is not allegory, Lewis insists, but it does suggest what an incarnation might be like if it were to occur in a place like Narnia. *Lion* is a tale of an evil witch, a greedy and treacherous little boy, and a major battle between the forces of good and the powers of evil. As the tale opens, four English children stumble upon the strange country of Narnia by walking through a magic wardrobe. Populated by mythological creatures and talking animals, Narnia is a land in which a little creature is discovered to have on its bookshelf a volume entitled *A Study in Popular Legend: Is Man a Myth?* Lucy, the first to arrive there, is befriended by a faun and told that the land has fallen under the influence of an evil White Witch, who makes it "always winter and never Christmas." But Lucy's brother Edmund meets this witch, who calls herself the Queen, and secretly agrees to bring his brother and two sisters to her, in exchange for some delicious, enchanted "Turkish Delight" and a promise that he can one day be king. The witch knows, as Edmund

---

[9] Two helpful guides for understanding Lewis' use of Arthurian material are Charles Moorman, *Arthurian Triptych* and Charles Williams, *Arthurian Torso*.

does not, that there is a prophecy in that land that her reign and her life will end when four human children sit on the thrones. She intends to see that this prophecy is thwarted as long as possible. Confronted later by Lucy's interpretation of the situation, however, Edmund is already "more than half on the side of the Witch" and chides his sister, "You can't always believe what Fauns say." Already regarded by the other children as too often beastly and nasty, Edmund becomes more vengeful toward the "pack of stuck-up, self-satisfied prigs" when the others discover that he has been lying to them. And learning that his own greediness has led to the arrest of Lucy's friendly faun, and the destruction of its home, Edmund attempts to cast suspicion on the other animals who are friendly to the children.

The four youngsters hear from Mr. Beaver that Aslan is on the move. Though they do not know at first who Aslan is, each child senses some enormous meaning at the very mention of his name. A strange feeling, like good news, again comes over them (except for Edmund) after dinner as Mr. Beaver tells them more about Aslan. Aslan is the great Lion, the King of Beasts. He is the Lord of the whole wood, though he is not often present. In fact, says Beaver, Aslan has never been here "in my time or my father's time." But word has come that Aslan is now returning to set things right. Somewhat nervous over a proposed meeting with Aslan, Susan is assured that her feelings are quite normal. "Then he isn't safe?" asks Lucy. "Course he isn't safe," retorts Beaver. "But he's good." The reader learns later that people who have never been to Narnia "sometimes think that a thing cannot be good and terrible at the same time." Mr. Beaver informs the children that they are to meet Aslan at the Stone Table.

After Edmund manages to slip away from the others to betray their plans to the Witch, Beaver notes that he recognized him as treacherous from the first, as one "who has been with the Witch and eaten her food." It is not that Edmund really wants his brother and sisters turned into stone by the Witch, but he does want to get the best of them. He tries to convince himself that the Witch probably is not as bad as her reputation, even though deep within he really knows her to be evil and cruel. Even before his betrayal is complete, Edmund begins reaping the bitter consequences of his decision. But as he becomes wet, cold, and bruised in his long journey through the forest to find the Witch, his hatred for the other children grows all the more. And he soon discovers, to his further misery, that the Witch is not at all concerned with his comfort and welfare as she sets out to overtake the others in their flight toward Aslan. Before she can intercept the children, however, it appears that the Witch's power has begun to fail. The weather grows warmer. Snow begins to melt, flowers begin to bloom, birds begin to sing. Even the Queen's dwarf-driver admits that her power is slipping: "This is Spring," he exclaims. "This is Aslan's doing."

Coming upon a Christmas party in the woods, the angry Witch turns to stone all the happy creatures present. Edmund begins to feel sorry for someone besides himself. Just as the Witch is preparing to slay Edmund, to assure that the prophecy about the reign of four children will not soon come true, the boy-traitor is rescued by the forces of Aslan. Taking him aside, Aslan talks for a long time with Edmund. Finally, the Lion brings him back to the others with the statement, "Here is your brother. . . . There is no need to talk to him about what is past." Aslan, apparently, is convinced that Edmund should be forgiven his treachery. This result may have been due in part to Peter's confession upon first meeting Aslan, as he attempted to explain Edmund's absence: "That was partly my fault, Aslan. I was angry with him and I think that helped him to go wrong."

Soon the Witch appears again, under a promise of safe conduct, to remind Aslan's party of the great "Law of Deep Magic," which was established in Narnia by the Emperor-Over-Sea at the very beginning —the law, indeed, which was engraved on the Table of Stone itself. According to this ancient law, every traitor becomes the Witch's property, and every treachery gives her the right to a kill. Confronted by this claim, Aslan realizes that the law will have to be fulfilled. He goes into a long, private conference with the Witch. At long last he returns to announce to the others, "I have settled the matter."

In a chapter entitled "The Triumph of the Witch," Peter receives instructions for continuing the battle against the Witch as Aslan hints mysteriously that he himself might not be present. Supper that evening is quiet and sad. Afterwards Lucy and Susan secretly follow the sad and lonely lion up the Hill of the Stone Table. Discovering them, he assures them that he is glad to have their company; but he insists upon going to the very top of the hill all alone. When he reaches the top, Aslan is set upon by a howling, torch-carrying crowd of hideous creatures from the Witch's crew. Lucy and Susan expect him to spring upon his enemies, but the lion makes no resistance and no noise as they bind him so tight that the cords cut his flesh. Then the Witch orders Aslan's beautiful mane shaved off. The crowd surges about him, jeering, kicking, hitting, spitting, and calling things like, "Puss, Puss! Poor Pussy!" and "How many mice have you caught today, Cat?" and "Would you like a saucer of milk, Pussums?" As the great lion is dragged to the Stone Table, the

Witch sharpens her knife. Aslan looks quietly at the sky, neither angry nor afraid, but sad. The distraught girls overhear the Witch speaking of a pact which Aslan has made with her, that through his death the Law of Deep Magic might be fulfilled. "But when you are dead," chortles the Witch, "what will prevent me from killing [Edmund] as well?" The children cannot bear to watch as the Witch's knife falls upon their beloved lion.

After the vile rabble has swept from the hilltop, the two girls, with many tears, manage (aided by some friendly mice) to loosen the ropes around Aslan's body. It is nearly morning when they decide to warm themselves by taking a walk. Suddenly there is a great cracking noise behind them. Returning to the Stone Table, they find it split in two. And Aslan has disappeared. To their amazement, the great Lion soon reappears, assuring them that he is dead no longer.

"What does it all mean?" asks Susan eventually, when they are more calm. Aslan tells them of a "Deeper Magic" of which the Witch has been ignorant. Back before the beginning of time, he says, there stood a different incantation—"that when a willing victim who had committed no treachery was killed in a traitor's stead, the Table would crack and Death itself would start working backwards."

In the hours which follow, Aslan restores to life many of the creatures whom the Witch had turned into statues, and a gigantic battle is waged between the creatures of Aslan and the company of the Witch. Edmund, though wounded in this battle, is himself instrumental in the final destruction of the remaining power of the Witch. The other children notice that Edmund has become "his real old self again and could look you in the face." (It is not clear whether Edmund ever fully realizes what Aslan has done on his behalf.) After a victorious battle, the ancient prophecy is fulfilled, and the four children are crowned the kings and queens of Narnia. Aslan slips quietly away, leaving the children to reign. Mr. Beaver had prepared them for this. "He'll be coming and going," he said. "One day you'll see him and another you won't. . . . He'll often drop in. Only you mustn't press him. He's wild, you know. Not like a *tame* lion." One familiar with Lewis' thought may here recall his distinction between magic and prayer. Magic attempts to *control* the supernatural. Prayer intends to make requests of the divine and to live in response to the divine. The God of the New Testament is not "tame"; he is not subject to control or manipulation.

Long and happy is the reign of the four children. Edmund comes to be known in the land as King Edmund the Just. There is finally an incident, however, which hurls the four back through the magic wardrobe. And they discover that their journey-of-years in Narnia has not taken an hour of ordinary English time. Their professor friend tells the children that this is to be expected, that any other world surely has its own kind of time.

It must be stressed here that theological content does not stand out as sharply in Lewis' story as it does in this abstract of his theme. It is possible in this day of theological illiteracy for some adults as well as children to read *Lion* as an exciting fantasy without recognizing any parallel between this material and the story of the Gospels. The material which I have discussed in detail here is concentrated in only four of the seventeen chapters of *Lion*. Although this theological dimension is present, it is blended with sparkling conversation, exciting adventures, and vivid natural descriptions in such a way that it does not appear particularly didactic to most readers.

The role of the professor in the book merits special attention. Before the rest of them have discovered the strange land of Narnia, the children come to their old friend about Lucy's claims to have been there. It is clear that this old professor is no materialist. "Well, sir," ventures Peter, "if things are real, they're there all the time." "Are they?" asks the professor. "But do you really mean, sir, that there could be other worlds?" "Nothing is more probable," says the professor. "I wonder what they *do* teach them at these schools." The old man warns the children that testimonies of unusual experience from usually reliable persons deserve careful consideration. "A charge of lying against someone who you have always found truthful is a very serious thing; a very serious thing indeed." Lewis seems here to be making the point, often emphasized by philosophers of religion, that the testimony of intelligent and saintly persons to the reality and significance of a spiritual dimension in life is not to be lightly dismissed by philosophers.

The professor assures the children following the end of their reign in Narnia that they will probably return there someday, but that the same route will never work twice. "Don't *try* to get there at all," he warns. "It'll happen when you're not looking for it." The professor here closely resembles the Prof. Lewis who has written so extensively in other books about the experiences of otherworldly *Joy*, which can never be captured through deliberate effort.

In another scene in *Lion*, it is Mr. Beaver who echoes Lewis' dread of the inauthentically human. Speaking of the White Witch, who looks human but really is not, Beaver advises, "When you meet anything that's going to be human and isn't yet, or used to be human once and isn't now, or ought to be human and isn't, you keep your eyes on it and feel for your hatchet."

Above all, *Lion* places in a simple children's narrative the idea that "grace" is superior to "law." The "Law of Deep Magic" is overcome by "Deeper Magic." The very table upon which the law is written is torn asunder and the law is abolished as the primary principle ruling Narnia. Narnian creatures can now live in the knowledge that Aslan, their Lord, has given himself in sacrificial love—a love which has the power, in a design older than time itself, to transcend the law and even to overcome death itself. The witch and her old ways are defeated, Edmund is forgiven and transformed, and the possibility of a new life opens before all the creatures of the land.

Both in theological exposition and in the genre of the novel, Lewis emphasizes his conviction that man has an inclination toward sin, and that at some particular point man has "tumbled down a moral cliff." In Lewis' early long poem, before he recognized the fruits of rebellion, Dymer enjoyed the anarchy of "the unfettered lands," out of the reach of the old laws. But in the long run, Lewis later admitted, man's freedom "is only a freedom of better or worse response." The soul's search for God is but an appearance of God's search for man. Everything derives from God; even the possibility of our loving him is a gift from him. Human evil results from man's misuse of God's good creation. Ransom describes Weston to the Green Lady as one who clings to "the wrong good." And the reader learns in *Magician's Nephew* that those who pluck good fruits at the wrong time or in the wrong way come to loathe them ever after. Still the temptation to "be like God" and to deny a creaturely status persists in every generation. The human race is both fallen and continually falling. The myth of the Fall points both to man's lofty origin and to the eternal temptation to respond to the Creator in rebellion and disobedience. As Lewis puts it in *Silver Chair,* those "Northern Witches" always mean the same thing, but they have a different plan for achieving it in each age.

VII

Man as He May Become: Redemption, with Fresh Images of New Men

Part I: New Men, Grace, Faith, and Love

Christianity and new men:

Compared with the development of man on this planet, the diffusion of Christianity over the human race seems to go like a flash of lightning—for two thousand years is almost nothing in the history of the universe. . . . Century by century God has guided nature up to the point of producing creatures which can (if they will) be taken right out of nature, turned into "gods." . . . Already the new men are dotted here and there all over the earth. Some, as I have admitted, are still hardly recognisable: but others can be recognised. Every now and then one meets them. Their very voices and faces are different from ours; stronger, quieter, happier, more radiant. They begin where most of us leave off. . . . I strongly suspect that they recognise one another immediately and infallibly, across every barrier of colour, sex, class, age, and even of creeds. In that way, to become holy is rather like joining a secret society. To put it at the very lowest, it must be great *fun*.

—*Mere Christianity*, pp. 186-88

People sometimes wonder what the next step in evolution might be. From the Christian point of view the human race is right now embarking upon its next major phase, as men change from being creatures of God to becoming sons of God. In a captivating vision of man's potential in *Mere Christianity*, Lewis claimed that the present process represents a sharp turn in nature. Far more than just another improvement in the species, this stage actually marks a transformation of human nature.

While all of these "new men" share in the life of Christ, there is no dull sameness about these individuals. Sameness, Lewis noted, predominates among natural men. The great saints have been more gloriously different from each other than have the great tyrants and conquerors of

140

history. Men are invited to forget their old natural selves and to move into this entirely new realm. Here they can begin to become what they were designed by their Creator to be. "Putting on Christ" is the whole task of a Christian. The process differs completely from the ordinary idea of "being good." For many people morality implies the meeting of certain demands or obligations in order to dismiss them and to get back to the main business of satisfying one's own desires. The natural self remains for them the central point of reference. But those who try to satisfy both conscience and self are headed for conflict, said Lewis. Torn between two competing sets of desires, eventually they will either give up trying to be good or make of themselves reluctant, grumbling martyrs.

According to Lewis, Christ comes to man announcing something like this: "I have not come to torment your natural self, but to kill it. I will give you a new self instead." The Christian life is in one sense very hard, while in another way it is very easy (as Christ himself noted). A person finds it difficult to surrender his whole self, his natural desires and interests. But once he does so, he is released from the burden of natural fussing and fretting. Human beings would often be glad to settle for some goal short of perfection, but God is not thus content. The command to be perfect is not "idealistic gas." It is the divine goal for every man, even though the task cannot be completed in this lifetime.

Man has a resemblance to God, a "shape" or a "likeness" of the divine. As the highest of the animals, he is the nearest resemblance to God that we know. If there are creatures more like the Creator in other worlds, we do not yet know about them. Man lives, loves, and thinks. Biological life has found its highest level in man. But men are not fully "sons of God" in their natural state. They can become such only by placing their confidence in Christ and by receiving the new life he makes available.

Lewis found it so confusing to use the word *life* for two very different realities that he adopted Greek terms to distinguish sharply between biological life and spiritual life. *Bios* represents the sort of life that comes to men through nature. It is the kind of life which tends always to run down and decay apart from the incessant subsidies from nature (air, water, food, etc.). *Zoe,* on the other hand, represents spiritual life. This is the type of life which man does not have at all in his natural condition. It is a higher kind of life which exists in God and which has been in him from all eternity. It is the kind of spiritual life which made the entire natural universe.

Christianity is concerned with the possibility of a man with *Bios* "coming to life" on the level of *Zoe*. If he will let God have his way, a person can come to share in this life of Christ, the unique Son of God. As men share in *Zoe*, they also become sons of God. Christ came into the world and became a man for this very purpose—that *Zoe* might be spread to others. The process of passing on *Zoe* may be viewed as a "good infection."

How can the act of a single person living a long time ago have anything to do with people living in the twentieth century? Lewis attempted to answer this question through his concept of the corporate nature of mankind. The concept seems to have been largely taken for granted in the early church, but the idea has been nearly absent from the thought of our individualistic era.

Human beings may appear to be separate because they walk around separately. In reality, however, they are not separate. From a divine point of view, humanity must look like a single growing thing—perhaps like a complex tree. In this one huge organism every individual is obviously connected with every other. The parts of the organism are related biologically, and they are related by the Divine Spirit that provides them all with simple life.

It is this gigantic human organism that the Christ-life has begun to affect. God took human form and was born into the world as an actual man. In him the natural life of human desire was killed. He allowed himself to be completely and perfectly taken up into the divine. When he was executed, the human creature united to the divine Son came to life again. The man in Christ rose again, and the world saw for the first time what a real man was like. Christ began to affect the whole human organism in a new way. And from that point the effect has continued to spread through all mankind. The good infection is still in process. The possibility of becoming a son of God, of passing from temporal biological life to timeless spiritual life, is now available to men. Salvation has already come to humanity in principle. Individuals must now appropriate what is potentially available if new life is to be theirs.

How does a person "come alive" to *Zoe*? What does one do to gain the "mind of Christ" or to be "born again"? Lewis recommended that one begin behaving as though he already possessed this quality of life, and that he try to be like Christ. The Son of God will begin to work upon the willing person in any number of ways: through nature, through his own body, through books, through "religious" experiences, and even through apparently anti-Christian experiences. Above all, Christ approaches persons through other persons. Christians often carry Christ to others. Sometimes the good infection is relayed by those who do not even recognize it themselves. It is very important, however, not to rely solely upon another human being, but to know the true source of this spirit. Other persons, subject to mistakes and to death as they are, cannot provide the firm foundation which is needed by faith.

When Christians speak of the presence of Christ, they mean a real living person. Christ comes interfering, said Lewis,

with your very self; killing the old natural self in you and replacing it with the kind of self He has. At first, only for moments. Then for longer periods. Finally, if all goes well, turning you permanently into a different sort of thing; into a new little Christ, a being which, in its own small way, has the same kind of life as God; which shares in His power, joy, knowledge and eternity. (*Mere Christianity*, p. 164)

Lewis offered in his imaginative works two memorable descriptions of the agony involved in becoming a "new man." There is in *Divorce* a ghost who has long struggled with a red lizard of Lust on his shoulder. Yet he declines to accept the necessary pain of having the flaming Angel come near enough to destroy the creature. He rationalizes: "Look, it's gone to sleep of its own accord. I'm sure it'll be all right now. . . . I think the gradual process would be far better than killing it." The lizard finally torments its victim so severely that the flaming spirit is allowed to approach. Following a moment of agony, the lustful ghost begins to grow solid enough to remain in heaven. And the lizard itself is transformed into a great stallion. An aspect of man that once was an enemy has become now a servant.

A further illustration of radical change is provided in a Narnia story. Eustace Scrubb, a dreadful little boy who likes bossing and bullying, has no friends and dislikes his Pevensie cousins. He slips away from his work and his companions on Dragon Island one day and comes upon the cave of a dead dragon. Having slept on its treasures, he awakens to find himself changed into a horrible creature. "Sleeping on a dragon's hoard with greedy, dragonish thoughts in his heart, he had become a dragon himself." Eustace feels relieved at first; now he has the power to terrorize others. But suddenly he realizes that he wants friends, not the life of a monster cut off from the human race. He begins to wonder whether he has been the fine person he has always thought. He flies back to the ship where the Pevensie children eventually guess the truth about the identity of the weeping beast. It is clear that Eustace's character has improved upon his becoming a dragon. He is actually eager now to help his shipmates.

Later on, Eustace becomes a boy again—a different kind of boy—

and he tells the others how he became un-dragoned. A huge lion had led him to a big round pool on the mountain top. As he attempted to undress for the bath, Eustace removed layer after layer of dragon skin. It finally became evident that only the lion could undress him properly. While the dragon lay on his back, the lion tore deep into his flesh, pulled off the skin, and then threw him into the water. Eustace was changed back into a boy and provided with new clothes. "I think you've seen Aslan," says Edmund. "Between ourselves, you haven't been as bad as I was on my first trip to Narnia. You were only an ass, but I was a traitor." Eustace sometimes has relapses after this experience, and he can still be very tiresome. But the cure has begun.

Lewis said in *Mere Christianity* that "the central Christian belief is that Christ's death has somehow put us right with God and given us a fresh start. Theories as to how it did this are another matter." Originally given as a series of BBC broadcast talks, the material in this book attempts to explain and defend central Christian beliefs which have been held by most Christians down through the ages. Lewis was concerned here only with the bare essentials—"mere" Christianity, as Baxter called it. Differences of belief should be discussed, Lewis felt only within the circle of those who already believe that Jesus Christ is the only Son of the one God. A *Christian*, briefly, is "one who accepts the common doctrines of Christianity." So used, the term is not at all one of praise or moral judgment. It is impossible to determine who is or is not close to "the spirit of Christ." Lewis followed, therefore, the original meaning of the term as it was used at Antioch to refer to those who accepted the teaching of the apostles and became disciples of Christ.

Christ was central in Lewis' theology, but he encouraged flexibility in interpreting the doctrines of the Incarnation and the Atonement. He noted in a letter that one can be a Christian even while saying, "I believe that Christ's death redeemed man from sin, but I can make nothing of the theories as to *how!*" Further, every person is loved individually by God, as though he were the only creature in existence. God is not like a government which deals with people only in mass. There is a sense in which God is present everywhere, acknowledged Lewis. But He is most likely to be known in Christ and the church. Lewis suggests in a poem that men know God best

> Not in Nature, not even in Man, but in one
> Particular Man, with a date, so tall, weighing
> So much, talking Aramaic, having learned a trade.

This "Particular Man," who came bringing God's offer of new life, figures occasionally even in the fantasies of Lewis. The Oyarsa of the planet Malacandra engages Ransom in an extensive discussion about "what Maleldil has done in Thulcandra." Following that conversation, Oyarsa is persuaded that the earth is not so fast shut against spiritual forces as he had formerly supposed. And the Green Lady of Perelandra notes that the eldila have had little power on earth since the Incarnation. Since "the great change," she says, nothing stands between man and Maleldil the Creator. Screwtape, of course, does not believe in God's grace, and he suspects that "all his talk about Love must be a disguise for something else. . . . We know that He cannot really love: nobody can; it doesn't make sense. If we could only find out what He is *really* up to!"

Lewis repeatedly made the point that man's salvation comes as a result of faith in God's grace, not as the product of human moral effort. He paid tribute to George Macdonald by saying that no one in modern times was more aware of the inevitable failure of mere morality, apart from the Gospel, than was this Scottish divine. Lewis explained in *Surprised* how his own schoolboy religion became an intolerable burden as he attempted to accomplish the impossible through willpower.

Night after night, dizzy with desire for sleep and often in a kind of despair, I endeavoured to pump up my 'realisations.' . . . The cold oilcloth, the quarters chiming, the night slipping past, the sickening, hopeless weariness. This was the burden from which I longed with soul and body to escape. It had already brought me to such a pass that the nightly torment projected its gloom over the whole evening, and I dreaded bedtime as if I were a chronic sufferer from insomnia. Had I pursued the same road much further I think I should have gone mad. (P. 54)

By "realisations" Lewis meant a sufficient vividness of imagination and affection. The above account resembles that of Martin Luther describing the days just prior to his justification-by-faith experience. But the immediate outcome for Lewis was quite different; he wrote, "I became an apostate, dropping my faith with no sense of loss but with the greatest relief."

Lewis further expressed dissatisfaction with the moralistic approach to life in *Regress*. The boy John early discovers the frustration of attempting to live by burdensome religious regulations. He finds that the rule card which he has received from the Landlord's Steward has one set of rules printed on the front and another set on the back. The second list of rules often contradicts the first. When Mr. Vertue is questioned

145

later about his destination, he admits that he is not clear about the goal; but he thinks the question rather unimportant. "These speculations don't make one a better walker," Vertue responds. "The great thing is to do one's thirty miles a day." Mr. Vertue declines Mother Kirk's offer of assistance for crossing the gorge. He can accept orders from no one, he says: he is determined to remain the captain of his own soul. He comes at last, however, to admit that there is a problem in his position: "If there is something to go to, it is a bribe, and I cannot go to it: if I can go, then there is nothing to go to." A scene in *Divorce* may serve as a summary of Lewis' attitude on this matter. A self-righteous ghost protests to one of "the bright people," "I'm asking for nothing but my rights. . . . I'm not asking for anybody's bleeding charity." The solid person quickly replies, "Then do. At once. Ask for the Bleeding Charity. Everything is here for the asking and nothing can be bought."

The Christian life begins in repentance for sin and trust in God's grace. Once a sin is repented and forgiven, said Lewis, it is annihilated. One may continue to be sorry for having been that sort of person, but there is no need to continue to seek pardon. Genuine repentance is more than disappointment or irritation at oneself. Lewis personally spoke with great appreciation of the voluntary arrangement provided for confession in the Anglican Church. The objective experience, he thought, helps many people actually to feel forgiven, and it strengthens their self-knowledge. Lewis distinguished between "guilt-feelings" and objective guilt. A person may have a pathological sense of guilt and not be guilty really. Or one may be guilty in an objective sense without any anguish of conscience. Lewis noted in *Surprised* that as a youth he felt no guilt for moral lapses except as an incident broke an honor code or stirred his pity. "It took me as long to acquire inhibitions as others (they say) have taken to get rid of them. That is why I often find myself at such cross-purposes with the modern world: I have been a converted Pagan living among apostate Puritans."

The term *faith* is used by Christians in two senses. In one sense, it means *belief*—that is, steadfastly regarding the doctrines of Christianity as true. This kind of faith is regarded traditionally as a virtue; for even after a man has made the best intellectual judgment of which he is capable, a battle continues to rage within his consciousness. Faith and reason become allied against the forces of emotion and imagination. Faith, then, is "the art of holding on to things your reason has once accepted, in spite of your changing moods." No one is expected to accept Christianity if his best reasoning finds the weight of evidence against it. And whatever additional evidence turns up will merit further rational attention. But the real problem arises from the fact that the mind is not ruled completely by reason. It will not go on automatically regarding a given belief as true after that belief has been worked out rationally. Wishes and desires mount a "blitz" against the logic of faith. Lewis claimed that a man can be neither a sound Christian nor a sound atheist unless he is willing to teach his moods "where they get off." Through daily reading, meditation, and prayer, one must reinforce in his own mind the main Christian doctrines, which he has already confessed to be true.

In another and more important sense, *faith* means *action*. It involves the attempt to put Christian belief into practice. If any person seriously tries to do this for a few weeks, he discovers certain facts about himself. For one thing, only those who earnestly try to resist temptation will find out how strong temptation can be; the man who gives in quickly does not know its full strength. But one also learns that his efforts to practice the Christian virtues are doomed to failure. He is unable to achieve them in his own power. Lewis thinks that no one can come into a proper relation with God until he has discovered his own moral bankruptcy. And a person does not know the depth of his own inadequacy until he fails even as he tries his hardest to fulfill God's law. There must come a time, before one can begin to have a right relationship with God, when a person recognizes the impossibility of attaining salvation through his own efforts. There comes a change from being full of confidence about one's own moral efforts to a state of despair over what one is able to accomplish. This change may come in a moment, or it may occur so gradually that one cannot point even to a particular year in which it happened. But the Christian finds himself turning to God for the gift of salvation which he is unable to merit, trusting that Christ will somehow make good his deficiencies and share with him His sonship.

Moral effort is not ended, of course, when one "turns to God" in failure or despair. While one cannot deserve God's love, to trust Christ means that one tries to do what He says—to take his advice, to obey him. Things are done now not in order to earn salvation, but because the process of salvation has already begun. The first faint gleam of heaven makes a person want to act in a proper way. There is little point in debating whether "good actions" or "faith in Christ" is more important. Both are essential, like two blades of a pair of scissors. When God and man work closely together, it is impossible to determine precisely what God does and what man does. But we can be certain that genuine faith in Christ involves trust and obedience—not just the intellectual acceptance of some theory about Christ.

Lewis elaborated further upon the nature of faith in his essay "On Obstinacy in Belief." It is inadequate, he stated here, to say that the scientist is concerned with knowledge while the Christian is concerned with belief. All men prefer knowledge to belief in those areas where knowledge is possible. And all men hold numerous beliefs in those areas of life where the scientific method does not apply. Belief is "assent to a proposition which we think so overwhelmingly probable that there is a psychological exclusion of doubt, though not a logical exclusion of dispute."

What is the role of evidence for the person considering Christianity? And why do Christians often encourage "firm faith" to withstand the blows and assaults of new evidence against religion? Lewis pointed out that these are actually two distinct questions: evidence is considered in one way prior to Christian commitment and in another way following such a commitment. Any man who accepts Christianity thinks that he bases his decision on good evidence. His evidence may be from history, religious experience, respected authority, or from any combination of these. No one is expected to accept beliefs in the absence of evidence or in the teeth of evidence, but the arguments against religion are not as firm as some suppose. In modern times theism may be "explained" in half a dozen different ways. And atheism is subject to similar explanations. If Christianity is interpreted as a "father-wish," for example, atheism can be interpreted as a non-father-wish. Nothing logically conclusive can be demonstrated from such arguments. A man is free to weigh all the pros and cons before making up his mind. After he makes a religious commitment, however, the situation is different. God's existence is no longer considered a speculative question (although works of apologetics may give this impression). When the question is answered in the affirmative, the Christian stands before God as a person. What might previously have been mere variations in opinion now become variations in personal attitude toward this person.

New evidence relating to faith is always rising. Some of it will be favorable to the primary commitment, and some unfavorable. Yet what appears to be a knowledge-by-acquaintance demands trust beyond some immediate bit of apparently contrary evidence. In fact, the believer anticipates that the operations of an infinitely wise God will not always be plain to him. (If his belief actually is a delusion, of course, this kind of reasoning may render it nearly incurable.) Why did Jesus once say to Thomas, "Blessed are those that have not seen and have believed"?

It should be remembered, Lewis said, that Jesus was speaking here to a particular person who had known him for a long time, who had seen him do many unusual things, and who refused to believe one thing more even though Jesus had often predicted it and it was vouched for by all his closest friends. This, said Lewis, was a rebuke not to philosophic skepticism, but to psychological suspicion. Once personal assent is given, belief is not to be proportioned to each fluctuation of apparent evidence. Faith becomes a matter of trusting the One who is deemed entirely trustworthy.

In spite of the obstinacy of his faith Lewis' writings also reflect a deep sensitivity to the perplexity which is one aspect of human experience and faith. *Malcolm* and *Grief* especially are noteworthy in this regard. Lewis alluded repeatedly to Pascal's famous statement: "The silence of those eternal spaces frightens me." Perhaps this sentence is mentioned throughout Lewis' works more often than any other single quotation.

From *Dymer* (in 1926) to *Faces* (in 1956), Lewis suggested in his imaginative works that human knowledge of the divine is limited and that many questions remain unanswered. Dymer asks a mysterious apparition why humans are lured on with whisperings at heart and soul-sickening gleams. "Must things of dust / Guess their own way in the dark?" he inquires. The shape replies, "They must." The Fox, the Greek slave in *Faces*, protests the paradoxical utterances of the priest of Ungit. The priest responds that nothing which is said clearly about the gods is the truth about them. "Holy places are dark places. It is life and strength, not knowledge and words, that we get in them." In the same story Psyche is compelled to say to Orual about the supernatural, "It's no use, Maia. . . . I see it and you don't. Who's to judge between us?" Lewis pondered in *Grief*, "Can a mortal ask questions which God finds unanswerable? Quite easily, I should think. All nonsense questions are unanswerable. How many hours are there in a mile? Is yellow square or round? Probably half the questions we ask—half our great theological and metaphysical problems—are like that."

If God exists, said Lewis, a person neither reaches him nor avoids him by traveling to Alpha Centauri. Some find God everywhere; others, nowhere. "Those who do not find Him on earth are unlikely to find Him in space." Some people conclude that the "voice" which speaks to them in conscience and in intense joy is their closest possible contact with the mystery of ultimate reality, and that this voice is to be trusted and obeyed, feared and desired, above all else. Other people do not draw this conclusion. For most, Lewis thought, belief or disbelief depends upon the prevailing tone of the circles they frequent. He warned further, "The world is full of impostors who claim to be disenchanted and are really unenchanted: mere 'natural' men who have never risen so high as to be in danger of the generous illusions they claim to have escaped from."

Many of Lewis' letters (now collected in *Letters*) comment upon the importance of maintaining the struggle for faith. He sent his "condolences and congratulations" to an adult convert and warned that the life just begun will not be without distress. In another letter he wrote, "How right you are when you say 'Christianity is a terrible thing for a lifelong atheist to have to face'! In people like us—adult converts in the 20th century—I take this feeling to be a good symptom." "Relying on God has to begin all over again every day as if nothing had yet been done," Lewis told another correspondent. In a letter to a Roman Catholic sister he said, "I now feel that one must never say one believes or understands anything; any morning a doctrine I thought I already possessed may blossom into this new reality." His letters sometimes note, as does *Screwtape,* that a psychological state of confidence fluctuates and "by no means always accompanies intellectual assent." Lewis wrote to a friend that while faith no longer presented him with intellectual difficulty, he sometimes had the feeling that there was nothing he disliked so much as religion. He found himself too prone to ask, "Do I believe? Am I enjoying this?" He reported in *Surprised* that he ceased being a Christian when "the Enemy" led him to think that nothing was to be believed unless it was either comforting or exciting.

Thus the life of faith is not without intellectual and emotional strain. Whatever one's religious position, Lewis says in *Reflections,* feelings will continue to assault that conviction. "As I well remember, the atheist too has his moments of shuddering misgiving, of an all but irresistible suspicion that old tales may after all be true, that something or someone from outside may at any moment break into his neat, explicable, mechanical universe." Lewis had even Screwtape confess himself sometimes nearly in despair, occasionally tempted toward the "silly nonsense and claptrap" of the Enemy. The major threat to faith, then, comes not from reason, but from such things as lust, terror, jealousy, boredom, or indifference. Genuine faith means "continuing to believe what we once honestly thought to be true until cogent reasons for honestly changing our minds are brought before us."

The God in whom Christians believe remains partially hidden in mystery, never subject to human control or total human comprehension. As Lewis wrote in *Malcolm,* "A *safe* God, a tame god, soon proclaims himself to any sound mind as a fantasy." This theme is echoed in the Narnia stories as we read again and again that Aslan is no *tame* lion. When Jill asks Aslan whether he will promise not to injure her, he replies, "I make no promise." "Do you eat girls?" she asks. The lion responds, "I have swallowed up girls and boys, women and men, kings and emperors, cities and realms." In *Horse and Boy*, Aslan reveals that he was the one who haunted the long journey. He refuses to tell Shasta why he has frightened and wounded Aravis, however. "I tell no-one any story but his own," the Large Voice gently explains.

In other words, Lewis insists upon maintaining a clear distinction between magic and religion. Genuine religion is more concerned with responding to the supernatural than it is with practicing control over the supernatural. Contrary to Freud's assumption, religious experience is not always in accord with human wishes. Biblical faith speaks of a God who, according to Buber, "does not let Himself be conjured." He is a good God, but He also remains "wild."

One final comment is necessary before departing from Lewis' understanding of faith. A *TLS* review of *Discarded Image* concludes with these startling words about Lewis: "Our last glimpse is not of a fideistic but of a profoundly sceptical mind." Lewis' thought was not as dogmatic and rigid as it has sometimes been represented. But neither was he in his later years any profound skeptic so far as the Christian faith was concerned. The skepticism which Lewis expressed near the conclusion of *Discarded Image* refers to the possibility of discovering any accurate "models" of the universe. World-pictures have changed through the centuries, and they continue to change as they reflect current scientific thinking. The *TLS* reviewer seems not to have understood that religious faith can exist quite independent of any particular world-picture. The worldview of Christianity may fit any of several pictures of the universe, and the Christian need not believe that any permanent world-picture is available to the limited understanding of man.

Another theme which Lewis stressed throughout his work is the utterly crucial nature of human choice. Too many people in our time, he thought, attempt to shuffle through life without making serious moral distinctions. It is a disastrous error to attempt "a marriage between heaven and hell," as did Blake. These great opposites are forever divorced. One's eternal destiny depends upon the central choice which he makes between God's will and self-will. As guide Macdonald says in *Divorce*, "There are only two kinds of people in the end: those who say to God, 'Thy will be done,' and those to whom God says, in the end,

'*Thy* will be done.' All that are in Hell, choose it. Without that self-choice there could be no Hell."

While many modern theologians (following I John 4) emphasize that there is no fear in love, Lewis was not averse to suggesting that fear plays a lowly but indispensable role in promoting the proper spiritual choices. He followed George Macdonald in believing that fear might take one's mind briefly off oneself, thereby granting a chance for salvation. Fear is not repentance, Lewis wrote, but it is a satisfactory introduction to repentance. It is better to be afraid prior to repentance than not to be afraid. He noted that his own schoolboy religion contained a great deal of fear. But he said, "I do not think there was more than was wholesome or even necessary. . . . I feared for my soul. . . . The effect, so far as I can judge, was entirely good. I began seriously to pray and to read my Bible and to attempt to obey my conscience." A certain "fear of the Lord" may be a desirable religious attitude. But Lewis made no attempt to distinguish between healthy and harmful feelings of fear, or between *filial* fear and *servile* fear. Reading the accounts of his boyhood religious experience in *Regress* and *Surprised,* one may even suspect some connection between the fearful religion of Lewis' youth and the eighteen years of atheism which followed it.

The conflicts between God-centeredness and self-centeredness, between the forces of good and evil, between God and Satan, are featured in many of Lewis' imaginative works. He suggests in *Mere Christianity* that the earth is now enemy-occupied territory. A battle motif permeates many episodes in the Narnia chronicles and in the science-fiction trilogy. One does not become good or carry out God's will effortlessly. Righteousness is always accompanied by struggle. It is impossible to remain neutral in the great battle. One is either wittingly or unwittingly the servant of God or of Satan. "Satan" may be represented in the avarice of a Devine (and Lord Feverstone) or in the false gods of Weston and Filostrato. Lewis suggested in a letter that God's grace inspires not only victory, but also struggle toward victory. "Is not this continued avoidance either of presumption or despair, this ever renewed struggle itself a great triumph of Grace?"

Salvation, according to Lewis, involves the universal principle of dying to live. Since the self is God's chief competitor, self-centeredness must die before human beings can become what they were created to be. In a Magadalen College sermon Lewis expounded upon the human "craving for limited liabilities." Lewis once found that he had prayed "so to pass through things *eternal* as not to lose the things *temporal.*"

It is human nature, he reflected, to consider reservations, to look eagerly for the minimum that God will accept—provided that the claims of religion are admitted at all. But "it is not so much of our time or so much of our attention that God demands; it is not even all our time and all our attention: it is our selves."

The struggle to overcome theological self-centeredness received prominent attention throughout Lewis' work. A double-meaning may be suspected behind John's words in *Regress* when he finally confesses to Mother Kirk, "I have come to give myself up." Screwtape concludes that the Enemy really does love human vermin—those "hairless bipeds." God wants men to lose their selves (their self-will) so that they can become more fully themselves than ever before. Lewis noted that Milton's Adam, confined to a small park on a small planet, has interests embracing all heaven and earth. But in the immensity of creation, Satan has found only one thing that interests him: Satan. A "monomaniac concern with himself and his supposed rights and wrongs is a necessity of the Satanic predicament." Those who refuse to be honest with themselves and others, Lewis suggested in *Divorce,* are like the seedy tragedian actor who cannot turn off his performance, but who grows smaller and smaller until he vanishes. In a poem, appropriately called "Legion," Lewis considers the multiple factions of the poet's consciousness as his "quarrelling selves."

Even the church has not sufficiently stressed the imperative nature of the great central choice, said Lewis. In *Regress,* Mr. Broad enjoys tea on the lawn and admits that he is inclined to set less store in orthodoxy as he grows older. To John's statement that he is trying to find an island in the West, Mr. Broad smiles: "That is a beautiful idea. . . . The seeking is the finding." John continues, "I want to know whether it is really necessary to cross the canyon." "My dear boy," replies Mr. Broad, "there is a very real danger at your age of trying to make these things too definite. . . . These great truths need re-interpretation in every age." Lewis appeared to think that the necessity for ultimate choice cannot be demythologized. Even Screwtape finds that some religion is a good thing, although one should observe moderation in everything. "A moderated religion is as good for us as no religion at all," the fiend chuckles, "and more amusing." Screwtape warns Wormwood against being overly eager to report spectacular wickedness in his patient. The patient may have an uneasy feeling that he has not been doing well recently, but he should be led to think that all his choices are trivial and revocable. "Indeed," notes Screwtape, "the safest road to Hell is the gradual one—the gentle slope, soft underfoot, without sudden turnings, without milestones, without signposts."

153

How does human choice relate to God's grace? "The real inter-relation between God's omnipotence and Man's freedom is something we can't find out," wrote Lewis. Conversion often seems, from within, to be wholly dependent upon God's grace. But it is impossible to make a general rule that is consistent with both the idea of divine justice and the responsibility of personal choice. The Calvinist question about free will and predestination is insoluble. Perhaps it is a meaningless question since it never arises in any concrete practical case. Even when influenced by grace, said Lewis, it remains *our* will. "What God does for us, He does in us. The process of doing it will appear to me (and not falsely) to be the daily or hourly repeated exercises of my own will." Man cannot by an effort of will abandon the "fatal reservation" of self-will; only God working in man can lead one to a renunciation of this cautious attitude. Even Weston is not compelled to become the incarnation of the Devil; he opens himself to that possibility gradually, choice by choice, until finally he cries out, "I call that Force into me completely. . . ." On the other hand, John begins to feel trapped by his formerly absent Landlord. After eating the flat-tasting bread the Man left for him, he knows that he is "caught into slavery again, to walk warily and on sufferance all his days, never to be alone; never the master of his own soul, to have no privacy, no corner whereof you could say to the whole universe: This is my own, here I can do as I please." As a Solid Person remarks in *Divorce,* "There are no private affairs."

A Christian commitment immediately involves one in responsible concern for his neighbors. Through Screwtape, Lewis poked fun at the kind of spiritual life which avoids the consideration of basic everyday human relationships. Religion can be so directed toward concern about the "inner life" and the "souls" of people that it wholly ignores real people all about. Lewis asked in a poem, "Who, that can love nonentities, would choose the labour / Of loving the quotidian face and fact, his neighbour?"

Christian morality is concerned with three things, said Lewis: (1) justice and harmony between individuals; (2) personal integrity; and (3) the purpose of life as a whole. Moral rules are for the purpose of keeping the human machine functioning properly. They exist to prevent unnecessary breakdown, strain, and friction. Every moral failure is a source of trouble, at least to the person primarily involved, and probably to other persons as well.

It is natural that the idea of morality is associated primarily with social relations. The results of poor performance in this sphere are everywhere so obvious. But morality inside the individual is equally important.

Men cannot be compelled to goodness by law, but without good men a good society is impossible. Furthermore, religious belief influences one's conduct, as differing interpretations of the universe lead to different responses. The Christian belief in immortality, for example, has considerable influence upon moral behavior. If one believes he is destined to live forever, he has a very different perspective on life than he otherwise would.

According to the Christian idea, a man's goodness is determined not so much by what he does as by what he does with what he has. Both Christianity and psychoanalysis make certain claims for putting the human machine right. It should be noted that two elements are always present in a moral choice—feeling and choosing. But these various feelings and impulses may be considered either normal or abnormal. In the latter case, psychoanalysts can help to remove unnatural feelings, giving a person better "raw material" upon which to base his acts of moral choice. Bad psychological material is a disease to be cured, not a sin. Morality is concerned only with the real, free choice of a man—whatever the material presented to him. Will he place his own advantage always first or not?

Here is the reason Christians are not to "judge" others. A man can criticize others for external actions, but God judges on the basis of what one does with the raw material which he has been provided. Some who appear very unworthy may have done much with the limited potential that was theirs. Most of a man's psychological makeup will probably perish with the body at death, said Lewis. The "real central man"—the thing that chose—alone will endure.

Christian morality is not simply a matter of keeping rules in anticipation of eventual reward. The results of moral choice have immediate built-in consequences. Every choice affects the real man, making one something a bit different than he was before.

And taking your life as a whole, with all your innumerable choices, all your life long you are slowly turning this central thing either into a creature that is in harmony with God, and with other creatures, and with itself, or else into one that is in a state of war and hatred with God, and with its fellow-creatures, and with itself. To be the one kind of creature is heaven: That is, it is joy and peace and knowledge and power. To be the other means madness, horror, idiocy, rage, impotence, and eternal loneliness. Each of us at each moment is progressing to one state or the other. (*Mere Christianity*, pp. 86-87)

If a man seriously turns to God in repentance, he can have "the twist" in his central man straightened out. And this right direction in life leads to knowledge as well as to peace. The man who is becoming better understands increasingly the evil that remains within. But the man who is getting worse understands his badness less and less.

Skeptics sometimes ask, "Why are not all Christians better persons than all non-Christians?" Several problems are raised by this question, said Lewis. It assumes, for one thing, that there is some clear way of distinguishing the two groups. Actually, some persons are consciously becoming Christians and others are ceasing to so identify themselves. Some belong to Christ without realizing it, and others are gradually drifting away from God almost unawares. The real world is filled with much confusion and many inconsistencies. There are to be found neither pure Christians nor pure non-Christians. This question, further, tends to overlook the complex factors which influence personality and behavior. A human being cannot know how much someone's pleasant disposition is dependent upon parental attitudes in childhood. God alone can make the necessary allowances in estimating a person's genuine moral potential. The label *Christian* should not be expected to produce wholesome, integrated personalities immediately and dramatically. It may even be true that social and psychological misfits are more attracted to Christianity than are persons who radiate health and self-confidence; the maladjusted may admit their need for divine assistance more rapidly. But after noting all of this, said Lewis, it remains true that a person who claims to be a Christian ought to be a better person than he was *before* he became a Christian, and a better person than *he* would be now if he were not a Christian.

The Christian is commanded to "love thy neighbor as thyself." This formula should help us understand how it is possible to hate what a man does without hating that person; human beings are able to accomplish this feat in regard to themselves. Said Lewis, "Just because I loved myself, I was sorry to find that I was the sort of man who did those things." We may despise cruelty and treachery while being sorry that a person should have done such things, hoping that he can be cured somehow and made fully human again. The Lord's Prayer, in fact, seems to suggest that one's own forgiveness is conditional upon his extending forgiveness to others: "Forgive us our sins as we forgive those that sin against us."

Christian love is the most difficult when it involves the duty of forgiving enemies. Indeed, many would regard this ideal with contempt. The Christian, however, is expected to show concern for the unlovable, even as God has loved him—not for his attractive qualities, but just because he is a part of creation. Should it become necessary to punish or to kill another human being, the Christian must carry out his duty without hatred or resentment toward this neighbor-enemy. The soldier has a perfect right to kill an enemy. Lewis has no sympathy for the sort of semipacifism which fills a soldier with shame for fighting and robs him of the gaity and wholeheartedness which are the natural accompaniments of courage. It may be that Lewis here parted company with his great mentor Augustine, who taught that Christians could engage in battle—when otherwise just—only in a "mournful mood." Lewis thought it possible to be genuinely loving even while killing. He wrote, "Even while we kill and punish we must try to feel about the enemy as we feel about ourselves—to wish that he were not bad, to hope that he may, in this world or another, be cured; in fact, to wish his good. That is what is meant in the Bible by loving him: wishing his good, not feeling fond of him nor saying he is nice when he is not."

Christian love (or charity) does not, of course, mean having affection for a person or liking him. It is a state of the will, not a state of the emotions. The Christian is not to bother about whether or not he feels love for his neighbor; he is to act as though he does. Affection often comes later as one finds himself liking more and more people he was not fond of in the beginning. "Good and evil both increase at compound interest," said Lewis. That is why small daily decisions are of such infinite importance.

What about man's love for God? Some people think they find no such feelings within themselves. Lewis recommended that men deliberately behave as though they do have love for God. It is no good trying to manufacture feelings. Simply ask, "If I did love God, what would I do?" Then go do it. God is not primarily concerned with human feelings. "Christian Love, either towards God or towards man, is an affair of the will." While human emotions may vary, men should remember that God's love for them does not change.

Lewis once wrote to a child in America, "Duty is only a substitute for *love* . . . like a crutch which is a substitute for a leg. Most of us need the crutch at times; but of course it is idiotic to use the crutch when our legs (our own loves, tastes, habits, etc.) can do the journey on their own." The test of every experience is this: does it make a person more God-centered and more neighbor-centered and less self-centered? If so, that is what the moral principle of Christian love requires.

The loves which Lewis discussed in *The Four Loves* are more varieties of human relationships than they are approaches to God. Anders Nygren is particularly concerned with the divine-human encounter in his mon-

157

umental *Agape and Eros,* a book for which Lewis had great appreciation. But the focus of Lewis' discussion here was somewhat different. His thesis was that natural loves are important but not self-sufficient. As he once wrote in a letter, "When I have learnt to love God better than my earthly dearest, I shall love my earthly dearest better than I do now. . . . When first things are put first, second things are not suppressed but increased."

Lewis opened *Four Loves* by distinguishing between gift-love, need-love, and appreciative love. Divine love is always gift-love, since God lacks nothing, and human gift-loves are God-like. Man's ordinary need-love, however, is more than mere selfishness; not to feel the need of others would be sheer egotism. Even human love for God is dominated by need-love. Appreciative love neither seeks nor gives but rejoices in the pleasure of beauty. It is neither based upon a specific desire, nor is it easily satisfied—as, for example, is the need-pleasure for food. Pleasure of appreciation is concerned with objects in their own right. While these three basic categories of love can be separated for analysis, it is doubtful that they exist for long in a pure and independent state in actual life, except perhaps need-love. A person's spiritual health is in direct proportion to his love for God; to give to human loves the sort of unconditional allegiance which belongs to God turns them into demonic idols which eventually become destructive.

Some loves are directed toward the subhuman; men speak of a love of nature or a love for country. Such pleasures and loyalties enrich life and are to be encouraged—provided only that they are not given a false transcendence. Without prior deep appreciation for nature, Lewis believed that he would have little meaning to bring to such an idea as the *glory* of God.

Affection is the first of the four loves represented in the title; the others are friendship, eros, and charity. Affection is a fondness for the familiar. It is undiscriminating and binds together those who happen to be in the same household or the same community. Affection may be very tolerant. But it can also become perverted. It may be too much taken for granted. It may resist change in the familiar behavior (or beliefs) of others, even if the change is for the better. It may pose as being generous when it actually conceals a ravenous need to be needed. Affection may attempt to dominant others through "sacrifice" for them. Lewis constructed characters with such warped affection in *Divorce* and *Faces.* And he satirized it in these lines of an epitaph: "Here lies one who lived for others; / Now she has peace. And so have they." If affection is absolutized in life, it becomes demonic. It produces happiness only when it is seasoned with reason, justice, and goodness.

Friendship was exalted in ancient and medieval times but has become marginal in modern life. It once represented a world of relationships freely and rationally chosen, even in independence or defiance of mere nature. Lewis felt that several causes had contributed to the decline of rational friendship—romanticism ("that great wallow of emotion"), this relationship's disinterest in "survival value," and perhaps a democratic hostility to selectiveness or exclusiveness. Lewis refuted the theory that every serious friendship is actually homosexual in nature. Friendship, as a matter of fact, is the least jealous of loves, he said. "Lovers are always talking to one another about their love; Friends hardly ever about their Friendship. Lovers are normally face to face, absorbed in each other; Friends, side by side, absorbed in some common interest." Genuine friendship, further, is not limited to two persons, but is best found in a small circle, limited only by the scarcity of kindred spirits, the size of rooms, and the audibility of voices. (One can hardly resist thinking of the Inklings as he reads this description.)

Friendship differs from companionship, the biologically important cooperation among those who hunt, fight, or work together. Friendship between two persons of the opposite sex can pass easily into erotic love, unless they are physically repulsive to each other or have romantic commitments elsewhere. But the deepest friendships (in this purely rational sense) will generally be between those of the same sex, whether men or women. The bond of friendship is such that an opinion from within the little circle outweighs that of a thousand on the outside. Friendship makes good men better—and bad men, worse. Authority often frowns on friendship, said Lewis, because such a relationship is a kind of secession or rebellion from the crowd. The circle must beware lest its necessity for some exclusiveness be turned into arrogance, a degrading pleasure in exclusiveness. God opens men's eyes to beauties in others through friendship. One's particular friends may differ little from other persons, but in friendship, eyes are opened. Lewis noted in *Surprised* that there are basically two types of friends: *the alter ego,* a person who shares one's special delights and reveals that one is not alone in the world, and the *anti-self,* a person who shares one's interests but has approached them all from a different angle. The anti-self has "read all the right books but has got the wrong thing out of every one. It is as if he spoke your language but mispronounced it." Owen Barfield represented this kind of friend for Lewis; the two seemed at times almost respectful enemies, but deep affection emerged from their perpetual argument.

A third kind of love is eros, or romantic love. Eros is not simply sexual experience. "Venus" can occur apart from romantic love, and eros includes more than sexual activity. Eros, it seems, usually begins with a delighted preoccupation with the beloved while the explicitly sexual element awakens later. Eros makes a man want, not just a woman, but a particular woman. It transforms a need-pleasure into the most appreciative of pleasures; eros sees the woman as intensely admirable in herself, beyond all relation to the lover's need. The identities of lovers become so merged in eros that the distinction between giving and receiving is obliterated.

Lewis reminded his readers that Paul warned the married against prolonged abstinence from Venus (I Cor. 7:5). Nevertheless, Lewis opposed the solemnization of sex which the present world seems to encourage. Men will never find the absolute in human flesh. The body is so often clumsy and mischievous—"Brother Ass," St. Francis called it— that there is reason to preserve a hint of playfulness about sex. When natural things appear most nearly divine, they are in danger of becoming demonic. Eros, like other loves, needs to be ruled by a greater principle.

Lewis dealt with a particular type of romantic love in his celebrated literary study *Allegory of Love*. Courtly love was a highly specialized kind of love, whose major characteristics included humility, courtesy, adultery, and "the Religion of Love." This type of love appeared quite suddenly at the end of the eleventh century, and it marks a rare change in human sentiment. Men of the age were prevented from connecting this new ideal of romantic, passionate love with marriage for two reasons: (1) marriages were not based upon love in the practice of feudal society; and (2) the "sexology" of the medieval church taught that passionate love was wicked, even in marriage. The final defeat of courtly love by the romantic conception of marriage is featured in Spenser's *The Faerie Queene*.

Natural loves are never self-sufficient. It is possible for natural loves to be rivals to love for God. But most people love others too little (and themselves too much) so that love for men is seldom a rival of love for God. Further, the natural loves themselves are incomplete without divine aid. Augustine, weeping over the death of a friend, advised against allowing happiness to depend upon anything that one might lose. But this advice, said Lewis, is more Stoic than Christian. "To love at all is to be vulnerable. Love anything, and your heart will certainly be wrung and possibly be broken." All natural loves can be inordinate, but it is unlikely that one ever loves another human being too much. He may love him too much in proportion to his love for God. "It is the smallness of our love for God, not the greatness of our love for the man, that constitutes the inordinacy."

Lewis closed *Four Loves* with a brief discussion of charity. This is a share of gift-love, which God communicates to men. It is a divine love which enables men to love what is not naturally lovable. God also bestows upon men two other supernatural gifts—a need-love for Himself and a need-love for one another. Men have a need for God's grace and for an unmerited love from their fellows as well. There is something in everyone which cannot naturally be loved. Eventually, concluded Lewis, we will discover that whatever was genuine love on earth was such because it had its source in God.

It is appropriate to discuss further at this point Lewis' beautiful and powerful book *Till We Have Faces*. As I understand this complex novel, it is a myth about love, faith, and divine mystery. There is little helpful criticism yet available on the book, but it is probably destined to be one of Lewis' most enduring volumes. The story is set vaguely in a semi-barbaric kingdom in the pre-Christian era.

One theme in *Faces* concerns the clash of possessive love with selfless love. Near the end of her life Queen Orual discovers that her relationships with others have been based upon "nine-tenths hatred, still calling itself love." Feeling an ownership of her younger sister, Orual had resented Psyche's leaving her for a god-husband. The Queen eventually concludes that those who proclaim love for others may be dangerous enemies, that mortals are jealous of the gods and "in league to keep a soul from being united with the Divine Nature." Orual discovers also that she has mistreated and neglected her sister Redival by pouring all of her affection upon Psyche. And she has killed the soldier Bardia, whom she secretly loved, by working him to death. The queen increases in self-knowledge when she finally admits that her concern for others has not been as generous as she has earlier supposed.

Another important theme in *Faces* concerns the "doubtings, fears, guessings, debatings, questionings" of religious belief. Is it possible, asks Orual, that some things are both real and unseeable? Her Greek slave, the Fox, thinks not; his rationalistic assumptions are based upon philosophy. But Bardia represents the simple faith of the queen's countrymen. Which view is correct? Psyche—free, fed, and happy—is a believer in the gods, but Orual is incapable of seeing persistently what Psyche claims to see. There have been brief moments when Orual thought she saw Psyche's god and his castle. But when confronted with both ambiguous evidence and the criticism of Greek reason, Orual's confidence in her own impressions is undermined. She prays for a sign, but she receives none. Hearing the sacred story of Istra, Orual protests,

> It's a story belonging to a different world, a world in which the gods show themselves clearly and don't torment men with glimpses, nor unveil to one what they hide from another, nor ask you to believe what contradicts your eyes and ears and nose and tongue and fingers. In such a world (is there such? it's not ours, for certain) I would have walked aright. (*Till We Have Faces*, pp. 243-44)

A third major theme in *Faces* concerns the mystery which lies at the heart of the supernatural. The gods provide "no answer" but do offer a personal encounter. Divine reality seems better discovered through obedience than through testing. Signs are given not at all or only very dimly. There seems to be a "brute aspect" to the supernatural, and the acceptance of doubt, uncertainty, and darkness appears essential for relating to the supernatural. The concluding lines of the book stress Orual's eagerness to have her reflections upon life and reality carried to Greece after her death. What urgent message does she think she has for the people there? Perhaps this: that sacrificial religion, with its sharing in anguish and death, is closer to life's reality than are the words and rational answers of the philosophers.

Orual comes to ask how the gods can meet men face to face "till we have faces." In other words, how can we expect to understand adequately divine nature when we so little confront and fathom the complexities of human nature? The queen comes to believe that the gods are not just, for "what would become of us if they were?" And recognizing the inseparable relationship which she has with Psyche and the suffering that the two have endured for each other, she concludes, "We're all limbs and parts of one Whole."

Any brief discussion of this profound and complex myth is certain to be inadequate. I cannot accept Clyde Kilby's interpretation, however, that Orual had known very well for forty years that the gods were real, but had willed otherwise. Even less can I agree with Martha Hook that the goddess Ungit, who is always found in darkness and fear, represents evil immorality, while the god of the mountain represents light and faith.[1] Miss Hook seems to have forgotten the comfort and joy which the peasants gain in their worship of Ungit, as well as the fact that Psyche's god-husband comes to her only in darkness and that she is

---

[1] "Christian Meaning in the Novels of C. S. Lewis," (M. A. thesis, Southern Methodist University, 1959), p. 84.

forbidden to see his face. Darkness and mystery surround both gods. A statement by Lewis in *Sixteenth Century* may be helpful in interpreting *Faces*: "Paganism is the religion of poetry through which the author can express, at any moment, just so much or so little of his real religion as his art requires." In some works, Lewis said, the gods are God *incognito,* and everyone is in on this secret.

Lewis provided in *Divorce* other illustrations of defective, possessive love and of a person destroying the happiness of another in the belief that he is acting in that person's best interest. There is the case of the nagging woman ghost who visits heaven insisting that the authorities return her husband to her, as she must have someone to do things to, someone to alter. There is the case of the mother who has been engaged in a ten-year ritual of grief for her son. As the wife admits to the tragedian ghost, "What we called love down there was mostly the craving to be loved." The spirits advise their visitors that no natural feelings are holy in themselves. Even mother love becomes a false god if it is set up independently. One cannot love a fellow human being rightly until he loves God since it is impossible for humans, all on their own, to make each other happy for long. Guide Macdonald says, "Every natural love will rise again and live forever in this country: but none will rise again until it has been buried." "The saying is almost too hard for us," complains his guest. "Ah, but it's cruel not to say it," responds Macdonald.

VIII

Man as He May Become: Redemption, with Fresh Images of New Men

Part II: Morality, Pain, Church, and Prayer

Moral law and moral relativity:

There have been differences between . . . moralities, but these have never amounted to anything like a total difference. . . . Selfishness has never been admired.

—*Mere Christianity,* p. 19

We turn now to a discussion of moral law in Lewis' thought. Lewis told of the shock he once received at discovering an Army buddy who took morality seriously. Until this time, Lewis had rarely encountered anyone of his own age and background who thought that virtues like strict veracity, chastity, and devotion to duty were really relevant to life. He noted in *Mere Christianity,* however, that whenever people quarrel, make excuses for their behavior, or blame others, they are assuming some kind of objective rule of fair play or decent behavior. This moral law has sometimes been called the *Law of Nature* (i.e., *human* nature): the idea of decent behavior was once thought to be so obvious to the race as a whole that men did not need to be instructed in it. Some may protest that the very idea of a law of nature is unsound in view of widespread cultural variation. But, insisted Lewis, moral differences have "never amounted to anything like a total difference." Men differ over what size group deserves their loyalty, but selfishness and cowardice have never been admired in any culture. This fact suggests that right and wrong are real, even when people are mistaken sometimes about the detailed content morality requires.

164

Can moral law be but a "herd instinct" based upon a natural desire to help? Sometimes, observed Lewis, one feels compelled to help another in trouble whether he wants to or not. It must be some other force that urges a man to suppress his impulse to run away from danger and to follow his impulse to help—some additional force which judges between the various instincts and decides which one should be encouraged. It is moral law, said Lewis, which directs the instincts, encourages some and discourages others, depending upon the occasion.

Might the moral law be only social convention—something derived from education? Nearly everything, of course, is learned from parents and teachers, friends and books. Some of the things men learn are mere conventions, which might have been arranged differently. But other things they are taught are more objectively true—the multiplication table, for example. To which class of things does the law of human nature belong?

Most men tend to believe that some moralities are better than others. If there were no true moral standards, why then should anyone prefer civilized morality to savage morality, or Christian morality to Nazi morality? Cultural variations abound, but the way in which men evaluate these differences supports the idea of genuine moral progress in human thought.

In nature a "law" simply describes what in fact happens to natural objects. But the law of human nature describes what ought to happen, rather than what does happen. It appears, then, that there is more than one kind of reality; there is, according to Lewis, "something above and beyond the ordinary facts of men's behaviour, and yet quite definitely real—a real law, which none of us made, but which we find pressing on us."

Can this moral law be a clue to the meaning of the universe? Since ancient times there have been two rival interpretations of the world. The materialist view claims that everything exists by accident; by "a sort of fluke" matter produced creatures who can think. The religious view claims that something like a mind—with consciousness, purposes, and preferences—created the universe. Science, of course, is unable to explore whether or not there is something behind the reality it observes; this kind of question cannot be settled by the scientific method. However, writes Lewis, there is a single thing in the universe which we can know more about than we could possibly learn from external observation: Man. "We do not merely observe men, we *are* men." External studies would never indicate a sense of moral law. Observations can show only what men do, not what they ought to do. But because we have "inside information," we know that men actually do feel they ought to obey a moral law which they did not make and which they cannot entirely forget.

In the human case, then, we discover something more in the universe than observable reality. Might not this fact be a genuine clue to the nature of the universe inself? There seems to be a Something—a power behind the facts, a director, or a guide—which operates the universe and which seems intensely interested in right conduct; in fair play, unselfishness, courage, good faith, honesty, and truth.

Such an interpretation of the universe raises a great problem. If the universe is not governed by absolute goodness, all human efforts are finally hopeless. But if this goodness is in charge, it must be admitted that much of what men do is in opposition to it; and the possibility of man's achieving moral perfection is also quite hopeless. Men fail to practice themselves the behavior that they expect from others. They make excuses for themselves, and to themselves. People do not in fact behave in the way in which they claim people should behave. It is at this very point that Christianity can begin to be meaningful. Persons need to become keenly aware of the moral law they have broken and the wrong relationship they have with the power behind that law. Only then will the Christian message of repentance and forgiveness begin to make sense on the human scene.

Lewis elaborates further upon this concept of moral law—or the *Tao*, as he often calls it—in *Abolition* and in *Reflections*. Walter Hooper calls *Abolition* "an all but indispensable introduction to the entire *corpus* of Lewisiana," and I would agree that this is one of Lewis' most significant books. The study of various ethical theories, as theories, tends to exaggerate the practical differences between them, Lewis said. "The number of actions about whose ethical quality a Stoic, an Aristotelian, a Thomist, a Kantian, and a Utilitarian would agree is, after all, very large." In some cases the principles of morality are expected to apply only to a restricted group, but the principles themselves are not unusual. Little significance need be attached to the diversity and eccentricity of savage codes (although even these are often exaggerated as to their variety) ; the savage has either not learned, or he has forgotten, what civilized man knows. Among civilized men, Lewis maintained, there are "far fewer differences of ethical injunction than is now popularly believed. In triumphant monotony the same indispensable platitudes will meet us in culture after culture." Christianity, of course, brings no new ethical code. Its founder came demanding repentance and offering forgiveness on the assumption that the moral law was already known.

In his essay "The Poison of Subjectivism," Lewis discussed two objections to a doctrine of objective value (the law of nature). Some suppose that mankind has "not one morality but a thousand." Others contend that the idea of an immutable moral code would cause men "to cut off all progress and acquiesce in stagnation." Lewis replied that it is "a good, solid, resounding lie" that cultures vary so widely that there is no common tradition. A few days spent in the library with the *Encyclopedia of Religion and Ethics,* he asserted, will demonstrate the truth of this claim. There is substantial agreement as well as considerable local difference in emphasis. As regards the second objection, Lewis believed that a permanent moral standard need not preclude progress. Real moral advances are always made *from within* an existing tradition.

Part of the task of education, said Lewis (following Plato and Aristotle), is to make pupils like and dislike what they ought. Most civilized communities have been concerned to produce good men through education. That is, teaching has included the interests of civil behavior and "right sentiment." Sentiments are related to the passions as habits are related to the body. Aristotle taught that education prepares men for leisure. But vocational training simply prepares pupils for work. Civilization means life in which the leisured activities of thought, art, literature, and conversation are man's natural end. Whenever training replaces education, civilization dies. There is value in knowledge for the sake of knowledge, said Lewis. This is something that a man of "radically servile character" can never understand, regardless of his leisure or fortune. "He will ask, 'But what *use* is it?' and finding that it cannot be eaten or drunk, nor used as an aphrodisiac, nor made an instrument for increasing his income or his power, he will pronounce it—he has pronounced it—to be 'bunk'." One may not assume the automatic spread of civilization, said Lewis; it is a rarity in history, attained with difficulty and easily lost.

Lewis wrote as follows in a letter: "The process of living seems to consist in coming to realize truths so ancient and simple that, if stated, they sound like barren platitudes. They cannot sound otherwise to those who have not had the relevant experience: that is why there is no real teaching of such truths possible and every generation starts from scratch." Lewis claimed that traditional poetry has played a valuable role in moral education.

The older poetry, by continually insisting on certain Stock themes—as that love is sweet, death bitter, virtue lovely, and children or gardens delightful— was performing a service not only of moral and civil, but even of biological,

167

importance. . . . That elementary rectitude of human response, at which we are so ready to fling the unkind epithets of "stock," "crude," "bourgeois," and "conventional," so far from being "given" is a delicate balance of trained habits, laboriously acquired and easily lost, on the maintenance of which depend both our virtues and our pleasures and even, perhaps, the survival of our species. (*A Preface to Paradise Lost*, pp. 56-67)

According to Lewis, an apprehension of moral law exists wherever civilization exists. But unless men continue to appreciate and to communicate the importance of the *Tao* to the young, civilization itself is threatened with decay.

When it came to discussing specific sins, Lewis followed Augustine in considering pride as the chief threat to Christian morality. Self-conceit is regarded as the main cause of misery throughout the earth since the world began. It is a sin which is purely spiritual in nature and does not come at all through the animal self. Pride is essentially competitive by nature; it takes pleasure not in the possession of a thing for its own sake, but in having more than another. Pride may infect even the religious life, making a person feel that he is better than someone else. The very opposite of humility, pride devours the possibility of love and contentment and common sense.

The concept of sinful pride needs to be guarded against some possible misunderstandings. Pride should be distinguished from the simple pleasure of being praised. A person who desires attention of this kind is still concerned with other people. But "black, diabolical Pride comes when you look down on others so much that you do not care what they think of you." Or we sometimes say that a person is "proud" of his son or of his school. This generally implies but a warmhearted admiration which is far from being sinful. God does not forbid pride because he is worried about his own dignity. Rather, he wants men to come to know him and to depend upon him. As this happens, pride is abolished and humility becomes natural. The really humble person does not acquire this virtue by fixing his attention upon it. He spends little time in thinking about himself at all.

Lewis spoke in *Surprised* of his own early resentment of authority and his "monstrous individualism" and lawlessness. "No word in my vocabulary expressed deeper hatred than the word *Interference*. But Christianity placed at the centre what then seemed to me a transcendental Interferer." He came to believe later that "a man who is eating or lying with his wife or preparing to go to sleep in humility, thankfulness, and temperance is, by Christian standards, in an infinitely *higher* state than one who is listening to Bach or reading Plato in a state of pride."

People who are not instructed in the Christian faith, he said, easily mistake the worse sins—spiritual sins—for virtues.

Screwtape notes that humility can be twisted if the demons can persuade a person to concentrate upon how humble he is becoming, leading him to take pride in his humility. Or humility may be used as a means for causing a person to take a low opinion of his own talents and character. The Lowerarchy attempts to cultivate "elaborate and self-conscious unselfishness" in its patients. Lewis treats pride and humility again in *Horse and Boy*. Bree, a talking horse, feels disgraced for running away from a scene of danger. The Hermit assures her that the loss of self-conceit is a good thing; "as long as you know you're nobody very special, you'll be a very decent sort of Horse, on the whole." When Rabadash, an enemy prince in the same story, angrily insists upon defending his pride, he is temporarily transformed into a donkey right before the eyes of the astonished Narnia children.

In "Screwtape Proposes a Toast," a satirical piece which appeared first in the *Saturday Evening Post* in 1959, Lewis protests the increasing loss of individualism, the leveling-down process of "democracy," and the pharisaism of the "religious." The scene is an annual dinner in Hell at which Screwtape is giving the speech. He apologizes at first for the poor quality of souls recently coming down. But he is consoled by the fact that the Enemy is doing no better. Persons of vivid and genial passions, he reports, have become scarce. With the loss of individualism, the material is lacking for developing either great saints or great sinners. Most who come now to Hell are grubby little nonentities who just drift in. Skillful tempters have helped to harden their choices so that they have rejected God's grace, but so many are suited neither for Heaven nor Hell. They have failed so miserably to make the grade that they really should be sent to Limbo, to sink forever into contented subhumanity.

The word *democracy*, says Screwtape, can be used increasingly for the purposes of Hell. The term should be used as an incantation and never given a clear, definable meaning. It will come to mean for many simply, "I'm as good as you." What used to be considered envy can be sanctioned then as democratic. The inferior can pull others down to their level. Any who might approach full humanity will come to avoid it for fear of being undemocratic. This principle applies also to education; "dunces and idlers must not be made to feel inferior to intelligent and industrious pupils." The policy will lead eventually to a nation of cocksure subliterates, a nation without great men, a nation where excellence is despised. A young female human, Screwtape announces, recently prayed: "Oh, God, make me a normal twentieth-century girl!" Thanks to the designs of the Lower Command, this means increasingly, "Make me a minx, a moron, and a parasite."

The banquet toast is made with old vintage *Pharisee,* a wine blended with types of Pharisee which were antagonistic on earth. Some had concentrated on "rules and relics and rosaries." Others had thought religion meant "drab clothes, long faces, and petty traditional abstinences." These had in common only their own self-righteousness, the belief that theirs was the only religion, and an infinite distance between themselves and the real desires of the Enemy. Screwtape concludes his toast with these words: "All said and done, my friends, it will be an ill day for us if what most humans mean by 'religion' ever vanishes from the Earth. It can still send us the truly delicious sins."

Christians share with all civilized people, said Lewis, the four "cardinal" virtues of prudence, temperance, justice, and fortitude. But to this list Christians add the "theological" virtues of faith, hope, and love. Prudence involves the application of common sense, making the effort to think through what one is proposing or doing. The Christian should not only be good but also as intelligent as possible. Temperance applies to every pleasure in life, requiring that a person remain within proper limits with any kind of indulgence. Individual Christians may abstain, if they wish, from all sorts of things for special reasons (marriage, meat, beer, or movies, e.g.) ; but they ought not to consider these things as bad in themselves or to become prideful about their particular abstinence. Lewis objected strongly to "the tyrannic and unscriptural insolence of anything that calls itself a Church and makes teetotalism a condition of membership." Screwtape notes that tempters in recent times have concentrated upon the gluttony of delicacy rather than the gluttony of excess. The belly and palate can still be used for a selfish indulging of the appetite, he says, often with the accompanying vices of querulousness, impatience, and uncharitableness.

The virtue of justice includes honesty, truthfulness, keeping promises, give and take, and all that is meant by "fair play," said Lewis. He noted in *Psalms* that one gains the impression in reading these old hymns that the Jews were a vindictive and vitriolic people. They took matters of right and wrong more seriously than did the Pagans. The Jews grew angry, not only because injustice was done to them, but also because such things were wrong and hateful to God as well as to the victims. One must be cautious not to think his own worst passions are holy, but God does demand that his servants practice justice. Fortitude, finally, includes both the kind of courage that faces danger and the kind that endures under pain ("guts"). Screwtape notes that men take pride in most of the vices at some time or other, but not in cowardice. "In the last war," he says, "thousands of humans, by discovering their own cowardice, discovered the whole moral world for the first time." From the tempter's point of view, it is dangerous to induce cowardice in men; they may immediately discover the self-knowledge and self-loathing which leads to humility and repentance. In the end, "courage is not simply *one* of the virtues, but the form of every virtue at the testing point."

"Virtue" is best interpreted as a quality of character, rather than a particular set of actions. The man who perseveres in performing acts of justice should become in the end a just man. God is not primarily concerned about obedience to a set of rules, regardless of personal attitudes involved. His main interest is in the internal quality, the character, the virtue of a man. As Lewis said, "He really wants people of a particular sort."

Screwtape advises that there is no harm in virtues so long as they are approved only by the intellect. They may be approved, loved, and admired, without any conflict whatsoever with the interests of Hell. Virtues cause problems for Hell only if they reach the human will and become embodied in habits. "Let him do anything but act," Screwtape writes concerning a human patient. "No amount of piety in his imagination and affections will harm us if we can keep it out of his will." It is also Screwtape who observes that nearly all of men's vices are rooted in prospects for the future. Gratitude looks to the past, and love to the present, but fear, avarice, lust, and ambition look ahead.

Lewis repeatedly emphasized the subtlety of temptation and sin.

No man, perhaps, ever at first described to himself the act he was about to do as Murder, or Adultery, or Fraud, or Treachery, or Perversion; and when he hears it so described by other men he is (in a way) sincerely shocked and surprised. Those others "don't understand". . . . With a wink or a titter, or in a cloud of muddy emotion, the thing has slipped into his will as something not very extraordinary. (*A Preface to Paradise Lost,* p. 126)

Uncle Andrew, in *Magician's Nephew,* is an example of a man who thinks he can dispense with the customary moral requirements. A dabbler in magic, he explains to the boy Digory that ordinary rules—which apply to boys, servants, women, and people in general—do not apply to a profound thinker like himself. Men of high destiny who possess hidden wisdom, he holds, must be free from common rules. As Uncle Andrew explains this, he looks so grave and noble and mysterious that Digory momentarily thinks that he is saying something fine. Soon, however, he makes his own translation of his uncle's words: "All it means is that he thinks he can do anything he likes to get anything he wants." This illustration of Lewis cannot be construed as an irrefutable answer to the question of situation ethics which is receiving so much theological attention in these days. But it might serve as a warning against the ever-present danger of rationalization as a chief reason for setting the rules aside.

We come now to a consideration of Lewis' views on sexual morality and marriage. Lewis noted in *Surprised* that people sometimes made a false identification between refinement and virtue. Unfortunately, Lewis himself occasionally slipped and used "virtue" in its popular sense of sexual purity. It is evident from the foregoing discussion that he generally gave the word its broader and more accurate meaning.

Chastity should not be confused with modesty, Lewis said. Ideas of propriety change according to the customs of a given social circle. Cultural rules suggest how much of the body may be displayed decently and how public discussion of sex is to be conducted. But the old Christian rule of chastity remains: "Either marriage, with complete faithfulness to your partner, or else total abstinence." Surely this is the most unpopular of the Christian virtues, he said. It is so difficult and so contrary to human instincts, he continued, that either Christianity is wrong or the sexual instinct has gone wrong.

Lewis proceeded to suggest ways in which the sexual instinct has gone awry. For one thing, the biological appetite is in ludicrous and preposterous excess for the biological purpose of producing children. And the popularity of the striptease does not indicate sexual starvation, as some have proposed, but suggests that the sexual appetite, like other appetites, grows by indulgence. Why is it, further, that sexual perversions are so numerous while perversions of other appetites are rare? People once held the theory that sex had become a mess because it was hushed up; now it has been chattered about for decades, and still it is in a mess. Modern Christianity has a positive outlook on sex and the body. Human reproduction and sexual pleasure are considered in themselves good elements of God's creation. But something has gone wrong. Human nature has been so warped through the generations that in our time it is difficult even to desire chastity, said Lewis—much less to achieve it. He mentioned in several letters the astonishment with which Oxford students greeted Charles Williams' lecture on chastity.

172

Lewis gave a number of reasons why complete chastity is so unpopular. For one thing, there is an enormous propaganda for unchastity sponsored by those "who want to keep our sex instinct inflamed in order to make money out of us." In poster, film, and novel, ideas of sexual indulgence are regularly associated with ideas of health, normality, youth, frankness, and good humor. But it is a lie to suggest that any sexual act to which one is tempted at any moment is simply healthy and normal. On the contrary, restraint is an important quality for genuine happiness, while "surrender to all our desires obviously leads to impotence, disease, jealousies, lies, concealment, and everything that is the reverse of health, good humour, and frankness." Many people think Christian chastity impossible, and therefore never attempt to achieve it. Lewis believed that it indeed cannot be attained by mere human effort. One must seek God's help. And a series of attempts and failures, he thought, might be spiritually helpful; the process of asking God's forgiveness and of trying again can cure one of illusions about himself and teach him to depend upon God. "We cannot trust ourselves even in our best moments, and . . . we need not despair even in our worst, for our failures are forgiven. The only fatal thing is to sit down content with anything less than perfection." A final reason why few desire chastity results from a confusion over what psychology teaches about repressions. "Repression" is a technical term applying to thoughts which are driven into the subconscious, to come before the mind later only in disguised forms. Repressed sexuality will not appear to a person to be sexuality at all. When one is engaged in resisting a conscious sexual desire, he is in no danger whatsoever of creating a repression. It is important to mental health, in fact, that certain ideas be suppressed, denied, and resisted.

Christian morality is not chiefly concerned with sex. Nor do Christians regard unchastity as the supreme vice. The sins of the flesh are bad enough, but the worst pleasures are purely spiritual. There are two selves within every man, competing with his potential human self— the animal self and the diabolical self. The latter is the worse. "A cold, self-righteous prig who goes regularly to church may be far nearer to hell than a prostitute. But, of course, it is better to be neither."

The Christian idea of marriage is based upon the words of Christ that a man and wife are a single organism ("one flesh") . This statement is regarded not as a sentiment, but as a fact—just as one might say that a lock and key make up a single mechanism. God has so designed humans that they combine in pairs, male and female. The kind of combination which is found on the sexual level is needed in other areas of life as well. The problem with sexual intercourse outside marriage is that it isolates sexual union from the total union of persons which is intended. Christian marriage is supposed to be permanent; this single-organism concept must regard divorce as a surgical operation, a cutting on a living body. Such surgery should be performed only in extreme cases, if at all.

What if the partners to a given marriage find that they are no longer "in love"? As a matter of fact, says Lewis, "the state called 'being in love' usually does not last." For awhile it is a glorious, noble, thrilling feeling. But it is only a feeling. And "no feeling can be relied on to last in its full intensity, or even to last at all. Knowledge can last, principles can last, habits can last; but feelings come and go." A married person can rather easily fall "in love" with someone else if he will let himself. And the person who moves from one partner to another soon finds the new love as cool as the former.

If a sound marriage is not based upon feelings, upon what is it founded? Upon promises, said Lewis. Justice demands that contracts and promises be honored, including the promise to remain faithful to one's partner till death. In fact, lovers have a natural inclination to bind themselves by promises, which represent more stability than momentary passion can offer. A solemn promise commits one to be true even if he ceases to feel himself in love. Ceasing to feel in love, of course, need not mean ceasing to love in the Christian sense. For Christian love

is a deep unity, maintained by the will and deliberately strengthened by habit; reinforced by the grace which both parents ask, and receive, from God. . . . This quieter love enables them to keep the promise. It is on this love that the engine of marriage is run: being in love was the explosion that started it. (*Mere Christianity,* p. 99)

To say that Pamela gets on Alan's nerves does not call for an attack upon the institution of marriage, said Lewis. This may be but a description of the general irritatingness of daily life, in this case as it occurs in the lives of married people.

"Falling in love" is not generally as irresistible as popular novels pretend. Personal choice is involved also in whether a given affair proves attractive or not. It is not for the church to legislate the rules of marriage for the nation. Two distinct kinds of marriage should be recognized, and the church should guide and govern only her own members in the institution of holy matrimony.

Readers of Lewis' remarks on sex and marriage in *Mere Christianity* frequently note that the words were written by a middle-aged bachelor. Lewis brought a number of important insights to the topic, but his tone here is sometimes more rationalistic and less sympathetic than it is in *Grief,* which was written following his own personal experience in marriage.

Lewis included a chapter on social morality in *Mere Christianity,* but he offered little guidance on specific social problems. He asserted the principle that the Christianizing process should advance on both the social level and the personal level. But he has little to say about either domestic politics or foreign policy. Chad Walsh pointed out that Lewis pictured himself as concerned more with the "spadework" than with the "blueprints" of a Christian society. He felt that detailed plans for application of Christian principles to the complexities of daily life must come from Christian specialists within the various fields. He expected his readers to go elsewhere for this kind of guidance.

Christ did not offer any brand new morality, and he presented no detailed political program, Lewis declared. Yet the church functions in society today through the whole body of its practicing members. Laymen must work out the application of Christian principles to the arts and crafts of the world. Christian statesmen and economists should direct their efforts toward putting the Golden Rule into action. In the end, men find that they cannot love their neighbors until they learn to love God; and they cannot learn to love God except by obeying him. Social matters, therefore, drive men to more religious matters. There can be no Christian society unless most of its members are Christian individuals.

The modern world offers two kinds of work, noted Lewis. One type of work is worth doing for its own sake. It brings delight to the laborer and would be worth doing even if it went unpaid. The other kind of work has the sole objective of earning money; it would not be performed unless it were paid. Good work is discouraged today because built-in obsolescence is considered an economic necessity. Lewis predicted that an artificially stimulated economy will likely collapse someday under its own internal contradictions, causing much suffering. But a complex economic situation cannot be cured by simple moral effort. Many jobs still remain in the first category although worthwhile and enjoyable labor is becoming a privilege for the fortunate few.

Lewis' remarks on government were brief and scattered. There are two possible reasons, he said, for believing in a democratic form of government. One may think that all men are so good that they deserve to share in their government and so wise that the government needs their advice. Or one may think that fallen men are so wicked that not one can be trusted with unlimited power over the others. The first idea is a false, romantic notion. The latter idea more nearly resembles the truth of man's actual situation. Theocracy, Lewis felt, is the worst possible type of government. The loftier the pretensions of any political system, the more meddlesome it will be. Political power is always a necessary evil, but it is least evil when its sanctions are modest. A government should operate with the limited objectives of usefulness and convenience for its citizens.

Lewis' reflections upon warfare are certain to strike many readers as inadequate, if not callous and uncompassionate. In his sermon "Learning in War-Time," Lewis contended that war creates no absolutely new situations. Life is always lived on the edge of the precipice, and war but aggravates the permanent human situation so that it can no longer be ignored. In many ways, life goes on as before; it is impossible for human creatures to suspend entirely their intellectual and aesthetic activities. War does, however, make death real. It is a good thing, Lewis said, for men to be aware of their own mortality.

A similar tone is reflected in *Screwtape*. Wormwood is warned that war encourages certain tendencies which are not in Hell's favor. Many turn to the Enemy in times of tribulation. Others have their attention diverted from themselves to values they consider more important than themselves. War enforces a continual remembrance of death, says Screwtape, so that the weapon of contented worldliness is rendered useless. Men die in places where they expected that they might. They often enter battle prepared for death. "In wartime not even a human can believe that he is going to live forever." Suffering does not necessarily destroy faith; Christians even consider suffering an essential part of redemption. Screwtape criticizes Wormwood for his "infantile rhapsodies about the death of men and the destruction of cities," suggesting that he may be infected with the human sentiment which regards death as the prime evil and survival as the greatest good. "Do not let us be infected by our own propaganda," Screwtape warns.

Lewis' view of war seemed to be dominated by an individualistic perspective, in which the major issue involved either private salvation or private damnation. Would it not be consistent with the purposes of Hell to have Screwtape rejoice at the destruction of cities, the despair of wounded and displaced millions, the crippled emotions and stunted morals of generations emerging from the shock of war? Lewis' imagery of war often suggests more nearly the chivalry of medieval battle than it does the horrors of modern warfare. He appears to have overlooked the fact that even death is never completely a private affair; it is also an event in the life of society. Mass death and destruction have enormous social consequences beyond the immediate loss of particular individuals who perish in the conflict. Lewis never concluded that war itself is a fundamental evil. He viewed battle as a rather neutral affair through which certain souls are dispatched to their ultimate destinies.

A number of Lewis' letters elaborate his attitude toward war. Like Reinhold Niebuhr he noted that a nation must be cautious about identifying the enemy with the forces of evil. He wrote, "I have no sympathy with the modern view that killing or being killed is a great evil." Surely he meant here that death is not the greatest evil—i.e., that *how* one lives is more important than *when* one dies. He sometimes spoke of the wastefulness of war. At the time of Munich, in 1938, Lewis confessed to Owen Barfield his horror at the threat of losing friends, books, and perhaps his own life in war. But even then he concluded that God does not give us these things to keep; one should learn to care for something else more. There is some reason (though it is difficult to feel this), he said, to be glad about war. It helps cure men of their worldliness. Lewis spoke of his experience in World War I as haunting his dreams for years. He even stated his belief that death would be preferable to living through another war. Yet, he added, whatever misery God permits "will be for our ultimate good unless by rebellious will we convert it to evil."

In my opinion, a great many other modern writers are more sensitive to the consequences of war than was Lewis. Charles I. Glicksberg writes in *Literature and Religion,* "We are witnessing today a progressive deterioration of religious faith. What modern literature reveals is largely what sensitive men are everywhere thinking and feeling. . . . It is the introduction of technological warfare on a global scale, with the grim prospect of wiping out the whole of civilization, that has made a hideous mockery of humanistic ideals." J. B. Priestley concludes his *Literature and Western Man* with these words:

It is doubtful if our society can last much longer without religion, for either it will destroy itself by some final idiot war or, at peace but hurrying in the wrong direction, it will soon largely cease to be composed of persons. . . . But I have no religion, most of my friends have no religion, very few of the major modern writers we have been considering have had any religion; and what is certain is that our society has none. No matter what it professes, it is now not merely irreligious but powerfully anti-religious. . . . So we have no religion and, inside or outside literature, man feels homeless, helpless, and in despair.[1]

[1] (New York: Harper and Brothers, 1960), pp. 444-45.

There are many persons who would not agree with Lewis that war makes a wholesome contribution to the spiritual welfare of mankind. There are others who would not want so blithely to conclude that God permits such misery for the potential benefit of his creatures. This topic, however, leads into our next major area of discussion—the problem of evil.

The "problem" of pain results from the Christian assurance that ultimate reality is righteous and loving even as men continue to suffer pain in their daily experience with the world. Religion does not, in fact, base its claims concerning the goodness and wisdom of the Creator upon the observation of events in this world. The origin of religion, with its identification of numinous power and moral obligation is in revelation.

It is to be expected that the genuine love of God will cause *some* pain. Not all pain is considered evil; it depends upon the intensity. Pains below a certain degree are neither feared nor resented by men. Further, there must be a neutral field upon which the free will of men can operate. Yet the fixed nature of the material world prevents it from being equally agreeable to every person, or even to a single person at different times. Accidents will happen, and human freedom will be misused. Nevertheless, a stability of nature is preferable to a world in which wrong actions would be impossible and in which freedom of will would be void. Lewis also noted that what seems good to us from a human perspective may not really be good from the divine point of view. Divine goodness differs from our ideas of it "not as white from black but as a perfect circle from a child's first attempt to draw a wheel."

In considering the relationship of a loving God to human suffering, we need to avoid a trivial meaning of the word *love*. It would be no kindness if God provided persons with lives undisturbed by difficulty or challenge. Genuine love is not indifferent toward the beloved; it desires his growth and perfecting. If we think we want something other than what God wants for us, however, we want that which cannot in fact make us happy. God knows, better than we do, what men most need and want. Lewis contended in *The Problem of Pain* that the results of suffering are not wholly bad. How mental and physical pain is interpreted and used depends upon the recipient. It may either be endured in patience and humility or it may be suffered in anger and cynicism.

The fact that wicked souls hurt one another probably accounts for four fifths of the world's suffering, said Lewis. But there remains much suffering which cannot be traced in any way to human decision. Such pain, Lewis believed, is God's "megaphone to rouse a deaf world." God "whispers to us in our pleasures, speaks in our conscience, but shouts in our pains." People do not attempt to surrender self-will when all seems to be well, but pain demands attention. Mortification, although painful in itself, is made easier by the presence of other pain. "To surrender a self-will inflamed and swollen with years of usurpation is a kind of death." Pain helps to shatter the illusion that all is well on the human scene.

Furthermore, said Lewis, pain can shatter the notion that what men possess is their very own and quite sufficient for them. Knowing that their true happiness rests in Him, God may need to remove some of the sources of false happiness. "The creature's illusion of self-sufficiency must, for the creature's sake, be shattered." Full surrender to God demands a certain amount of pain. It is impossible to surrender the self by doing exactly what one likes.

Lewis was aware that his arguments which attempt to justify suffering would provoke bitter resentment. "I am not arguing that pain is not painful," he said. "Pain hurts. . . . I am only trying to show that the old Christian doctrine of being made 'perfect through suffering' is not incredible." Nevertheless, many readers will be disturbed that Lewis so directly traced the miseries of the world to the designs of God. And they may be startled that Lewis undertook so fully to explain a problem which remained essentially a mystery for Job and Jesus. It is one thing to assert that pain can be used redemptively when it comes, and quite another to suggest that God causes pain for the potential benefit of mankind. John M. Moore, in a *Journal of Bible and Religion* review, raises the key question about this aspect of Lewis' thought: "Can all pain be justified as a means of perfecting human character?"

In Lewis' fiction, the *hrossa* of the planet Malacandra appear to have a wholesome appreciation of danger and death. Speaking of the vicious *hnéraki*, the aquatic monsters, Hyoi confesses, "I do not think the forest would be so bright, nor the water so warm, nor love so sweet, if there were no danger in the lakes." A few deaths do not make a *hnau* so miserable or blacken the world so much as would a "bent" *hnau*. In other words, on Malacandra "natural evil" is not considered nearly as bad as "human evil." Contrary to a suggestion of Corbin Carnell, I do not think that the *hnéraki* are in any way associated with moral evil. Furthermore, there seems to be no genuine "problem of evil" on that planet. The *hnéraki* are dangerous, but they are also considered a great delight. Whenever a satisfying explanation for apparent evil can be provided, genuine and permanent evil disappears, and the real "problem" of evil has vanished.

If suffering is spiritually helpful, should it be pursued rather than

179

avoided? No, said Lewis. There is a paradox about tribulation. Suffering is not good in itself, even though it can be used for good. There is no question but that Christians are to work for the removal of suffering in society. Since tribulation is necessary for redemption, it can never be wholly overcome by any human scheme. Nevertheless, Christians should work to remove evils even though a perfect heaven on earth is an impossible dream.

Lewis wrote *Pain*, he claimed, to solve the intellectual problem raised by suffering, not to teach fortitude and patience. When pain must be borne, courage helps more than knowledge. To get a real pain while composing a book on pain neither explodes the doctrine nor demonstrates its truth. The experience, the author said, remains quite separate from the theory. Lewis at first considered writing this book anonymously. But his editor suggested that he explain in the preface that he did not live up to his own principles. "You would like to know how I behave when I am experiencing pain, not writing books about it?" he asks. "I am a great coward." There is always a problem about fitting one's general beliefs on suffering to any particular tribulation. The particular, when it arrives, appears especially intolerable. One spot in which Lewis captures imaginatively this experience of a particular "thundering pain" is in *Dymer*:

> That for a time he could not frame a thought
> Nor know himself for self, nor pain for pain,
> Till moment added on to moment taught
> The new, strange art of living on that plane,
> Taught how the grappled soul must still remain,
> Still choose and think and understand beneath
> The very grinding of the ogre's teeth.

Richard Cunningham considers *Pain* to be one of Lewis' best books. Clyde Kilby also praises it highly. Lewis is aware that he has not solved all the problems entailed in pain and evil, says Kilby, "yet it is hard to conceive how in so small a volume they could be faced more squarely or treated more honestly or effectively." I myself must agree, however, with Austin Farrer's judgment that Lewis' answer on pain is not the whole truth, nor perhaps half of it: "Pain cannot be related to the will of God as an evil wholly turned into a moral instrument." I find the book quite deficient. It all too easily explains and "justifies" suffering, too readily interprets pain as the work of God. Lewis tended too quickly to accept evil (even war) as spiritually useful. It would be unfortunate, further, should anyone identify the highly personal speculations of the final two chapters of *Pain* with traditional Christianity. Lewis admitted in his preface that this material is speculative, but the reader may forget this reservation before reaching the end of the book.

Leslie Weatherhead points out in his excellent little book on pain that Jesus did not say, "I have explained the world." What he said was, "I have overcome the world." [2] Paul Hessert writes about pain, "In simple terms, the problem of evil involves aspects of our experience that do not make sense. We must recognize this at the outset, lest we despair over our inability to understand what, by definition, defies meaning." [3] Some evil is only apparent. But other incidents of evil may be genuine, far-reaching, and inexplicable. Charles Williams, in discussion with Lewis, once compared Job's comforters to "the sort of people who write books on the Problem of Pain." Lewis seems to have appreciated this remark.

When Lewis dealt with the theme of suffering in *A Grief Observed*, which was published under a pseudonym following the death of his wife, his tone was less rationalistic and more compassionate. He observed, in fact, that prior to Helen's death his interpretation of pain had been too intellectualistic—"an imaginary faith playing with innocuous counters labelled 'illness,' 'pain,' 'Death' and 'Loneliness.'" It might be said of the Lewis who wrote this book what his Orual once said when the Fox broke down in tears over Psyche: "His love got the better of his philosophy."

Lewis cried out in *Grief*, "Cancer, and cancer, and cancer. My mother, my father, my wife. I wonder who is next in the queue." After some speculation on the purposes of God, he asked, "Aren't all these notes the senseless writings of a man who won't accept the fact that there is nothing we can do with suffering except to suffer it? Who still thinks there is some device (if only he could find it) which will make pain not to be pain." "Where is God?" Lewis wondered during the early hours after his wife's death. One goes to God in desperate need and finds a door slammed in his face, with "a sound of bolting and double bolting on the inside." Reflected Lewis, "Was it ever inhabited? It seemed so once. And that seeming was as strong as this. What can this mean?" Several days later, he reported that the great door no longer seemed shut and bolted. Are extremities of suffering really necessary for people, he wondered. "If they are unnecessary, then there is no God or a bad one. If there is a good God, then these tortures are necessary. For no even moderately good Being could possibly inflict or permit them if they weren't." Even in *Grief* the attempt completely "to solve the intel-

[2] *The Will of God* (Nashville: Abingdon Press, 1944), p. 31.
[3] *Introduction to Christianity* (Englewood Cliffs, N. J.: Prentice-Hall, 1958), p. 234.

lectual problem raised by suffering" occasionally reappears. In my opinion, Lewis' effort went beyond the usual Christian affirmation that good can come from apparent evil. He bordered at times upon hoping and attempting to solve the insoluble.

Lewis captured something of the "tether and pang of the particular" in two poems which deal with painful memories. He wrote in "Scazons,"

> Passing to-day by a cottage, I shed tears
> When I remembered how once I had dwelled there
> With my mortal friends who are dead. Years
> Little had healed the wound that was laid bare.

"Joys That Sting," I think, is especially moving:

> *Oh doe not die,* says Donne, *for I shall hate*
> *All women so.* How false the sentence rings.
> Women? But in a life made desolate
> It is the joys once shared that have the stings.
>
> To take the old walks alone, or not at all,
> To order one pint where I ordered two,
> To think of, and then not to make, the small
> Time-honoured joke (senseless to all but you) ;
>
> To laugh (oh, one'll laugh) , to talk upon
> Themes that we talked upon when you were there,
> To make some poor pretence of going on,
> Be kind to one's old friends, and seem to care,
>
> While no one (O God) through the years will say
> The simplest, common word in just your way.

Another sphere of interest and concern in the Christian life involves social relationships. One of the dominant desires of life is to be on the inside of some select group, to gain the intimacy and conveniences of belonging to "the inner ring." The status of achieving such recognition may be cherished even more than the money, the power, and the privilege of evading certain rules and duties, involved in the position. But, warned Lewis, the passion to belong can turn one who intends no evil into a regular scoundrel. If a man is to resist the pressures to compromise which come as a temptation from the desire to get "in," he will need to make a conscious and continuous effort in another direction. If one makes vocational excellence his chief end, he will become a sound craftsman and thus belong to the only inner circle in the profession which really matters. Genuine friendship, further, can be better found apart from the struggles of professional rivalry.[4]

[4] "The Inner Ring," *Transposition,* pp. 55-64.

Lewis asked in *Psalms* how Christians should behave in the presence of people who are bad and powerful, prosperous and impenitent. It is not simply a matter of accepting poor outcasts, he noted; these persons are received in society with great cordiality. Perhaps the Christian should tend to avoid close social relationships with people who are lascivious, cruel, dishonest, and spiteful. In a day of intense reaction against priggery, it is unlikely that the ordinary Christian will consider himself "too good" for such company. He is probably not good enough, however, to cope with the temptations to condone, to connive, and to consent through words and looks and laughter. One may sometimes remain silent in such situations, and it may be possible to express disagreement without appearing priggish. But occasionally a protest must be registered against accepted evil. Said Lewis, "If we are strongly tempted not to do so, we are unlikely to be priggish in reality."

Lewis observed that Kipling shows a particular fascination with the "inner ring" theme in his books. Kipling's characters often operate within the warm intimacy of a closed circle. This "poet of work" recognized the inescapable bond of shared experience, especially shared hardship. But the inner-ring spirit is in itself morally neutral, Lewis claimed. It can serve either valor and public spirit, or cruelty and dishonesty. Kipling had unusual insight into the power of group intimacy, Lewis concluded, but it is important to go beyond him and to evaluate the ends toward which sacrificial energy is directed.[5]

The inner-circle theme also appears several times in *Screwtape*. Through hunger for approval or popularity a man may assume all sorts of cynical or skeptical attitudes which are not really his own, writes Screwtape. Eventually the looks and tones, the laughs and silences tend to become one's own. A man can lead parallel lives for awhile only, becoming a different person for each circle he frequents. "All mortals tend to turn into the thing they are pretending to be." Certain types of humor are especially valuable to Hell. Almost any act can get itself accepted with admiration, rather than with disapproval, if it is presented as a joke. Flippancy—the ability to talk as if virtue were funny—is particularly cherished by the Lowerarchy.

A *leitmotif* of *Hideous Strength* concerns the desperate eagerness of young sociologist Mark Studdock to belong to an "inner ring." This goal involves his being seen with the right people, being able to talk their language, avoiding association with "outsiders," and sometimes overlooking moral principles. In momentary despair, Mark displays his

[5] "Kipling's World," *Paper,* pp. 72-92.

disgust for pretense and asks himself when he has ever done what he really wants. But his yearning to be in on "big stuff" dominates his life. When N.I.C.E. asks Mark to undertake an assignment he clearly knows to be criminal,

the moment of his consent almost escaped his notice; certainly, there was no struggle, no sense of turning a corner. . . . It all slipped past in a chatter of laughter, of that intimate laughter between fellow professionals, which of all earthly powers is strongest to make men do very bad things before they are yet, individually, very bad men. (*That Hideous Strength*, p. 130)

In the end, it becomes evident to Mark that his lifelong eagerness to belong to an inner circle has driven him toward the wrong circle. His wife Jane has found the right one—a circle relaxed and free, sensitive to beauty, full of easy laughter.

One of the proper circles for shaping outlook, character, and values, Lewis believed, was the church. A Christian is called neither to individualism nor to collectivism, but to membership, he said. There is no such thing as solitary religion. And collectivism is an outrage against human nature. In the church, however, persons are members of one another. That is, they are to be organs—"essentially different from, and complementary to, one another." One is invited by baptism not into a collective but into a body.

The life of the collective is always lower in status than personal life. Economics, politics, laws, armies, and institutions have no value for Lewis except as they serve the private life and the happy home. Excessive claims by the collective should be countered with the reminder that *it* is mortal, while individuals live forever. Persons are assured of "eternal self-identity and shall live to remember the galaxies as an old tale." It is not, of course, that each human soul is in itself of infinite value; Christ died, after all, for sinners. Neither the isolated individual nor the whole community can inherit eternal life—neither a natural self nor a collective mass—but a new creature. Christianity defends the collective, not through isolation, but by giving status to every organ in the mystical body of Christ.

God has so arranged things that the new life of Christ is to be spread particularly through the means of baptism, belief, and Holy Communion, Lewis affirmed. It may seem strange that these special things should be conductors of new life. But Jesus taught his followers that the new life was to be communicated in this way. It seems as wise to depend upon a reliable authority in this matter as to turn to a generally trustworthy scientist or historian for authoritative guidance in other areas of life. Like natural life, the new life must be nurtured if it is to be maintained. The Christ-life dwells within, offering forgiveness and making repairs. Taken together, Christians are the physical organism through which Christ acts on earth. Christ-life is not merely a mental or moral quality. Its growth is more than the spreading of an idea; it is more like a biological or super biological fact of evolution. Man is not intended by God to be a purely spiritual creature; the new life is nourished by material things like bread and wine.[6]

Lewis spoke of his early attitude toward the church in *Surprised*. "I had as little wish to be in the Church as in the zoo. It was, to begin with, a kind of collective; a wearisome 'get-together' affair. I couldn't yet see how a concern of that sort should have anything to do with one's spiritual life. To me, religion ought to have been a matter of good men praying alone and meeting by twos and threes to talk of spiritual matters." His later appreciation for the church was expressed in many of his letters. It seems to be a law of creation, he said, that the thing we know already and have told ourselves many times can become suddenly operative when it is said by someone else. It appears, as Charles Williams suggests, that "no one can paddle his own canoe but everyone can paddle someone else's." Lewis came to believe that the Bible helps to bring men to Christ when it is read in the proper spirit and under the guidance of informed teachers. Passages must be interpreted in context, and in light of the purpose and nature of the books in which they are found. When one makes decisions with the intention of pleasing God, the Holy Spirit is present for internal guidance, Lewis taught. The Spirit does not operate only from within; he speaks also through Scripture, church, Christian friends, books, and in other ways.

Lewis once wondered why religious people were always insisting that men "praise" God. He came to see that enjoyment spontaneously overflows in praise unless for some reason it is blocked. Men spontaneously praise whatever they cherish, and they urge others to join them in praise. In fact, "praise not merely expresses but completes the enjoyment"; delight is not complete until it is expressed. It appears to be in this mood that Lewis concluded *Perelandra* with a great dance suggesting the ultimate order and purpose of all created things.

Lewis was an advocate of church unity throughout most of his adult Christian life. In a 1939 letter to a Roman Catholic priest, he expressed the need for a united Christendom as a challenge to paganism. He recommended that churches engage in vigorous cooperation even while

[6] *Mere Christianity*, pp. 62-66.

acknowledging their differences. An experienced unity on some things, he proposed, might lead to confessional unity later. Lewis hoped that his *Mere Christianity* might help to make clear why Christians ought to be reunited. He remarks in this book that modern churchmen are still "early Christians." He considered wicked and wasteful divisions between Christians a disease of infancy.

"God has his own way with each soul," asserted Lewis. He objects in *Mere Christianity* to those sects which have a uniform program of conversion for everyone. God never deals with men in mass, he writes. "When Christ died, He died for you individually just as much as if you had been the only man in the world." Lewis himself prefers a fixed form for public worship, feeling that permanent structure sets devotional life free. Extempore prayers, he thinks, tend to become provincial—if not phony or heretical. Since it is difficult to be at the same time both critical and devotional, it is best to follow a regular form. While he finds the sectarian custom of plastering the landscape with religious slogans personally distasteful, Lewis admits that the practice may suit the taste of some people. His attitude toward individualistic expression in religion is summarized thus in one letter: "My model here is the behaviour of the congregation at a 'Russian Orthodox' service, where some sit, some lie on their faces, some stand, some kneel, some walk about, and *no one takes the slightest notice of what anyone else is doing*. That is good sense, good manners, and good Christianity. 'Mind one's own business' is a good rule in religion as in other things."

Lewis' reflections on the church are found occasionally in his imaginative work. Screwtape reports that Hell encourages the cultivation of "religion" as a means to some other end. "Once you have made the World an end, and faith a means," he writes, "you have almost won your man, and it makes very little difference what kind of worldly end he is pursuing." The Church can be used as an ally of Hell, notes Screwtape. The patient's mind should be made to flit between the notion of "the body of Christ" and the actual faces in the next pew. "Provided that any of those neighbours sing out of tune, or have boots that squeak, or double chins, or odd clothes, the patient will quite easily believe that their religion must therefore be somehow ridiculous." A person should be taught to avoid the question, "If I, being what I am, can consider that I am in some sense a Christian, why should the different vices of those people in the next pew prove that their religion is mere hypocrisy and convention?" Is it possible to keep such an obvious thought from the human mind? Screwtape rejoices, "It is, Wormwood, it is!"

John's trip to the Landlord's Steward in *Regress* exposes some of the artificiality, duplicity and contradiction common in religious instruction. The Steward, normally a jolly and kind gentleman, puts on a mask and talks in a queer singsong voice when it comes time to discuss the Landlord. Handing John a card with an impossible set of rules on it, the Steward informs him that if he ever breaks any, he may be shut up forever in a black hole filled with snakes and scorpions. But, adds the Steward after removing his mask, "I shouldn't bother about it all too much if I were you." The interview ends with the Steward's pointing out that the Landlord is extraordinarily kind and loving toward his tenants —and will certainly torture them to death at the slightest pretext.

In the same allegory, John and Vertue come to a great chasm on their journey. An old woman seated in a rocker on the edge of the precipice declares that neither can cross unless they allow her to carry them down. Vertue recognizes the old lady as "Mother Kirk" and whispers to John, "Some of the country people say she is second-sighted, and some that she is crazy." John discovers that the old woman not only believes in the Landlord, but claims even to be his daughter-in-law. John and Vertue agree that they can come back to Mother Kirk for aid, if worst comes to worst, but they hope it will not come to that. In the end, they do return and find Mother Kirk waiting for them, significantly, beside a pool of water.

Although Lewis had little use for classical mysticism, he regarded prayer as an important part of the Christian life. As he pointed out in *Letter to Malcolm: Chiefly on Prayer,* prayer involves the awareness that one's material surroundings, and one's own "self," are not rock-bottom realities. Lewis endorsed patterns of permanence and uniformity for worship in *Malcolm.* Language ought to be modernized for intelligibility, he said, but it would be best if any new liturgy would represent a united church and would reflect genuine literary talent. The ideal church service should demand little conscious attention. One's attention should be fastened upon God—not upon novelties within the service or upon a "liturgical fidget" of a celebrant. Lewis was quite flexible in recommending types of prayer for private devotion. It takes all sorts to make a church, he said; Heaven encourages more variety than Hell. Prayer without words is best, but this practice is often difficult. Prayers in one's own words are also desirable. Neither should formal, "ready-made," prayers be neglected in private devotion. These keep a person in touch with sound doctrine, are comprehensive in their concerns, and provide a helpful ceremonial element. The times and places for prayer are, of course, widely varied. Bedtime is the worst possible hour for concentration, and church buildings often prove distracting spots for private prayer. Since the body should engage in prayer as well as the soul, it is well to kneel; but many other things are more important than posture.

What should a Christian pray about? Does not God know everything anyway? Are not human concerns likely to appear trivial to him? We move in prayer, continued Lewis, from the category of objects known by God to personal relationships with him. We tell and show and offer ourselves to view. It may be that our desires are at times stronger than their trivial objects deserve. Yet things which are in our thoughts should be also in our prayers, whether in penitence or petition or both. "I fancy we may sometimes be deterred from small prayers by a sense of our own dignity rather than of God's."

Lewis further noted in *Malcolm* that the word *religion* seldom appears in the New Testament. The term seems to suggest a department of life, alongside economic, social, intellectual, recreational, and other concerns. "But that whose claims are infinite can have no standing as a department. Either it is an illusion or else our whole life falls under it. We have no non-religious activities; only religious and irreligious." A "sacred" department of life can become an end in itself—a love of observances and organization which obscures the love of God and neighbor. Genuine religion is more than a system of beliefs or one interest among others in a well-balanced life. Even so, it is valuable to have specific holy days, places, and things, to serve as reminders that God is all about us.

Petitionary prayer is important, as well as acts of penitence and adoration. Determinists reject as illusion "our spontaneous conviction that our behaviour has its ultimate origin in ourselves," Lewis noted. But like everyone else, they still ask others to pass them the salt, and they continue to act as though men were at least partially self-determining. We do not live in a fully predictable universe; the purposive action of both man and God shape the future. Alexander Pope penned the maxim: "The first Almighty Cause / Acts not by partial, but by general laws." But Lewis found this concept of God subtly and disastrously "anthropomorphic." By precept and example, he said, men are taught to pray. But prayer would be meaningless in the impersonal universe pictured by Pope.

The New Testament contains some extravagant promises about what prayer can accomplish. Yet "every war, every famine or plague, almost every death-bed, is the monument to a petition that was not granted." It is not difficult to understand intellectually why prayers made in ignorance must be refused, even though it is hard for the will to accept. For most Christians it is proper to add the reservation, as Jesus did in Gethsemane, "if it be Thy will." Lewis noted a difficult problem concerning petitionary prayer in *Reflections*. Christianity seems to teach two inconsistent patterns of petitionary prayer, he observed. On the one hand, it appears that all requests are to be subjected to the condition "Thy will be done"; men are to pray in the full knowledge that they may not receive what they ask. On the other hand, they are instructed to pray with a confident faith that whatever is asked for will be received. Lewis concluded that this remained for him a problem without an answer.

Lewis admits in *Last Night* that while a Christian is convinced that God answers prayer, empirical proof (or disproof) for this belief is impossible. The believer prays, and events occur which seem to him to validate his prayer. But how can he demonstrate that these things might not have happened anyway? Or even if a miracle occurs, how can a causal connection be proved between the prayers and the subsequent event? Men can establish no experiment to test the results of prayer— for example, praying diligently for the patients in one hospital and neglecting to pray for those in another. In ancient times it was said that God refused thus to be "tested." Such an experiment would have as its primary goal not the relief of suffering but the demonstration of some theory; the real purpose and the nominal purpose of the experiment would vary. The assurance that God hears prayer grows, not out of laboratory-like proof, but out of a kind of personal relationship with Him. Prayer is not magic; the Christian does not expect invariable success in prayer, perhaps even controlling nature in ways contrary to the wisdom of God. Prayer is a request, submitted to the will and judgment of God.

Why should men suppose that God pays any attention to their prayers? Why would he modify his action in response to human suggestions? In other areas of life, said Lewis, men exercise free will to share in God's work. Perhaps God could sustain life miraculously without food, spread knowledge without schools, convert others without missionaries. But the will of man participates in the execution of God's will. Christ has instructed his followers to pray. Is it any more strange that these prayers should affect the course of nature than other actions undertaken by men? All that is said on subjects such as prayer, Lewis concludes in *Last Night,* must remain analogical and parabolic. Pure reality is incomprehensible by human faculties, so we continue to work with mental models and symbols. The best that men can do is to attempt to get rid of poor analogies and bad parables.

Lewis often referred to prayer in his letters and in his more imaginative work. He replied to a correspondent that spiritual healing is promised in Scripture, although any particular instance of purported healing may be real, chance, or fraud. Any such claim may be true, said Lewis, and it is not his business to render a decision whether or not it is. There is no reason why prayer should not be for actual things, he told another correspondent. "How very odd it would be if God in His actions towards me were bound to ignore what I did (including my prayers). . . . Why should my asking or not asking not be *one* of the things He takes into account?" Lewis places this idea about prayer in a poem. It is not strange, he declares, if God momentarily enfeebles His power,

> . . . if His action lingers
> Till men have prayed, and suffers their weak prayers indeed
> To move as very muscles His delaying fingers.

Kidnapped and carried to the planet Malacandra, Ransom continues his daily prayers in a normal way. On the planet Perelandra, Ransom is discovered quietly saying grace over his meals. One rarely finds in contemporary literature a character who takes prayer more seriously. Prayer figures prominently also in *Dawn Treader*, when the crew of the ship faces a terrible crisis and Lucy seeks supernatural aid. A shrewd Screwtape observes that prayer for daily bread in a "spiritual sense" is just as crudely petitionary as any other kind. He suggests, further, that a patient can be kept from serious prayer either by encouraging him to repeat, parrotlike, the prayers of his childhood, or by the cultivation of a vaguely devotional mood in which will and intelligence have no part. The patient's intentions can be misdirected by causing him to watch his own reactions and feelings, rather than to concentrate upon the "Enemy Himself." "Teach them to estimate the value of each prayer by their success in producing the desired feeling," Screwtape writes, "and never let them suspect how much success or failure of that kind depends on whether they are well or ill, fresh or tired, at the moment."

John Haigh says of the Narnia chronicles that "Lewis's skill lies in presenting virtue as more real and exciting than sin." Some readers will agree that Lewis is equally successful in achieving this goal as he considers the nature of redemption in his theological and imaginative works. Lewis attempts to present a dazzling vision of human potential, of the "new life" lived on the basis of grace, faith, and love. There is certain to be ample room for criticism of anyone who undertakes an extended discussion of such huge topics as Christian morality, the problem of evil, and the means of grace. But all in all, it seems to me, Lewis creates an attractive vision—perhaps even an exhilarating vision—of what human life on this planet is intended to be. The range of his vision and the depth of his insight are truly remarkable.

190

IX

Man as He Is Yet to Be: Eschatology, with Fresh Images of Human Destiny

Concerning time and destiny:

We are so little reconciled to time that we are even astonished at it. 'How he's grown!' we exclaim, 'How time flies!' as though the universal form of our experience were again and again a novelty. It is as strange as if a fish were repeatedly surprised at the wetness of water. And that would be strange indeed; unless of course the fish were destined to become, one day, a land animal.
—*Psalms*, p. 138

"I can understand a man coming in the end, and after prolonged consideration, to the view that existence is not futile," wrote Lewis. "But how any man could have taken it for granted . . . beats me." In popular thought "evolution" is taken to mean "improvement." Actually, says Lewis, it means only "change." He cites J. B. S. Haldane as saying that progress is the exception in evolution, while degeneration is the rule. Against a background of "huge tracts of empty space and the enormous masses of uninhabitable matter," mankind stares out on principles of entropy, degradation, and disorganization. "Everything suggests that organic life is going to be a very short and unimportant episode in the history of the universe. Organic life is only a lightning flash in cosmic history. In the long run, nothing will come of it."

In view of the approaching end of organic life, how can life be meaningful? For Lewis, man's participation in reason and morality indicates that something else beyond the natural world is real. Both reasonable and moral judgments are often expressed imperfectly. But to suggest that they need correction also implies that they are something more than sub-

191

jective facts about ourselves. "Either there is significance in the whole process of things as well as in human activity, or there is no significance in human activity itself."

Although it is widely ignored by the modern world, the doctrine of the Second Coming is an integral part of the Christian faith, Lewis declared in *Last Night*. In fact, it is probably impossible to retain belief in the Christian revelation while abandoning the promise and threat of Christ's Return. Donne's question remains forever relevant: "What if this present were the world's last night?"

There are several reasons for embarrassment over this doctrine which prevent modern men from giving it the attention it deserves. Some people have reacted to Dr. Albert Schweitzer's tendency to exaggerate the "apocalyptic" element as the essence of Christ's teaching. Others feel that this material in the Gospel message is accounted for or excused by the discovery that it belongs to a class of apocalyptic predictions common to the thought of first-century Palestine. A valid teaching, however, is not totally discredited if it is spoken with exaggeration. And the question remains whether the expectation of a catastrophic, divinely ordered end of this world is valid or not. Some suppose that the apocalyptic beliefs of the New Testament have already been demonstrated false. Did not Jesus prophesy that these things would happen in "this generation"? That verse, said Lewis, is the most embarrassing in the Bible. But it is followed hastily by another verse which insists that no man, even Jesus himself, knows the exact time for the return.

Whether conscious of the reason or not, some people feel that the idea of the Second Coming is out of character with the dominant emphasis today upon evolution and gradual development. Assuming Darwinian biology to be correct, there is, of course, no general law of progress in biological history. And certainly there is none in ethics or culture or social history. Various theoretical concerns deter some from taking the doctrine of the Second Coming seriously, but other persons are embarrassed by it for practical reasons. They are acquainted with the mass hysteria and folly which have sometimes accompanied particular attempts to predict the moment of return (in spite of Jesus' warning that such prediction is impossible).

What did Jesus himself have to say about his return, and what can this doctrine mean for modern man? Lewis claims that Jesus' teachings on the matter consist of three ideas: (1) that he certainly will come again; (2) that no one can possibly know in advance when; and (3) that his followers should remain always alert for the time of his coming. While Lewis does not think it desirable to banish all fear from religion, it is not the purpose of this doctrine to excite fear. In fact, it is impossible to sustain fear, or any other emotion, over a long period of time.

The doctrine of the Second Coming has two important implications for modern life. First, it encourages men continually to take the end into account. It is wise to remember that the whole life of humanity is precarious, temporary, and provisional. "All achievements and triumphs, in so far as they are merely this-worldly achievements and triumphs, will come to nothing in the end." Further, the return is a judgment as well as an end. In that day, every human soul will be revealed for what it actually is, and the clear truth about every man will be made evident before the entire universe. Why is God not yet landing in the enemy-occupied world in force? Lewis stated in *Mere Christianity* that He is going to invade, but is delaying in order to give men the chance to join His side freely. When the invasion comes, it will be the end, and none will have any choice left. It will be too late then to choose sides.

Edgar Boss attributes to Lewis the belief that "Jesus is literally, personally coming again." In the reference which Boss gives to document this statement, however, I am unable to find in Lewis anything to support this apparent fundamentalist position. I do not know what Boss means by "literally" when it is used in this sense, but this terminology will not be found in Lewis' discussion of eschatology.

William Butler Yeats had an unusually lofty poetic vision of the universe. He saw not only individual lives as fleeting, but man's greatest civilizations also rising and perishing in a brief time-span. Yeats wrote, "Egypt and Greece, good-bye, and good-bye, Rome! / Hermits . . . know / That day brings round the night, that before dawn / His glory and his monuments are gone." [1] Although Yeats's perspective was large indeed, Lewis assumed an even greater one: his eschatology led him to envision the death of planets and solar systems.

The interplanetary trilogy and the Narnia stories especially provide Lewis a framework for expressing imaginatively his grand perspective. He mentions in a letter that he views "Westonism" as a real danger. Many people, he thought, suppose that improving and perpetuating the human race through interplanetary colonization is the goal which gives the entire universe its meaning. Weston, a monomaniac obsessed with planetary imperialism in the science-fiction trilogy, has the wild dream that mankind should discover his immortality by dominating the universe, planet after planet, galaxy after galaxy. Ransom considers this idea "the sweet poison of the false infinite." Weston is convinced that he is

[1] "Meru."

justified in doing anything at all, as Ransom says, "on the off chance that some creatures or other descended from man as we know him may crawl about a few centuries longer in some part of the universe." The rights or life of one person or of a million, Weston admits, have not the slightest importance in comparison with this tremendous goal. Further, he contends, all "educated opinion"—classics, history, and "such trash" aside—agrees with him.

The creatures of Malacandra, in contrast with Weston, contentedly acknowledge the transitory nature of their existence. The *sorn* replies to Ransom's query about the extinction of the ancient birdlike creatures in the petrified forests of that planet: "A world is not made to last for ever, much less a race; that is not Maleldil's way." Ransom goes to sleep wondering what it would be like to live always within sight of a land which has become uninhabitable. Later, when Oyarsa questions Ransom about his travel-partner Weston, Ransom confesses that Weston wants men from earth to leap from world to world so that the race will last forever. "Is he wounded in his brain?" asks Oyarsa. "Does he think Maleldil wants a race to live for ever?" "He does not know there is any Maleldil," replies Ransom.

In the Narnia stories Digory and Polly are drawn into Charn, a world which appears to have been deserted for thousands of years. A great red sun, bigger and older than ours, hangs near the end of its life "weary of looking down upon that world." The pair learn from the revived Witch that she has used her secret of the Deplorable Word to destroy every living thing in that world, "for reasons of State." What would be wrong for common people, she contends, is not wrong for a great Queen with the weight of the world on her shoulders. She has felt herself free from petty rules because hers is a high and lonely destiny. It is evident in *Last Battle* that the world of Narnia itself is destined to draw one day to an end. Only Aslan's own country, the real Narnia, can endure forever. All the others are shadowlands—mere copies of something in Aslan's real world. "It's all in Plato, all in Plato," Lord Digory explains. As the end of Narnia approaches, the great Time-giant stretches out his arm, grasps the sun, and squeezes it like a orange. Instantly, the world beyond the Door is plunged into total darkness.

Lewis proclaimed himself a desperate skeptic on any philosophy of history. "I don't know whether the human tragi-comedy is now in Act I or Act V; whether our present disorders are those of infancy or of old age." He wrote in *Reflections*, "The philosophy of history is a discipline for which we mortal men lack the necessary data." Men cannot say what history means, or what its total pattern is. They tend to find meanings in those historical periods they have studied the least. But modern man knows next to nothing about the past, "a roaring cataract of billions upon billions of . . . moments: any one of them too complex to grasp in its entirety, and the aggregate beyond all imagination." The quantity of "selections" which we have from the past are as a single word compared with the library of the British Museum, Lewis noted. Christians believe they have divine comment on certain great events. The creeds make plain so much of their significance as men need. But on most events mortal men can register no significant comment.

Lewis wrote in *Torso*, "Again and again something arises which seems to be 'beyond history, holding history at bay'. . . . Nothing is further from the truth than the picture of history given in Keats's *Hyperion* where each perfection is ousted by 'a new perfection' treading on its heels. The movement is not from lovely Titans to still more lovely Gods, but from Augustus to Tiberius, from Arthur to Mordred, from Voltaire to Vichy." Lewis asked in *Sixteenth Century* why men should assume that the conservation of cultures is normal and that their death is an abnormality to be explained. Arts and cultures, as well as men and women, he said, are subject to accident and violent death. The best does not always survive. "An art, a whole civilization, may at any time slip through men's fingers in a very few years and be gone beyond recovery."

Perhaps the archetypal image of our age misleads men about the nature of history. A dominant image of our time is the picture of old machines being superseded by new and better machines. The major milestones of life for a family may be the automobiles and other machines which they own at various stages along their life pilgrimage. But the coming of machines has altered man's place in nature and has placed between present and past a chasm which marks the greatest change in the history of Western Man. The birth of machines has furnished man with *a new archetypal image*. "Permanence" in our age suggests "stagnation." "Primitive" suggests inefficiency, clumsiness, or barbarity; for our ancestors the same word sometimes connoted "purity." A study of the literature and culture of the past, in Lewis' thought, liberates men from the present. One can come to view his own time as a period with its own peculiarities and idols. But a knowledge of history also liberates from the past. The unhistorical, said Lewis, are often unconsciously enslaved to a fairly recent past.

Lewis suggested in a variety of ways that one's perspective largely determines his interpretation of events. Confused by blurred masses of color when he first arrives on a strange planet, Ransom observes, "You cannot see things till you know roughly what they are." In *Last Battle* a band of dwarfs decline participation in a grand banquet because they refuse to be "taken in." And when the friendly beasts of Narnia descend upon Uncle Andrew with noises of cheerful interest, he is certain that he is under attack from a herd of dangerous wild animals. What you see and hear, notes Lewis, depends a great deal upon where you are standing and upon what sort of person you are. No matter how beautifully Aslan sings, Uncle Andrew always persuades himself that the sound is nothing but a roar. What one finds in the drama of life and history also depends upon one's eschatological perspective. What is the purpose of life itself, and where is the universe headed?

Not only is the universe itself destined to die one day, but each person born moves inevitably toward his own death. Compared with the attitudes of the Stoics or Hobbes, the Christian view of death is ambivalent. The Stoics taught that death does not matter; it should be treated with indifference. Hobbes considered death the greatest of all evils, and he erected a system on that basis. For Christians, however, death is both holy and unholy—"our supreme disgrace and our only hope." Lewis set down the following words a few days after the death of his wife:

It is hard to have patience with people who say 'There is no death' or 'Death doesn't matter.' There is death. And whatever is matters. And whatever happens has consequences, and it and they are irrevocable and irreversible. You might as well say that birth doesn't matter. I look up at the night sky. Is anything more certain than that in all those vast times and spaces, if I were allowed to search them, I should nowhere find her face, her voice, her touch? She died. She is dead. Is the word so difficult to learn? (*A Grief Observed*, p. 16)

A lonely husband asks himself in *Grief* whether he can now honestly believe that Helen is anything. While he had prayed for other dead in the past, he finds that he cannot do so for Helen; there is only "a ghastly sense of unreality, of speaking into a vacuum about a nonentity." Later he records, "You never know how much you really believe anything until its truth or falsehood becomes a matter of life and death." What does it mean to say that Helen is now "at peace," Lewis asks. How can the separation which agonizes the lover left behind be painless to the lover who departs? Lewis remembers that during Helen's illness there was one temporary recovery that might even be considered a miracle. But time after time, when God appeared most gracious, "He was really preparing the next torture," Lewis protested. He later noted that his grief had driven him to express this idea as "a yell rather than a thought."

Lewis expressed sensitivity to the harsh fact of death in several of his letters. "What a grim business even a happy human life is when you read it rapidly through to the inevitable end," he wrote. One should not pretend that death is not real. Perhaps only one who has lived fully can fully appreciate the threat of death. Some men are not so much in love with life as is commonly thought; they attempt to reduce much of it to near the level of nonlife, through the use of drugs, sleep, irresponsibility, and amusement. Many might seek death if they could be sure it would not hurt. The first severe personal loss to death for Lewis was the death of his friend Charles Williams. This event, he reported, gave undreamed-of corroboration to his belief in immortality. "What the idea of death has done to him is nothing to what he has done to the idea of death," wrote Lewis.

The inevitable reality of death is confronted also in Lewis' more imaginative work. John hears in *Regress* that his disreputable old uncle has received sudden notice from the Landlord "to quit." The whole family had assumed that his lease was to run on for several years more, but the Landlord retains the right to turn anyone out without advance notice. The Steward assures Uncle George that he is being turned out only in order to be made more comfortable elsewhere. Everyone wears masks for the moments of farewell. Uncle George's mask keeps slipping off. He crosses a little brook, never to be seen again. "Will the Landlord put Uncle George in the black hole?" asks John. "Of course he won't," answers his mother; "Your Uncle George was a very good man." "You never told me that before," replies John.

The creatures of Malacandra know that Maleldil does not make them long-livers. Yet the weakest of them does not fear death. Only the Bent One, they think, causes men to waste their lives fleeing from what they know will finally overtake them. Says Oyarsa, "If you were subjects of Maleldil you would have peace." The inhabitants of the planet use this sacred ritual for dissolving the bodies of their dead:

Let it go down; the *hnau* rises from it. This is the second life, the other beginning. Open, oh coloured world, without weight, without shore. You are second, and better; this was first and feeble. . . .

Let us scatter the movements which were their bodies.
So will Maleldil scatter all worlds when the first and feeble is worn. (*Out of the Silent Planet,* p. 132)

The Greek slave in *Faces* argues that men are but resolved into the natural elements at death. But when Wormwood's patient is hit by a bomb and dies, he enters directly into "joy." The Hermit of the Southern March summarizes the precarious situation of life for Hwin, a talking horse of Narnia. Hwin inquires anxiously about the welfare of a friend, but the Hermit can only reply, "I do not know whether any man or woman or beast in the whole world will be alive when the sun sets to-night." Perhaps Prince Rilian of Narnia echoes the mood of Paul when he concludes, "Whether we live or die Aslan will be our good lord." Death is undeniably real, but there is also another Reality capable of dealing with death.

Lewis has sometimes been represented as so exclusively concerned with immortality that some readers may be surprised to hear him speak occasionally of the danger of being overly concerned about eternal destiny. Happiness and misery beyond death—in themselves alone—are not even religious subjects, he wrote in *Psalms*. When hopes and anxieties center on oneself, God is not central. God should not be thought to exist only for the sake of something else, even immortality. Lewis said in *Miracles* that conceptions of Heaven are important to Christians, but they are not among those things which are the most important. "If you find that they so distract you," he advised, "think of them no more. . . . It is of more importance for you or me to-day to refrain from one sneer or to extend one charitable thought to an enemy than to know all that angels and archangels know about the mysteries of the New Creation."

Lewis stated in *Surprised,* further, that immortality should not be made the central doctrine of religion; a preoccupation with it is corrupting, he noted. Genuine goodness is not self-seeking, and much concern about reward or punishment contaminates the will. Union with God is bliss. Separation from him is horror. This is the meaning of heaven and hell. But these concepts should not be hypostatised as though they had a substantial meaning apart from God. To do this corrupts the doctrine and the persons who hold it. Lewis said that the question of immortality did not occur to him for nearly a year following his conversion to Christianity. Although belief in the next world is not the central or most important concern of the Christian faith, Lewis concluded in *Malcolm* that interest in this dimension of reality can hardly be slight, if it is believed in at all.

As an Oxford student, Lewis found the idea of immortality disgusting. Yet in a 1921 letter to his father he expressed the thought that death itself is rather incredible. It was not that he had any faith in immortality, he hastened to add. It was just that it is hard to believe that something turns into nothing. Lewis reported in *Surprised* that for more than fifty years he felt no horror at the possibility of annihilation at death. Only after he had been long reconverted, after he had begun to appreciate what life really might be, did he feel some anxiety at the idea of becoming a nonentity. He thought it quite unlikely that wishful thinking had anything whatsoever to do with the wavering of his own materialistic faith. For one thing, a person always has wishes on both sides. And any rational conception of reality tends to favor some wishes and to frustrate others.

Lewis admitted that it is a debatable question whether man should continue to be "a noble animal, splendid in ashes and pompous in the grave." But he concluded, "I think he should." Walter Hooper thinks the central premise of all of Lewis' theological works is the conviction that *all* men are immortal. Lewis might protest that this is not *the* center of his theology, but he does say in *Mere Christianity* that every person is destined to live forever. The individual, therefore, is incomparably more important than any given state or civilization, which will last for but a moment of time.

While Lewis believed strongly in a life after death, he also insisted that the precise character of this life remains unimaginable. The Bible, he notes, "seems scrupulously to avoid any *description* of the other world, or worlds, except in terms of parable or allegory." Lewis said in a letter that he believed in resurrection, but that the state of the dead prior to this eschatological event could not be pictured. He noted in *Malcolm* that the doctrine of "the resurrection of the body" is concerned more with a resurrection of the senses or memory than it is with some future state of "matter." Why, he asked, should heaven seem unreal to modern man when we know that our present "real world" differs so much from the real world described by physics? Lewis thought that the body in which we shall live in the new mode will by both like and unlike the present body. It will be differently related to space, and probably to time as well. But it will not be cut off from all time-space relations. Lewis noted in *Miracles* that Jesus' disciples failed immediately to recognize the risen Christ on three separate occasions (Luke 24:13-31; John 20:15, and 21:4). The theory of hallucination appears to break down if a figure was observed first and only later recognized to be Jesus. The Christian does not expect the resurrection body to be composed of the same particles of matter which it has had during this life, of course. Even if such an idea were not denied in Scripture, Lewis noted, there would not be enough material particles to go around. We all live in "second-hand suits," he said. "There are doubtless atoms in my chin which have served many another man, many a dog, many an eel, many a dinosaur." Humans can know very little about the promised "spiritual body." It is not the task of the Christian imagination to forecast on this matter, but simply to make room for "circumspect agnosticism."

199

In his discussions of life after death, Lewis repeatedly employed one expression that will puzzle some readers. He wrote in *Grief* that God's grand enterprise is to create spiritual animals and then to challenge them to become *gods*. He said in *Last Night* that God makes *gods* out of nothing. Near the end of *Divorce* one reads, "The Lord said we were gods." It is not customary for theologians of the West to refer to human beings as *gods*. It is particularly surprising that Lewis used this term so often since he clearly named as the Original Sin the persistent human temptation to "be like gods." There is a clue to Lewis' special understanding of this term, however, in *Discarded Image*. The conceptions of *god* and *immortal*, he said there, are interchangeable in all classical thought. Lewis' reflections on life after death are in several ways more dependent upon Greek categories of thought than they are upon biblical thought. But to refer to people as *gods*, I think, is bound to prove more confusing than helpful.

Lewis said in his sermon "The Weight of Glory,"

It is a serious thing to live in a society of possible gods and goddesses, to remember that the dullest and most uninteresting person you talk to may one day be a creature which, if you saw it now, you would be strongly tempted to worship, or else a horror and a corruption such as you now meet, if at all, only in a nightmare. All day long we are, in some degree, helping each other to one or other of these destinations. . . . There are no *ordinary* people. You have never talked to a mere mortal. (*The Weight of Glory*, pp. 14-15)

In this oft-reprinted Oxford sermon Lewis affirmed his belief that men are created for the destiny of heaven. The desire for this far-off country exists in people even now, although it may not yet be attached to its proper object and may even appear as a rival to that destination. The desire may be identified with a nostalgic, romantic, or aesthetic response. But men pine for that which no natural happiness can satisfy, because the real human goal is elsewhere. Mankind has but "the scent of a flower we have not found, the echo of a tune we have not heard, news from a country we have never yet visited."

The desire for the reward of heaven is not bad in itself, Lewis continued. Indeed, the New Testament is filled with staggering promises of rewards. In this case the reward is not arbitrarily "tacked on" to an independent activity; it is the natural consummation of Christian living. Many people today suppose that complete unselfishness is the highest virtue. But unselfishness often proves a negative ideal which carries with it the suggestion of personal abstinence more than the securing of good things for others. Self-denial is never a proper end in itself. One should desire heaven for himself and recognize that the weight of his neighbor's glory—his destiny—is also laid upon him.

Modern education has neglected the persistent, inner voice, charged Lewis in "The Weight of Glory." Philosophies have been contrived to persuade men that human good is to be found on earth. But we know, too, that nothing which can be done on this planet will either "delay the senility of the sun or reverse the second law of thermodynamics." The real goal of man lies somewhere else. The sacred books offer a symbolical account of man's far-off destination. "Heaven is, by definition, outside our experience, but all intelligible descriptions must be of things within our experience. . . . Heaven is not really full of jewelry any more than it is really the beauty of Nature, or a fine piece of music." Yet the Scriptural imagery bears a certain authority. It comes from men close to God and has met the test of generations of Christian experience. Any given symbol is like the reality to which it points in some respects, and unlike it in other ways. Each symbol, therefore, needs to be set among other symbols for its own refinement and correction.

Nature is mortal, said Lewis, and men shall outlive her. When suns and nebulae are no more, every person created by God will live on. The heavenly aspiration is not to dwell with a risen body in numb insensibility, but to live "in glory" with the Creator. Each day a man walks on the razor edge between these two incredible possibilities: he can either be banished from God's presence to be ignored in eternity, or he can prepare to be welcomed to a glory and honor which will finally heal that old deep ache.

A human being's eternal destiny depends upon the central choice of his life, as well as upon the numerous lesser choices which follow in the train of that crucial decision. Lewis dramatized the nature of this key choice in *Divorce*, a fantasy which concerns a bus trip from the "Grey Town" to the "High Countries." In the Grey Town neighbors are so quarrelsome that people keep moving about, getting further and further apart. Some persons are already astronomical distances away—millions of miles apart—and they occasionally move further still. Even in these dark circumstances, one character remains optimistic, insisting that there is no evidence that the twilight of Hell will eventually turn into night. "What we now see in this subdued and delicate half-light," he proposes, "is the promise of the dawn."

In contrast with the Grey Town, the landscape of the High Countries is so substantial that the visitors there seem transparent ghosts by comparison. The grass and trees are so solid there that the visitors seem but stains on the bright air. The bus passengers are greeted by Solid People

201

who try to persuade them to remain. A choice is still possible. Any visitor can remain as long as he wishes, or even choose never to return to the Grey Town. In the end, however, all the passengers but one are so bound to petty self-interest that they are unable to make the break necessary to stay. They board the bus and travel back to the Grey Town.

In his preface to *Divorce,* Lewis emphasized that the transmortal conditions he describes here are but fantasy. They represent neither a guess nor speculation about the future life, but are only "imaginative supposal." Blake wrote of the marriage of Heaven and Hell. But Lewis insisted upon their divorce. He considered it a disastrous error to attempt to embrace both alternatives, as though reality never presents men with an "either-or." Lewis said, "If we insist on keeping Hell (or even earth) we shall not see Heaven: if we accept Heaven we shall not be able to retain even the smallest and most intimate souvenirs of Hell." For those who choose earth instead of Heaven, said Lewis, even earth turns out to be but a region of Hell. But if earth is placed second to Heaven, then earth itself becomes a beginning of Heaven.

Clyde Kilby observes about Lewis' view of judgment, "Sin violates not simply the commands of God but the very principle of life. 'Be sure your sins will find you out' is not an edict from outside or the capricious decree of God but rather a law at the center of creation. The world is so constructed that this world as well as the next pays off for ill conduct." [2] Lewis recognized that there is no complete correlation between goodness and good fortune (or between badness and misfortune) in the present world. The next world, therefore, must be the locus for final judgment in a moral universe.

Lewis' concept of a diminishing choice moving toward final judgment is reflected in several of his imaginative accounts. As the time for the end of Narnia approaches in *Last Battle,* the animals begin to stream toward a huge doorway presided over by Aslan—an entrance to a world "farther in and higher up." The beasts who look at Aslan with hatred suddenly cease to be Talking Beasts. They swerve from the door and disappear in the darkness. Those who love Aslan enter in at the Door. Dimble observes in *Hideous Strength* that "good is always getting better and bad is always getting worse: the possibilities of even apparent neutrality are always diminishing. The whole thing is sorting itself out all the time, coming to a point, getting sharper and harder."

There is no point in discussing whether all men will ultimately be saved, says guide Macdonald. The ideas of Universalism may be true.

[2] *Christian World,* p. 190.

But men cannot know that such is the case, and "it's ill talking of such questions." Within time, he affirms, the answer is clear: the choice of ways remains open. The guide in *Regress* tells John, "You must not try to fix the point after which a return is impossible, but you can see that there will be such a point somewhere." In one dramatic illustration, Macdonald indicates that a grumbler may finally become a grumble. A person at first may be distinct from his grumbling moods and be able to criticize them and to repent of them. But eventually one can become so absorbed in his moods that he is no longer able to criticize and to escape them.

"Is judgment not final? Is there really a way out of Hell into Heaven?" the author's ghost asks Macdonald in *Divorce*. "It depends on the way ye're using the words," the guide replies. "If they leave that grey town behind it will not have been Hell. To any that leaves it, it is Purgatory. And perhaps ye had better not call this country Heaven. Not *Deep Heaven,* ye understand. . . . Ye can call it the Valley of the Shadow of Life. And yet to those who stay here it will have been Heaven from the first." According to Macdonald, Hell is a state of mind only—the product of a creature shut up within itself. But Heaven is reality itself. "Is there a real choice after death?" his guest asks. "Ye cannot fully understand the relations of choice and Time till you are beyond both," the guide replies. "And ye were not brought here to study such curiosities. What concerns you is the nature of the choice itself." There is always something that a "lost soul" insists on retaining, even at the cost of much misery—something he prefers to joy and reality. In one sense, a lost soul is not "real" and "human" at all. Perhaps it should be referred to as the "remains" of what once was a man. What enters hell is an ex-man —a "damned ghost." Most of the ghosts in *Divorce* are incapable of breaking with some dominant sin of pride or self-centeredness; treasuring their sin more than all the joys of Heaven, they cannot remain in the High Countries.

According to Edgar Boss, in Lewis' thought "consignment to the particular places called Heaven and Hell is but the eternal confirmation on a state already begun on earth." While Lewis certainly believed in the continuity of experience between this world and the next, it may be somewhat misleading to speak in terms of "consignment" and "places." Kilby also reports that Lewis believed heaven and hell to be final. Lewis stressed the urgency of present choice, but I do not think he ever committed himself to the position that no choice is possible beyond the grave. It seems to me that he left open the question of universalism, even as he recommended against relying upon its conclusions. He stated that if additional chances after death will do any good, God will provide them. Although he had little to say about possible future states between heaven and hell, Lewis occasionally referred to limbo and purgatory. Limbo, he said, is for souls already lost. Purgatory provides an opportunity for purification and purgation prior to the entry of Heaven itself.

A *Time* magazine cover-feature article on Lewis reported that he regarded Heaven as "a state as real as Sunday morning breakfast." [3] Heaven is not merely a state of mind, he said in *Miracles*. It has its own kind of reality. The faint and uncertain inklings which so tantalize human life are the promises of fulfillment beyond this time and place. John Haigh observes that modern literature provides many interpretations of Hell, from Baudelaire's "Un Saison en Enfer" to Sartre's "Huis Clos." Huxley, Orwell, and Golding provide other examples. But Lewis brings to contemporary literature something that is relatively rare— visions of Heaven. According to Charles Moorman, Lewis' contrast between the reality of Heaven and the illusion of ordinary reality as it exists on earth and in Hell, sounds distinctly like Charles Williams. It also sounds like Plato. I am unable to find meaningful, however, the concept of "timeless eternity" which Lewis got from Plato and elaborated at various places in his writing. Richard Cunningham also cites this concept as a weakness in Lewis' thought and thinks that he should have read Oscar Cullman and the later Karl Barth on the nature of time.

Lewis' Narnia is not to be identified with heaven. Narnia belongs to the "third world"—the world of the imagination. The real Narnia is beyond that Narnia, just as the real earth is beyond this earth. This is the meaning of Digory's words and the final scenes of *Last Battle*.

The lead ghost in *Divorce* asks his teacher about the idea that the loss of one soul can destroy the joy of those who are saved. Behind this idea, Macdonald replies, is "the demand of the loveless and the self-imprisoned that they should be allowed to blackmail the universe: that till they consent to be happy (on their own terms) no one else shall taste joy: that theirs should be the final power; that Hell should be able to *veto* Heaven." Macdonald maintains that the balance of power lies in the opposite direction. "Either the day must come when joy prevails and all the makers of misery are no longer able to infect it: or else for ever and ever the makers of misery can destroy in others the happiness they reject for themselves. I know it has a grand sound to say ye'll accept no salvation which leaves even one creature in the dark outside. But

---

[3] "Don v. Devil." *Time*, September 8, 1947, p. 66.

watch that sophistry," he warns, "or ye'll make a Dog in a Manger the tyrant of the universe."

Lewis acknowledged in *Pain* that not all suffering is redemptive. Pain may also provoke unrepented rebellion against God. Jesus' utterances about Hell, he noted here, were not designed to satisfy intellectual curiosity, but were directed to the human conscience and will. Probably these sayings have done all that was intended of them if they spur men into action by convincing them of a terrible possibility. It is true that many tragedies in life have come from belief in a doctrine of Hell. But, asked Lewis, are not the tragedies which come from ignoring the concept just as great?

God is so merciful, said Lewis, that He is willing to die by torture to save His creatures. But he is unwilling (if not unable) to coerce a response from men. He will not capture men against their will. The doctrine of Hell is not tolerable, but it is morally sound. Indeed, there exists an ethical demand that right eventually be asserted, and that evil be exposed for what it is. Who would truly desire a life of cruelty and treachery to continue unchallenged and unchecked forever? The man who admits no guilt cannot truly accept forgiveness. While God's love is willing to forgive the worst of sinners, He cannot be expected to overlook and condone the sin of one who desires not to change his evil ways. The judgment which eventually befalls such a person may be considered not so much a retributive punishment inflicted by God as a natural consequence of total self-centeredness.

Some persons object that transitory sin ought not require eternal damnation, or that one should be given a "second chance" even after death. If a million chances would do any good, Lewis believed that they would be given. But, he warned, finality must come eventually. God knows when it is useless to extend the time for repentance further, even as a teacher knows when it is useless to continue giving a certain boy a particular examination repeatedly. It may be that additional time but carries a person continually further from the real possibility of making any change.

Lewis said that a Christian is meant to live in continual anticipation of his "true country" in the eternal world. Men find themselves with desires which no experience in this world can possibly satisfy. Yet is it customary in nature for each human desire to be matched with a potential satisfaction. Perhaps unsatisfied desires exist as the best evidence that man is created for some world other than the one he knows at present.

The main object of a man's life, Lewis wrote, in *Mere Christianity*, is "to press on to that other country and to help others to do the same."

205

The heavenly goal is far more important than most moderns are willing to allow. "If you read history," Lewis said, "you will find that the Christians who did most for the present world were just those who thought most of the next. . . . It is since Christians have largely ceased to think of the other world that they have become so ineffective in this."

Lewis acknowledged the difficulty most people in the modern world have in desiring heaven at all, except that they might like to meet again their deceased dear ones. Modern education is completely preoccupied with the things of this world. Even when a "real want for heaven" comes—an acute desire for something not available in this world—men do not tend to identify it in religious terms. Some men spend their lives searching the earth over for an effective means to satisfy that deep longing. But every hobby, vacation, and wife fails to satisfy completely; and the earthbound quest ends forever in disappointment. Other men recognize the futility of expecting contentment from the world and abandon the search. Disillusioned and "sensible," they attempt to scale down their hopes and dreams to those which actually can be fulfilled within their immediate environment. But what if the Christians are right? What if men have been created to live forever, and the fulfillment of unsatisfied longings is precisely what heaven is intended to provide? Belief in such a reality would certainly make a difference in one's outlook on the universe.

Lewis developed a special appreciation for the poetry of William Morris because of the balance it expresses between a piercing passion for immortality and an opposite feeling that "such desire is not wholly innocent, that the world of mortality is more than enough for our allegiance." [4] Lewis contended that the work of Morris is not a "poetry of escape," but that his invented world has genuine intellectual and emotional relevance to the world in which men live. A poet needs to supplement his love for the natural world with a sense of this world's incompleteness, said Lewis.

Morris, in honest Pagan spirit, does not state the ultimate significance of those impulses which lead men quite inevitably beyond the visible world. He neither justifies these impulses, as would a Christian, nor represses them, as would a materialist. He presents them in unresolved tension. He notes that the present value of life both tempers the desire for some Acre of the Undying and aggravates the sting of human mortality. It is happiness—not unhappiness—which makes men "more mindful that the sweet days die." The idyllic expression is not simply an escape;

[4] *Rehabilitations,* p. 45.

it is an expression of the tension between the conviction that vigorous enjoyment and improvement of life are infinitely worthwhile even though the mortal nature of man is fundamentally unsatisfactory. Morris is not particularly afraid of death; he is instead driven by a passionate thirst for immortality.

In *The Well at the World's End,* the Innocent folk say, "The gods have given us the gift of death lest we weary of life." The idea is similar to Berdyaev's statement that "if there were no death in our world, life would be meaningless." There are no conclusions in Morris about these mysteries. He remains content to raise the questions—questions which it is the task of theology to attempt to answer. There are those who pretend that it does not matter "that the race and the planet themselves must one day follow the individual into a state of being which has no significance—a universe of inorganic homogeneous matter moving at uniform speed in a low temperature." But poets like Morris, Yeats, and Lewis have difficulty believing in this condition as the final goal toward which the universe has been moving for so long. Lewis concluded,

No full-grown mind wants optimism or pessimism—philosophies of the nursery where they are not philosophies of the clinic; but to have presented in one vision the ravishing sweetness and the heartbreaking melancholy of our experience, to have shown how the one continually passes over into the other, and to have combined all this with a stirring practical creed, this is to have presented the *datum* which all our adventures, worldly and other-worldly alike, must take into account. (*Rehabilitations,* p. 55)

Lewis believed that non-Christian religions contain at least a portion of God's truth. It is not necessary for a Christian to believe that all other religions are wholly wrong, he said. As in arithmetic, some wrong answers may be closer to the right one than others. Christians believe that no one can be saved except through Christ, but this does not necessarily mean that only those who consciously know Christ can be saved through Him. Some are acquainted with God *incognito.* Lewis dealt with the theme of the virtuous unbeliever in a number of his letters. Actions based upon a false hypothesis surely lead to less satisfactory results than actions based upon a true hypothesis. Christians, therefore, consider it their duty to do what they can to convert unbelievers. But Christians are not informed of God's detailed plans for non-Christians. It is certain that God will deal with these persons in justice and mercy. It does appear, Lewis believed, that the Western world is partially saved in a way that the East is not, with all its temple prostitution, infanticide, torture, and political corruption. The East seems still to be living in B.C.

207

Lewis regarded monotheism not as the rival of polytheism but as its maturity. "Where you find polytheism, combined with any speculative power and any leisure for speculation," he wrote, "monotheism will sooner or later arise as a natural development."

Prayers made sincerely to false gods then, or to an imperfectly conceived true God, are accepted by God. "Christ saves many who do not think they know Him." Christ is dimly present in the good aspects of inferior teachers. "Our anxiety about unbelievers is most usefully employed," Lewis concluded, "when it leads us, not to speculation but to earnest prayer for them and the attempt to be in our own lives such good advertisements for Christianity as will make it attractive." The conflict between the true and the false gods is illustrated in *Last Battle*. It is said that Tash wears the head of a vulture and demands human sacrifice. The ape Shift tries to persuade the other animals that Tash and Aslan are but two different names "for you know Who." But the inhabitants of Narnia discover that the truth is more complex than this. And one result of the ape's setting up a false Aslan is that people stop believing in the real Aslan. Nevertheless, Aslan himself explains in the end, "If any man swear by Tash and keep his oath for the oath's sake, it is by me that he has truly sworn, though he know it not, and it is I who reward him. And if any man do a cruelty in my name, then, though he says the name Aslan, it is Tash whom he serves and by Tash his deed is accepted." The realities of religious truth are deeper than the superficial labels which men place upon them.

In a Narnian chapter entitled "The Unwelcome Fellow Traveller," Shasta discovers that it was not bad luck after all that his trip was apparently plagued by lions. Actually, there was but one lion: Aslan presided over the journey as an unknown guardian, driving away jackals and frightening the horses to spur them on to greater strength during the last miles. Aslan is no *tame* lion. To his enemies, he is even considered "a demon of hideous aspect and irresistible maleficence." But to those who call him a friend, he is Somebody who can say, "You would not have called to me unless I had been calling to you."

In his 1954 Cambridge inaugural address, Lewis spoke of the culture of the post-Christian era and noted, "Christians and pagans had much more in common with each other than either has with a post-Christian. The gap between those who worship different gods is not so wide as that between those who worship and those who do not." Langmead Casserley objects to the current vogue term of "post-Christian" on the grounds that there never has been an age which was overwhelmingly

Christian. In a sense, says Casserley, it would be just as meaningful to refer to the present—or to any age gone by—as "pre-Christian." But there was once a time, Lewis observed, when religious belief and practice were the norm; now they are the exception. Post-Christian man has by no means "lapsed into Paganism." He is, rather, cut off from both the Christian past and the more ancient (and often noble) pagan past.

Lewis declared himself in this lecture to be more a native of the "Old Western order" than of the modern age. Alluding to his own training in classics and his natural appreciation for Medieval and Renaissance literature, he advised his colleagues, "I may yet be useful as a specimen. . . . There are not going to be many more dinosaurs." Austin Farrer views this ironical description as a trick of rhetoric "to gain a hearing for an exposition of medieval literature from a medieval point of view." Is it perhaps something more? Does the illustration also reflect Lewis' delight in taking an unpopular position, in which "we few" stand together against something very powerful? Does it illustrate Lewis' impatience with all that labels itself "progress" while ignoring basic questions of reality and truth? Whether or not Lewis intended to suggest so much in this lecture, his choice of words manages to express much that is true to the Lewis spirit. Throughout his life, Lewis preferred to stand for the truth as he saw it—nearly alone and facing the threat of extinction—rather than to compromise with superficial, popular thought whose chief asset is that it calls itself "modern."

Screwtape reports in a key passage that the satanic Lowerarchy has developed a special technique for isolating modern scholars from the learned men of former generations. Called the "Historical Point of View," this diabolical attitude prevents a student from asking whether the words of an ancient author are *true,* says Screwtape. Instead, the scholar considers questions of literary influence, internal consistency, philosophical development, schools of interpretation, etc. Without all this diversion, Screwtape admits, "there is always the danger that the characteristic errors of one [generation] may be corrected by the characteristic truths of another."

Whether in matters of literary criticism or in matters of philosophy and theology, it is more important to inquire about the essential value of ideas than it is to revere their modernity. It is "chronological snobbery," warned Lewis, to accept or reject ideas solely upon the basis of current fashion. There is a difference, he observed, between "a mature and travelled man's love for his own country and the cocksure conviction of an ignorant adolescent that his own village (which is the only one he knows) is the hub of the universe and does everything in the Only Right Way. . . . Our own age, with all its accepted ideas, stands to the vast extent of historical time much as one village stands to the whole world." [5]

It remains important to ask about the Gospel, not "is it popular?" but "is it true?" On matters of eschatology, it is essential to consider not only the ideas that are currently in vogue but the validity of New Testament concepts as well. With measured strokes in broad perspective and with dramatic style, Lewis challenged the present generation to consider deeply again the question of ultimate human destiny.

[5] *Studies in Literature,* p. 138.

Conclusion

On theology and communication:

Any fool can write *learned* language. The vernacular is the real test. If you can't turn your faith into it, then either you don't understand it or you don't believe it.[1]

According to critic Chad Walsh, in the two decades following the 1942 publication of *Screwtape Letters* the books of C. S. Lewis had an impact upon American religious thinking and imagination "which has been very rarely, if ever, equalled by any other modern writer." At least half a dozen of Lewis' more imaginative books, Walsh predicts, will assume a position among the classics of religious literature. Roger Lancelyn Green, a British author of nearly a dozen volumes in the field of juvenile fiction, thinks that the Narnia stories will have a permanent place among the great works of children's literature. Green considers Lewis to be among the half dozen best writers for children in the present century.

As one who was an atheist for eighteen years of his young adult life and who finally became "a reluctant convert" to Christianity, Lewis was particularly sensitive to the intellectual difficulties which a modern man faces when considering the Christian faith. As a Christian apologist and myth-maker, Lewis has provided readers (as Edmund Fuller observes) with some of "the great symbolic visions of ultimate reality which reveal to us that we are more—and a part of more—than the data of our senses can record." Through nearly fifty books Lewis exhibits "an unabashed spiritual joy, confident and aggressive exercise of reason, and a belief in objective values."[2]

[1] C. S. Lewis, Letter to the Editor, *The Christian Century*, LXXV (December 31, 1958), 1515.
[2] John Haigh, "The Fiction of C. S. Lewis," p. 361.

Richard Cunningham notes that "as a master of satire, sarcasm, caricature, and the shock technique, Lewis often overstates his case, paints issues in stark black and white, and warns of danger without extolling values." Walsh speaks of the "static" quality of Lewis' theology and concludes, "His religious thinking is strong on clarity, strong on the 'either-or' challenges of the Christian faith, but edged at times with too shrill and simple a moralism, and inadequate awareness of the paradoxes of the Christian life and the ways in which God often works through those who apparently least succeed in living by the rulebook." [3]

There is no denying that something of these tendencies is to be found in Lewis. But he also sounds at times as "modern" as any twentieth-century theologian. He concluded *The Four Loves*, for example, by saying, "If we cannot 'practice the presence of God,' it is something to practice the absence of God, to become increasingly aware of our unawareness." Lewis' enormous respect for the intellectual accomplishments of past ages, however, did cause him to slight contemporary literature, theology, and biblical criticism in favor of those books and ideas which have already met a test of time.

Dr. Hugh R. Macintosh notes in *Types of Modern Theology* that typically German theology "is prone to advance in a zigzag manner, tacking from one extreme to another, enveloping all in a fierce spirit of party, equipping each new school with the penetrating power of a one-sided fervour as well as with the practically effective slogan which calls men round a newly erected banner." C. S. Lewis would have agreed with Dr. Macintosh, I think, that a less exciting arena produces a theology of far sounder judgment. Lewis was no theological extremist of any variety. He deliberately avoided identifying himself with current schools of theological debate. It is possible, therefore, that the partisans of various camps will find his thought suspect. But it is also probable that his theological contribution will prove more lasting than those of most theological faddists in the current decade.

Lewis presented a comprehensive view of human nature, shaped by classical Christian doctrines of Creation, the Fall, Redemption, and Echatology. He demonstrated that he was capable of penetrating to the core of these traditional concepts, of separating the essential from the inessential, and of creating new images to convey theological truth to modern men. The prolific imagination of C. S. Lewis has generated a multitude of powerful scenes and symbols which interpret Christianity in a way that is remarkably unforgettable.

[3] "The Elusively Solid C. S. Lewis," *Good Work: Quarterly of the Catholic Art Association,* XXX (Winter 1967), 20-22.

Anything more than a superficial reading of his now-completed work is bound to shatter the widespread impression that Lewis was inclined toward theological fundamentalism. While he has been so classified both by conservative and liberal theologians and by many reviewers, this judgment represents a failure to take seriously the nature of literature and the nature of theological language, even as Lewis himself understood them. Far from being a theological literalist, Lewis developed a sophisticated theory of religious language and presented an extensive discussion on literary theory in his own works. For more than forty years Lewis produced imaginative literature reflecting his keen understanding of myth and metaphor as the essential language of religion. C. S. Lewis was a Christian remythologizer par excellence.

Appendixes

1

ORIGINAL PUBLICATION DATES OF LEWIS' MAJOR WORKS

1. Spirits in Bondage, 1919
2. Dymer, 1926
3. The Pilgrim's Regress, 1933
4. The Allegory of Love, 1936
5. Out of the Silent Planet, 1938
6. Rehabilitations and Other Essays, 1939
7. The Personal Heresy (with E. M. W. Tillyard), 1939
8. The Problem of Pain, 1940
9. The Screwtape Letters, 1942
10. A Preface to "Paradise Lost," 1942
11. The Case for Christianity, 1942
12. Christian Behaviour, 1943
13. Perelandra, 1943
14. The Abolition of Man, 1943
15. Beyond Personality, 1944
16. That Hideous Strength, 1945
17. The Great Divorce, 1946
18. George Macdonald: An Anthology, 1946
19. Miracles, 1947
20. Arthurian Torso (with Charles Williams), 1948
21. The Weight of Glory and Other Addresses, 1949
22. The Lion, the Witch and the Wardrobe, 1950
23. Prince Caspian, 1951
24. Mere Christianity, 1952
25. The Voyage of the "Dawn Treader," 1952
26. The Silver Chair, 1953
27. The Horse and His Boy, 1954

28. English Literature in the Sixteenth Century, 1954
29. The Magician's Nephew, 1955
30. Surprised by Joy, 1955
31. The Last Battle, 1956
32. Till We Have Faces, 1956
33. Reflections on the Psalms, 1958
34. The Four Loves, 1960
35. Studies in Words, 1960
36. The World's Last Night and Other Essays, 1960
37. A Grief Observed, 1961
38. An Experiment in Criticism, 1961
39. They Asked for a Paper, 1962
40. Letters to Malcolm: Chiefly on Prayer, 1964
41. The Discarded Image, 1964
42. Poems, 1964
43. Screwtape Proposes a Toast and Other Pieces, 1965
44. Studies in Medieval and Renaissance Literature, 1966
45. Letters of C. S. Lewis, 1966
46. Christian Reflections, 1967
47. Of Other Worlds, 1967
48. Letters to an American Lady, 1967
49. Spenser's Images of Life, 1967

2

GENERAL CLASSIFICATION OF BOOKS BY C. S. LEWIS

LITERARY CRITICISM

The Allegory of Love, 1936
Rehabilitations and Other Essays, 1939
The Personal Heresy (with E. M. W. Tillyard), 1939
A Preface to "Paradise Lost," 1942
Arthurian Torso (with Charles Williams), 1948
English Literature in the Sixteenth Century, 1954
Studies in Words, 1960
An Experiment in Criticism, 1961
They Asked for a Paper, 1962
The Discarded Image, 1964
Studies in Medieval and Renaissance Literature, 1966
Of Other Worlds, 1967
Spenser's Images of Life, 1967

THEOLOGY AND PHILOSOPHY

The Problem of Pain, 1940
The Case for Christianity, 1942
Christian Behaviour, 1943
The Abolition of Man, 1943
Beyond Personality, 1944
George Macdonald: An Anthology, 1946
Miracles, 1947
The Weight of Glory and Other Addresses, 1949
Mere Christianity, 1952
Surprised by Joy, 1955
Reflections on the Psalms, 1958

The Four Loves, 1960
The World's Last Night and Other Essays, 1960
A Grief Observed, 1961
Letters to Malcolm: Chiefly on Prayer, 1964
Screwtape Proposes a Toast and Other Pieces, 1965
Letters of C. S. Lewis, 1966
Christian Reflections, 1967
Letters to an American Lady, 1967

IMAGINATIVE WORKS: Fantasies, Chronicles of Narnia, and Verse

The Pilgrim's Regress, 1933
Out of the Silent Planet, 1938
The Screwtape Letters, 1942
Perelandra, 1943
That Hideous Strength, 1945
The Great Divorce, 1946
Till We Have Faces, 1956

The Lion, the Witch and the Wardrobe, 1950
Prince Caspian, 1951
The Voyage of the "Dawn Treader," 1952
The Silver Chair, 1953
The Horse and His Boy, 1954
The Magician's Nephew, 1955
The Last Battle, 1956

Spirits in Bondage, 1919
Dymer, 1926
Poems, 1964

3

A Chronology
Some Major Events in the Life of C. S. Lewis

1898 Clive Staples Lewis is born (November 29), in Belfast, Northern Ireland.

1905 The family moves to the "New House" in the country.

1908 The mother of "Jack," now age 9, and Warren, age 12, dies of cancer. Jack begins his formal education in Hertfordshire, England (at "Oldie's," in Belsen).

1910 His education continues briefly at "Campbell College," in Belfast.

1911 He attends Malvern Preparatory School ("Chartres" in "Wyvern") and there abandons Christianity.

1912 At age 13, Jack produces his first complete novel (unpublished).

1913 He wins a scholarship to Malvern College, in Worcester (Wyvern).

1914 Private tutoring begins under W. T. Kirkpatrick in Great Bookham, Surrey.

1917 Lewis enters Oxford, but soon enlists in the Army and spends nineteenth birthday in frontline trenches.

1918 Wounded in France, he is hospitalized briefly and discharged from the Army.

1919 Lewis returns to his Oxford studies at University College and publishes his first book (*Spirits in Bondage*).

1924 He receives temporary appointment at Oxford as lecturer in philosophy.

1925 He is elected a fellow of Magdalen College, Oxford, and tutor in English literature, a position he holds for thirty years.

1929 Converted to Theism, Lewis soon becomes a Christian.

1942 *The Screwtape Letters* is published, to become Lewis' best-known work.

1946 He receives an honorary Doctor of Divinity degree from St. Andrews University, Scotland.

1954 Lewis becomes professor of Medieval and Renaissance English at Cambridge University, and a fellow of Magadene College.

1957 Lewis is married to Joy Davidman Gresham, in hospital bedside ceremony.

1960 His wife Joy, at age 45, dies of cancer.

1963 Lewis, at age 64, dies (on November 22).

4

A Glossary for *Out of the Silent Planet*

Planets: *Malacandra*—the old planet
   Thulcandra—the "silent" world

The *hnau* of Malacandra:
   Hross, hrossa (e.g., Hyoi)
   Sorn, séroni (e.g., Augray)
   Pfifltrigg, Pfifltriggi

The other life of Malacandra:
   Hnakra—evil monster
   Hmān—man
   Eldil, eldila (or *eldils*) —"invisible" beings
   Oyarsa—the great eldil, ruler

Geographic terms:
   Harandra—the highland
   Handramit—the lowland
   Meldilorn—the sacred island

Theological terms:
   Maleldil the Young—Creator and Ruler
   The Old One

5

Professor J. R. R. Tolkien

Oxford 61639

76 Sandfield Road
Headington
Oxford

11th September, 1967.

Dear Mr. White,

I can give you a brief account of the name *Inklings*: from memory. The Inklings had no recorder and C. S. Lewis no Boswell. The name was not invented by C.S.L. (nor by me). In origin it was an undergraduate jest, devised as the name of a literary (or writers') club. The founder was an undergraduate at University College, named Tangye-Lean,—the date I do not remember: probably mid-thirties. He was, I think, more aware than most undergraduates of the impermanence of their clubs and fashions, and had an ambition to found a club that would prove more lasting. Anyway, he asked some 'dons' to become members. C.S.L. was an obvious choice, and he was probably at that time Tangye-Lean's tutor (C.S.L. was a member of University College). In the event both C.S.L. and I became members. The club met in T.-L.'s rooms in University College; its procedure was that at each meeting members should read aloud, unpublished compositions. These were supposed to be open to immediate criticism. Also if the club thought fit a contribution might be voted to be worthy of entry in a Record Book. (I was the scribe and keeper of the book).

Tangye-Lean proved quite right. The club soon died: the Record Book had very few entries: but C.S.L. and I at least survived. Its name was then transferred (by C.S.L.) to the undetermined and unelected circle of friends who gathered about C.S.L., and met in his rooms in Magdalen. Although our

221

habit was to read aloud compositions of various kinds (and lengths!), this association and its habit would in fact have come into being at that time, whether the original short-lived club had ever existed or not. C.S.L. had a passion for hearing things read aloud, a power of memory for things received in that way, and also a facility in extempore criticism, none of which were shared (especially not the last) in anything like the same degree by his friends.

I called the name a 'jest', because it was a pleasantly ingenious pun in its way, suggesting people with vague or half-formed intimations and ideas plus those who dabble in ink. It might have been suggested by C.S.L. to Tangye-Lean (if he was the latter's tutor); but I never heard him claim to have invented this name. *Inkling* is, at any rate in this country, in very common use in the sense that you quote from C.S.L.'s writings. [I remember that when I was an undergraduate there was, briefly, an undergraduate club called the *Discus*, suggesting a round-table conference, and *discuss*: it was a discussion club.]

With best wishes,

Yours sincerely,

(signed) J. R. R. Tolkien.

William Luther White,
Chaplain,
Illinois Wesleyan University,
Bloomington,
Illinois,
U.S.A.

Bibliography

Primary Works

The Abolition of Man: or Reflections on Education with Special Reference to the Teaching of English in the Upper Forms of Schools. New York: Collier Books, 1962.

The Allegory of Love: A Study in Medieval Tradition. Galaxy ed.; New York: Oxford University Press, 1958.

(With Charles Williams). *Arthurian Torso: Containing the Posthumous Fragment of the Figure of Arthur by Charles Williams and a Commentary on the Arthurian Poems of Charles Williams by C. S. Lewis.* New York: Oxford University Press, 1948.

Christian Reflections, ed. Walter Hooper. Grand Rapids: Eerdmans Publishing Co., 1967.

The Discarded Image: An Introduction to Medieval and Renaissance Literature. New York: Cambridge University Press, 1964.

Dymer. New edition with preface. New York: The Macmillan Co., 1950.

English Literature in the Sixteenth Century, Excluding Drama. The Oxford History of English Literature, vol. III. New York: Oxford University Press, 1954.

(Ed., with a preface). *Essays Presented to Charles Williams.* Grand Rapids: Eerdmans Publishing Co., 1966.

An Experiment in Criticism. New York: Cambridge University Press, 1961.

The Four Loves. New York: Harcourt, Brace & World, 1960.

(Ed., with a preface). *George Macdonald: An Anthology.* London: Geoffrey Bles, 1946.

The Great Divorce. Macmillan paperbacks ed.; New York: The Macmillan Co., [1946] 1963.

A Grief Observed. New York: Seabury Press, 1963.

The Horse and His Boy. New York: The Macmillan Co., 1954.

The Last Battle. New York: The Macmillan Co., 1956.

Letters of C. S. Lewis, ed. W. H. Lewis. New York: Harcourt, Brace & World, 1966.

Letters to an American Lady, ed. Clyde S. Kilby. Grand Rapids: Eerdmans Publishing Co., 1967.

Letters to Malcolm: Chiefly on Prayer. New York: Harcourt, Brace & World, 1964.

The Lion, the Witch and the Wardrobe. New York: The Macmillan Co., 1951.

The Magician's Nephew. New York: The Macmillan Co., 1955.

Mere Christianity: A revised and enlarged edition, with a new introduction, of the three books The Case for Christianity, Christian Behaviour, *and* Beyond Personality. Macmillan paperbacks ed.; New York: The Macmillan Co., 1960.

Miracles: A Preliminary Study. Macmillan paperbacks ed.; New York: The Macmillan Co., 1947.

Of Other Worlds: Essays and Stories, ed. Walter Hooper. New York: Harcourt, Brace & World, 1967.

Out of the Silent Planet. Macmillan paperbacks ed.; New York: The Macmillan Co., [1943] 1965.

Perelandra. Macmillan paperbacks ed.; New York: The Macmillan Co., 1965.

(With E. M. W. Tillyard). *The Personal Heresy: A Controversy.* Oxford paperbacks ed.; New York: Oxford University Press, 1965.

The Pilgrim's Regress: An Allegorical Apology for Christianity, Reason and Romanticism. Eerdmans pocket ed.; Grand Rapids: Eerdmans Publishing Co. [1943] 1958.

Poems, ed. Walter Hooper. New York: Harcourt, Brace & World, 1965.

A Preface to Paradise Lost. Galaxy ed.; New York: Oxford University Press, 1961.

Prince Caspian: The Return to Narnia. New York: The Macmillan Co., 1951.

The Problem of Pain. Macmillan paperbacks ed.; New York: The Macmillan Co., 1962.

Reflections on the Psalms. New York: Harcourt, Brace & World, 1958.

Rehabilitations and Other Essays. New York: Oxford University Press, 1939.

The Screwtape Letters and Screwtape Proposes a Toast. Macmillan paperbacks ed.; New York: The Macmillan Co., 1962.

Screwtape Proposes a Toast and Other Pieces. London: Fontana Books, 1965.

The Silver Chair. New York: The Macmillan Co., [1953] 1963.

Spenser's Images of Life., ed. Alastair Fowler. New York: Cambridge University Press, 1967.

Spirits in Bondage: A Cycle of Lyrics. London: William Heinemann, 1919 (under the pseudonym of Clive Hamilton).

Studies in Medieval and Renaissance Literature, ed. Walter Hooper. New York: Cambridge University Press, 1966.

Studies in Words. New York: Cambridge University Press, 1960.

Surprised by Joy. New York: Harcourt, Brace & World, 1956.

That Hideous Strength: A Modern Fairy-Tale for Grown-ups. Macmillan paperbacks ed.; New York: The Macmillan Co., 1965.

They Asked for a Paper: Papers and Addresses. London: Geoffrey Bles, 1962.

Till We Have Faces: A Myth Retold. Eerdmans paperback ed.; Grand Rapids: Eerdmans Publishing Co., [1957] 1964.

Transposition and Other Addresses. London: Geoffrey Bles, 1949.

The Voyage of the Dawn Treader. New York: The Macmillan Co., 1952.

The World's Last Night and Other Essays. New York: Harcourt, Brace & World, 1960.

SECONDARY SOURCES

Books and Dissertations

Beattie, Sister Mary Josephine, RSM. "The Human Medievalist: A Study of C. S. Lewis' Criticism of Medieval Literature." Ph. D. diss., University of Pittsburgh, 1967.

Boss, Edgar W. "The Theology of C. S. Lewis." Th.D. diss., Northern Baptist Theological Seminary, Chicago, 1948.

Carnell, Corbin S. "The Dialectic of Desire: C. S. Lewis' Interpretation of *Sehnsucht.*" Ph.D. diss., University of Florida, 1960.

Courtney, Charles R. "The Religious Philosophy of C. S. Lewis." M.A. thesis, University of Arizona, 1955.

Cunningham, Richard B. *C. S. Lewis: Defender of the Faith.* Philadelphia: Westminster Press, 1967.

Fisher, Margery. "The Land of Faerie," in *Intent Upon Reading.* First American ed.; New York: Franklin Watts, 1962. Pp. 69-96.

Foulon, Jacqueline. "The Theology of C. S. Lewis' Children's Books." M.A. thesis, Fuller Theological Seminary, 1962.

Fuller, Edmund. *Books with Men Behind Them.* New York: Random House, 1962.

Gibb, Jocelyn, ed. *Light on C. S. Lewis.* New York: Harcourt, Brace & World, 1966.

Green, Roger Lancelyn. *C. S. Lewis.* London: The Bodley Head, 1963.

———. "New Wonderlands," in *Tellers of Tales: British Authors of Children's Book from 1800 to 1964.* First American ed.; New York: Franklin Watts, 1965. Pp. 269-79.

Haigh, John D. "The Fiction of C. S. Lewis." Ph.D. diss., Leeds University, England, 1962.

Hamilton, G. Rostrevor. *Hero or Fool?: A Study of Milton's Satan.* London: G. Allen and Unwin, 1944.

Hart, Davney Adams. "C. S. Lewis's Defense of Poesie." Ph.D. diss., University of Wisconsin, 1959.

Highet, Gilbert. "From World to World," in *People, Places and Books.* New York: Oxford University Press, 1953. Pp. 130-37.

Hoey, Sister Mary Amy, RSM. "An Applied Linguistic Analysis of the Prose Style of C. S. Lewis." Ph.D. diss., University of Connecticut, 1966.

Hook, Martha Boren. "Christian Meaning in the Novels of C. S. Lewis." M.A. thesis, Southern Methodist University, 1959.

Kilby, Clyde S. *The Christian World of C. S. Lewis.* Grand Rapids: Eerdmans Publishing Co., 1964.

Lawlor, John, ed. *Patterns of Love and Courtesy: Essays in Memory of C. S. Lewis.* Chicago: Northwestern University Press, 1967.

Lee, Ernest George. *C. S. Lewis and Some Modern Theologians.* Booklet No. 2 in the series "Religion in a Changing World: Unitarians State Their Faith." London: Lindsey Press, 1944.

Longaker, Mark and Bolles, Edwin C. *Contemporary English Literature.* New York: Appleton-Century-Crofts, 1953.

Moorman, Charles. *Arthurian Triptych: Mythical Material in Charles Williams, C. S. Lewis, and T. S. Eliot.* Los Angeles: University of California Press, 1960.

————. *The Precincts of Felicity: The Augustinian City of the Oxford Christians.* Gainesville: University of Florida Press, 1966.

Norwood, William Durward, Jr. "The Neo-Medieval Novels of C. S. Lewis." Ph.D. diss., University of Texas, 1965.

Nott, Kathleen. *The Emperor's Clothes.* Bloomington: Indiana University Press, 1958.

Reilly, Robert J. "Romantic Religion in the Work of Owen Barfield, C. S. Lewis, Charles Williams and J. R. R. Tolkien." Ph.D. diss., Michigan State University, 1960.

Russel, Mariann Barbara. "The Idea of the City of God: Allegory in C. S. Lewis, Tolkien and C. Williams." Ph.D. diss., Columbia University, 1965.

Schmerl, Rudolf Benjamin. "Reason's Dream: Anti-Totalitarian Themes and Techniques of Fantasy." Ph.D. diss., University of Michigan, 1960.

Starr, Nathan Comfort. *C. S. Lewis's Till We Have Faces.* New York: Seabury Press, 1968.

Stillwell, Kathryn A. "The Lion of Judah in Never-Never Land: The Theology and Philosophy of C. S. Lewis Expressed in His Fantasies for Children." M.A. thesis, Long Beach Teachers College, 1957.

Wain, John. "Oxford," in *Sprightly Running.* New York: St. Martin's Press, 1963. Pp. 98-157.

Walsh, Chad. *C. S. Lewis: Apostle to the Skeptics.* New York: The Macmillan Co., 1949.

Wright, Marjorie E. "The Cosmic Kingdom of Myth: A Study in the Myth-Philosophy of Charles Williams, C. S. Lewis, and J. R. R. Tolkien." Ph.D. diss., University of Illinois, 1960.

Journal and Periodical Articles

Allen, E. L. "The Theology of C. S. Lewis," *Modern Churchman,* XXXIV (March 1945), 317-24.

Anderson, George C. "C. S. Lewis: Foe of Humanism," *The Christian Century,* LXIII (December 25, 1946), 1562-63.

Bailey, George. "My Oxford Tutor, C. S. Lewis," *Reporter,* XXX (April 23, 1964), 37-40.

Barrington-Ward, Simon. "The Uncontemporary Apologist," *Theology.* LXVIII (February 1965), 103-8.

Bertram, James. "C. S. Lewis," *Comment: A New Zealand Quarterly Review,* V (April 1964), 11-12.

Brady, Charles A. "Finding God in Narnia," *America,* XCVI (October 27, 1956), 103-5.

————. "Introduction to Lewis," *America,* LXXI (May 27, 1944), 213-14 and (June 19, 1944), 269-70.

Brooke, N. S. "C. S. Lewis and Spenser: Nature, Art and the Bower of Bliss," *Cambridge Journal* (April 1949), 420-34.

Cassell, George F. "Clive Staples Lewis," a lecture presented November 28, 1949. Chicago Literary Club, 1950.

Chambers, Whittaker. "The Devil," *Life*, XXIV (February 2, 1948), 76-85.

Churchill, R. C. "Mr. C. S. Lewis as an Evangelist," *Modern Churchman*, XXXV (March 1946), 334-42.

Clarke, Arthur C. "Space and the Spirit of Man," *Horizon*, I (January 1959), 27-31, 122-23.

Crouch, Marcus S. "Chronicles of Narnia," *The Junior Bookshelf*, XX (November 1956), 244-53.

Davies, Horton. "C. S. Lewis and B. L. Manning: Lay Champions of Christianity," *Religion in Life*, XXXI (Autumn 1962), 598-609.

Deasy, Philip. "God, Space, and C. S. Lewis," *Commonweal*, LXVIII (July 25, 1958), 421-23.

"Defender of the Faith," *Time*, LXXXII (December 6, 1963), 57.

"Don v. Devil" (cover feature), *Time*, L (September 8, 1947), 65-74.

Donaldson, E. Talbot. "The Myth of Courtly Love," *Ventures*, VI (Fall 1965), 16-23.

Driberg, Tom. "Lobbies of the Soul," *New Statesman and Nation*, XLIX (March 19, 1955), 393-94.

Egoff, Sheila A. "Tomorrow Plus X: Some Thoughts on Science Fiction," *Ontario Library Review*, XLVI (May 1962), 77-80.

Fowler, Albert. "The Lost Relevance of Religion," *Approach: A Literary Quarterly*, XXXII (Summer 1959), 3-7.

Fowler, Helen. "C. S. Lewis: Sputnik or Dinosaur," *Approach: A Literary Quarterly*, XXXII (Summer 1959), 8-14.

Fuller, Edmund. "The Christian Spaceman—C. S. Lewis," *Horizon*, I (May 1959), 64-69, 125-27.

————. "Speaking of Books," *New York Times Book Review*, January 12, 1964, p. 2.

Furlong, Monica. "Second Thoughts on Screwtape," *John O'London's*, IV (March 16, 1961), 288.

Gardner, Frank M. "Carnegie Medal Award for 1956," *Library Association Record*, LIX (May 1957), 168-69.

Gardner, Helen. "Clive Staples Lewis," *Proceedings of the British Academy*, LI (1965), 417-28.

Gilbert, Allan H. "Critics of Mr. C. S. Lewis on Milton's Satan," *South Atlantic Quarterly*, XLVII (April 1948), 216-25.

Glasson, T. Francis. "C. S. Lewis on St. John's Gospel," *Theology*, LXXI (June 1968), 267-69.

Green, Roger Lancelyn. "C. S. Lewis: 1898-1963," *Aryan Path*, XXXV (March 1964), 98-103.

Greenley, Andrew M. "A Chap in His Place," *Reporter*, XXXVI (January 12, 1967), 64.

Grennan, Margaret R. "Lewis Trilogy: A Scholar's Holiday," *Catholic World*, CLXVII (July 1948), 337-44.

Haldane, J. B. S. "Auld Hornie, F. R. S.," *Modern Quarterly*, N.S. I (Autumn 1946), 32-40.

227

Hamm, Victor. "Mr. Lewis in Perelandra," *Thought: Fordham University Quarterly,* XX (June 1945), 271-90.

Hart, Jeffrey. "The Rebirth of Christ," *National Review,* XVII (December 28, 1965), 1192-96.

Higgins, James E. "A Letter from C. S. Lewis," *Horn Book,* XLII (October 1966), 533-39.

Hilton-Young, Wayland. "The Contented Christian," *Cambridge Journal,* V (July 1952), 603-12.

Hough, Graham. "The Screwtape Letters: How Well Have They Worn?" (London) *Times,* February 10, 1966, p. 15.

Irwin, W. R. "There and Back Again: The Romances of Williams, Lewis, and Tolkien," *Sewanee Review,* LXIX (Autumn 1961), 566-78.

Kilby, Clyde S. "C. S. Lewis and His Critics," *Christianity Today,* III (December 8, 1958), 13-15.

———. "C. S. Lewis: Everyman's Theologian," *Christianity Today,* VIII (January 3, 1964), 313-15.

Kruener, Harry H. "A Tribute to C. S. Lewis," *Religion in Life,* XXXIV (Summer 1965), 451-61.

Kuhn, Helmut. "C. S. Lewis: Der Romancier der unerbittlichen Liebe," *Wort und Wahrheit* (Freiburg), X (February 1955), 113-26.

Loomis, Roger Sherman. "Literary History and Literary Criticism: A Critique of C. S. Lewis," *Modern Language Review,* LX (October 1965), 508-11.

McCulley, Dale. "C. S. Lewis: An Unorthodox Champion of Orthodoxy," *Christian Herald,* LXX (November 1947), 69-71.

Masterman, Margaret. "C. S. Lewis: the Author and the Hero," *Twentieth Century,* CLVIII (December 1955), 539-48.

Milne, M. "Dymer: Myth or Poem?" *The Month,* N.S. VIII (September 1952), 170-73.

Moorman, Charles W. "Space Ship and Grail: The Myths of C. S. Lewis," *College English,* XVIII (May 1957), 401-5.

Myers, Edward D. "The Religious Works of C. S. Lewis," *Theology Today,* I (January 1945), 545-48.

Norwood, W. D., Jr. "C. S. Lewis, Owen Barfield, and the Modern Myth," *Midwest Quarterly,* VIII (April 1967), 279-91.

———. "Unifying Themes in C. S. Lewis' Trilogy," *Critique,* IX (November 1965), 67-80.

"Obituary," New York *Times,* November 25, 1963, p. 19.

"Obituary Notes," *Publishers' Weekly,* CLXXXIV (December 9, 1963), 28.

Phelan, John M. "Men and Morals in Space," *America,* CXIII (October 9, 1965), 405-7.

Pittenger, W. Norman, "Apologist versus Apologist: A Critique of C. S. Lewis as 'Defender of the Faith,'" *The Christian Century,* LXXV (October 1, 1958), 1104-7.

"Professor C. S. Lewis: Scholar and Christian Apologist" (obituary), (London) *Times,* November 25, 1963, p. 14.

Robson, W. W. "C. S. Lewis," *The Cambridge Quarterly,* I (Summer 1966) 253-72.

Sale, Roger, "England's Parnassus: C. S. Lewis, Charles Williams, and J. R. R. Tolkien," *Hudson Review,* XVII (Summer 1964), 203-25.

Samaan, Angele Botros. "C. S. Lewis, the Utopist, and His Critics," *Cairo Studies in English,* 1963-1966, pp. 137-66.

"The Scholar's Tale" (lead article), *Times Literary Supplement,* January 7, 1965, pp. 1-2.

Shumaker, Wayne, "The Cosmic Trilogy of C. S. Lewis," *Hudson Review,* VIII (Summer 1955), 240-54.

Smith, Lillian H. "News from Narnia," *Horn Book,* XXXIX (October 1963), 470-73.

Soper, David W. "An Interview with C. S. Lewis," *Zion's Herald,* CXXVI (January 14, 1948), 28; (January 21, 1948), 60.

"Space, History and God" (editorial), *Life,* XLIV (April 7, 1958), 37.

Spacks, Patricia Meyer. "The Myth-Maker's Dilemma: Three Novels by C. S. Lewis," *Discourse,* II (1959), 234-44.

Starkman, M. K. "The Militant Miltonist; or The Retreat from Humanism," *ELH: Journal of English Literary History,* XXVI (June 1959), 209-28.

Stoll, Elmer Edgar. "Give the Devil His Due: a Reply to Mr. C. S. Lewis," *Review of English Studies,* O.S. XX (April 1944), 108-24.

Utley, Francis Lee. "Anglicanism and Anthropology: C. S. Lewis and John Speirs," *Southern Folklore Quarterly,* XXXI (March 1967), 1-11.

Wain, John. "C. S. Lewis," *Encounter,* XXII (May 1964), 51-56.

————. "Leavis on Lawrence," *Spectator,* CXCV (October 7, 1955), 457-59.

Walsh, Chad. "Aldous Huxley and C. S. Lewis: Novelists of Two Religions," *Journal of Bible and Religion,* XIV (August 1946), 139-43.

————. "C. S. Lewis, Apostle to the Skeptics," *Atlantic Monthly,* CLXXVIII (September 1946), 115-19.

————. "C. S. Lewis: Champion of Reason," *The Christian Century,* LXVI (January 19, 1949), 76-77.

————. "C. S. Lewis and the Christian Life," *Catholic World,* CLXVIII (February 1949), 370-75.

————. "The Elusively Solid C. S. Lewis," *Good Work: Quarterly of the Catholic Art Association,* XXX (Winter 1967), 17-24.

————. "Last Things First Things: the Eschatology of C. S. Lewis," *Theology Today,* I (1949), 25-30.

————. "Pros and Cons of C. S. Lewis," *Religion in Life,* XVIII (1949), 222-28.

Wilhelmsen, Marie. "Realisme, Romantikk, Mystikk," *Samtiden,* LXVII (1958), 546-56.

Book Reviews

Adams, E. W. *Hibbert Journal,* XLII (January 1944), 145-51. Rev. of *Pain.*

Allen, D. C. *English Language Notes,* II (December 1964), 133-35. Rev. of *Discarded Image.*

Ames, Alfred C. "A Prominent Christian Tells of His Pagan Youth," *Chicago Sunday Tribune,* February 5, 1956, p. 3. Rev. of *Surprised.*

"The Analysis of Love," *Times Literary Supplement,* April 15, 1960, R.B.S. p. ix. Rev. of *Four Loves.*

Auden, W. H. "Red Lizards and White Stallions," *Saturday Review of Literature,* XXIX (April 13, 1946), 22-23. Rev. of *Divorce.*

Bacon, Leonard. "Confusion Goes to College," *Saturday Review of Literature,* XXIX (May 25, 1946), 13-14. Rev. of *Hideous Strength.*

———. "Critique of Pure Diabolism," *Saturday Review of Literature,* XXVI (April 17, 1943), 20. Rev. of *Screwtape.*

———. "The Imaginative Power of C. S. Lewis," *Saturday Review of Literature,* XXVII (April 8, 1944), 1, 9. Rev. of *Perelandra.*

Bergonzi, Bernard. "Open to Books," *Spectator,* November 17, 1961, p. 718. Rev. of *Criticism.*

Blissett, William. *Canadian Forum,* XXXVI (January 1957), 238-39. Rev. of *Faces.*

———. *Canadian Forum,* XLII (July 1962), 93. Rev. of *Criticism.*

Bloesch, Donald G. "Love Illuminated," *The Christian Century,* LXXVII (December 14, 1960), 1470. Rev. of *Four Loves.*

Bradbrook, M. C. "Medieval Model," *New Statesman,* LXVIII (April 7, 1964), 188. Rev. of *Discarded Image.*

Brody, Mary P. *Catholic World,* CLXXXIII (May 1956), 156-57. Rev. of *Surprised.*

Brunini, John G. *Commonweal,* XL (May 12, 1944), 90-91. Rev. of *Perelandra.*

Burrow, John. "The Model Universe," *Essays in Criticism,* XV (April 1965), 207-11. Rev. of *Discarded Image.*

Coblentz, Stanton A. "The Songs of Love in the Middle Ages," *New York Times Book Review,* July 5, 1936, p. 12. Rev. of *Allegory.*

"Continual Cerebration," *Times Literary Supplement,* July 28, 1966, p. 654. Rev. of *Letters.*

Cooke, Alistair. "Mr. Anthony at Oxford," *New Republic,* CX (April 24, 1944), 578-80. Rev. of *Christian Behaviour* and *Perelandra.*

Curley, T. F. "Myth into Novel," *Commonweal,* LXV (February 8, 1957), 494-95. Rev. of *Faces.*

D'Arcy, Martin. "These Things Called Love," *New York Times Book Review,* July 31, 1960, p. 4. Rev. of *Four Loves.*

Daiches, David. "Just How Should a Critic Approach a Book?" *New York Times Book Review,* December 17, 1961, p. 6. Rev. of *Criticism.*

Davie, Donald. "Entering Into the Sixteenth Century," *Essays in Criticism,* V (April 1955), 159-64. Rev. of *Sixteenth Century.*

Davis, Robert G. "Cupid and Psyche," *New York Times Book Review,* January 13, 1957, p. 5. Rev. of *Faces.*

Deane, A. C. "A Nightmare," *Spectator,* CLXXVI (January 25, 1946), 96. Rev. of *Divorce.*

Deasy, Philip. "Critic of Our Age," *Commonweal,* LXXI (March 4, 1960), 632. Rev. of *Last Night.*

Dock, E. K. T. "Mr. Lewis's Theology," *Scrutiny,* XIV (Summer 1946), 53-59. Rev. of *Divorce.*

"Dream of the After-World," *Times Literary Supplement,* February 2, 1946, p. 58. Rev. of *Divorce.*

Duchene, Anne. "Fatal Interview," *Manchester Guardian,* October 7, 1955, p. 10. Rev. of *Surprised.*

Empson, William. "Love and the Middle Ages," *Spectator,* CLVII (September 4, 1936), 389. Rev. of *Allegory.*

"The End of a Saga," *Times Literary Supplement,* May 11, 1956, Children's Books Section, p. v. Rev. of *Last Battle.*

Evans, Bergen. "But What Does It Mean?" *New York Times Book Review,* November 13, 1960, p. 38. Rev. of *Studies in Words.*

Falle, George. *Canadian Forum,* XLI (December 1961), 209. Rev. of *Studies in Words.*

Farber, Marjorie. "Imperfect Paradise," *New York Times Book Review,* March 26, 1944, p. 4. Rev. of *Perelandra.*

"Final Achievement," *Times Literary Supplement,* February 27, 1964, p. 173. Rev. of *Malcolm.*

Fremantle, Anne. "Truth, Terror, Thrills," *New York Herald Tribune Weekly Book Review,* June 2, 1946, p. 12. Rev. of *Hideous Strength.*

———. "The Universe Rang True When Fairly Tested," *Commonweal,* LXIII (February 3, 1956), 464-65. Rev. of *Surprised.*

———. *Commonweal,* XLII (September 14, 1945), 528-29. Rev. of *Beyond Personality.*

"The Function of Criticism," *Times Literary Supplement,* November 3, 1961, p. 790. Rev. of *Criticism.*

Gardner, Helen. "Learning and Gusto," *New Statesman and Nation,* XLVIII (October 30, 1954), 546. Rev. of *Sixteenth Century.*

Gill, Theodore A. "Not Quite All," *The Christian Century,* LXXIII (May 9, 1956), 585. Rev. of *Surprised.*

Glauber, Robert H. "C. S. Lewis in Happily Familiar Form," *New York Herald Tribune Book Review,* February 21, 1960, p. 7. Rev. of *Last Night.*

———. "Circles Within Circles," *The Christian Century,* LXXIV (March 20, 1957), 362-63. Rev. of *Faces.*

"Grete Clerke of Oxford," *Times Literary Supplement,* July 16, 1964, p. 632. Rev. of *Discarded Image.*

Hailsham, Lord. "Dr. Lewis's Pilgrimage," *Spectator,* CXCV (December 9, 1955), 805-6. Rev. of *Surprised.*

Harris, Sydney J. "Shafts from a Christian Marksman," *Saturday Review of Literature,* XLIII (March 5, 1960), 21-22. Rev. of *Last Night.*

Harrison, Charles T. "The Renaissance Epitomized," *Sewanee Review,* LXIII (Winter 1955), 153-61. Rev. of *Sixteenth Century.*

Hart, Jeffrey. "C. S. Lewis: 1898-1963," *National Review,* XVI (March 24, 1964), 240-43. Rev. of *Malcolm.*

Hartshorne, Charles. "Philosophy and Orthodoxy," *Ethics,* LIV (July 1944), 295-98. Rev. of *Case for Christianity.*

Hazelton, Roger. "C. S. Lewis: No Further than Gethsemane," *New Republic,* CLVI (February 18, 1967), 25-27. Rev. of *Letters.*

Hough, Graham. "*The Screwtape Letters:* How Well Have They Worn?" (London) *Times,* February 10, 1966, p. 15.

"In Defense of Shelley and Morris," *Times Literary Supplement,* April 1, 1939, p. 190. Rev. of *Rehabilitations.*

Joad, C. E. M. "Mr. Lewis's Devil," *New Statesman and Nation,* XXIII (May 16, 1942), 324. Rev. of *Screwtape.*

Johnson, Talmage C. "The Meaning and Use of Pain," *The Christian Century,* LX (December 1, 1943), 1400. Rev. of *Pain.*

Kermode, Frank. "Against Vigilants," *New Statesman*, LXII (November 3, 1961), 658-59. Rev. of *Criticism*.

Kilby, Clyde S. "C. S. Lewis and the Long Road He Took to Christianity," *New York Herald Tribune Book Review*, February 5, 1956, p. 5. Rev. of *Surprised*.

Knight, Jackson. "Milton the Christian," *Spectator*, CLXIX (November 13, 1942), 460. Rev. of *Preface*.

Knights, L. C. "The Academic Mind on the Seventeenth Century," *Scrutiny*, VII (June 1938), 99-103. Rev. of "Donne and Love Poetry in the Seventeenth Century."

————. "Milton Again," *Scrutiny*, XI (December 1942), 146-48. Rev. of *Preface*.

Leon, Philip. *Hibbert Journal*, XLII (April 1944), 280. Rev. of *Abolition*.

"Letters from Hell: Truth by Paradox," *Times Literary Supplement*, February 28, 1942, p. 100. Rev. of *Screwtape*.

"Lewis's Faith," *Times Literary Supplement*, March 17, 1966, p. 228. Rev. of Kilby's *Christian World*.

"Little Hmān, What Hnau?" *Time*, XLII (October 11, 1943), 100. Rev. of *Silent Planet*.

MacLure, Miller. *Canadian Forum*, XXXV (July 1955), 94. Rev. of *Sixteenth Century*.

McNaspy, C. J. *America*, CX (February 15, 1964), 321. Rev. of *Malcolm*.

McSorley, Joseph. *Catholic World*, CLXIII (June 1946), 277-78. Rev. of *Hideous Strength*.

Maddocks, Melvin. "C. S. Lewis Reworks a Myth," *Christian Science Monitor*, January 10, 1957, p. 7. Rev. of *Faces*.

Mascall, E. L. *Theology*, XXXVIII (April 1939), 303-4. Rev. of *Silent Planet*.

Masterman, Margaret. "C. S. Lewis: the Author and the Hero," *Twentieth Century*, CLVIII (December 1955), 539-48. Rev. of *Surprised*.

Matthews, T. S. "Then Signals from Another World," *New York Times Book Review*, February 5, 1956, p. 5. Rev. of *Surprised*.

Maud, Ralph. "C. S. Lewis's Inaugural," *Essays in Criticism*, V (October 1955), 390-93. Rev. of "De Descriptione Temporum."

"Medieval Medley," *Times Literary Supplement*, July 14, 1966, p. 616. Rev. of *Studies in Literature*.

"Milton's Riches," *Times Literary Supplement*, November 28, 1942, p. 582. Rev. of *Preface*.

"Miracles Rationalized," *Times Literary Supplement*, June 14, 1947, p. 298. Rev. of *Miracles*.

"A Modern Epic," *Times Literary Supplement*, January 13, 1927, p. 27. Rev. of *Dymer*.

Moore, John M. *Journal of Bible and Religion*, XII (May 1944), 123-24. Rev. of *Pain*.

Myres, John L. *Nature*, CLX (August 30, 1947), 275-76. Rev. of *Miracles*.

Neider, Charles. *New York Herald Tribune Weekly Book Review*, October 3, 1943, p. 12. Rev. of *Silent Planet*.

Novak, Michael. "The Way Men Love," *Commonweal*, LXXII (August 19, 1960), 430-31. Rev. of *Four Loves*.

O'Brien, Kate. "Fiction," *Spectator*, CLXX (May 14, 1943), 458. Rev. of *Perelandra*.

"Occasions," *Times Literary Supplement,* September 15, 1966, p. 860. Rev. of *Other Worlds.*

Parris, Robert. "Psyche's Double-Exposure," *New Republic,* CXXXVI (January 21, 1957) , 19. Rev. of *Faces.*

Peel, Robert. "Wit and Orthodoxy," *Christian Science Monitor,* February 11, 1960, p. 11. Rev. of *Last Night.*

"Personal Orthodoxy," *Times Literary Supplement,* March 23, 1967, p. 246. Rev. of *Reflections.*

"Professor Lewis on Linguistics," *Times Literary Supplement,* September 30, 1960, p. 627. Rev. of *Studies in Words.*

"Provençal Sentiment in English Poetry," *Times Literary Supplement,* June 6, 1936, p. 475. Rev. of *Allegory.*

Raven, C. E. "Can Miracles Happen?" *Spectator,* CLXXVIII (May 16, 1947) , 566. Rev. of *Miracles.*

Redman, Ben R. "C. S. Lewis's Magnificent Fantasy," *Saturday Review of Literature,* XXVI (October 16, 1943) , 52. Rev. of *Silent Planet.*

———. "Love Was the Weapon," *Saturday Review of Literature,* XL (January 12, 1957) , 15. Rev. of *Faces.*

"Religion in Literature," *Journal of Bible and Religion,* XIV (November 1946) , 252. Rev. of *Divorce.*

"The Reluctant Convert," *Time,* LXVII (February 6, 1956) , 98. Rev. of *Surprised.*

Reynolds, Horace. "Rocket to Mars," *New York Times Book Review,* October 3, 1943, p. 16. Rev. of *Silent Planet.*

Saurat, Denis. "Milton's Christianity," *New Statesman and Nation,* XXIV (November 14, 1942) , 325-26. Rev. of *Preface.*

Sayers, Dorothy L. "Chronicles of Narnia," *Spectator,* CVC (July 22, 1955) , 123. A letter.

"The Scholar's Tale," *Times Literary Supplement,* January 7, 1965, pp. 1-2. Rev. of *Poems.*

Scott, N. A. "Dialogue with Deity," *Saturday Review of Literature,* XLVII (March 7, 1964) , 41. Rev. of *Malcolm.*

Scrutton, Mary. "Confused Witness," *New Statesman and Nation,* L (October 1, 1955) , 405. Rev. of *Surprised.*

Shuster, George N. "Discipline," *New York Herald Tribune Weekly Book Review,* December 26, 1943, p. 6. Rev. of *Pain.*

Singleton, Charles S. "The Universe of C. S. Lewis," *New York Review of Books,* II (July 30, 1964) , 10-12. Rev. of *Discarded Image.*

[Skillin, Edward, Jr.] "Short but Neat," *Commonweal,* XXXVII (March 5, 1943) , 498. Rev. of *Screwtape.*

———. "Smart Writing," *Commonweal,* XXXIX (October 22, 1943) , 17-18. Rev. of *Case for Christianity.*

Smith, G. D. "Nature and Spirit, According to a Recent Work," *Clergy Review,* XXV (1945) , 62-69.

Smith, Stevie. "The Simple Psalms," *Spectator,* September 12, 1958, p. 352. Rev. of *Psalms.*

Smith, T. V. "Holy Logic," *Saturday Review of Literature,* XXXI (January 31, 1948) , 28-29. Rev. of *Miracles.*

Southron, Jane S. "The Pilgrim's Regress and Other Works of Fiction," *New York Times Book Review,* December 8, 1935, p. 7.

Spencer, Theodore. "Symbols of a Good and Bad England," *New York Times Book Review,* July 7, 1946, p. 10. Rev. of *Hideous Strength.*

Sprott, W. J. H. "Would You Believe It?" *New Statesman and Nation,* XXXIII (May 31, 1947), 398-99. Rev. of *Miracles.*

Stephenson, George R. "Holiday from Hades," *New York Times Book Review,* March 17, 1946, p. 6. Rev. of *Divorce.*

———. "Of Faith and Reason," *New York Times Book Review,* May 18, 1947, p. 22. Rev. of *Abolition.*

Sugrue, Thomas. "Terrifying Realities of the Soul," *New York Herald Tribune Weekly Book Review,* March 3, 1946, p. 4, Rev. of *Divorce.*

Telfer, Dorothy. "History and Meaning," *ETC.,* XXII (March 1965), 103-7. Rev. of *Studies in Words.*

"Theme and Variations," *Times Literary Supplement,* November 17, 1950, Children's Books Section, p. vi. Rev. of *Lion.*

"Theology as Discovery," *Times Literary Supplement,* October 21, 1944, p. 513. Rev. of *Beyond Personality.*

"Time Disciplined," *Times Literary Supplement,* March 25, 1955, p. 181. Rev. of "De Description Temporum."

Tucker, Martin. "The Face of Love," *Chicago Review,* XI (Summer 1957), 92-94. Rev. of *Faces.*

Turner, W. J. "The Devil at Work," *Spectator,* CLXVIII (February 20, 1942), 186. Rev. of *Screwtape.*

"Understanding the Psalms," *Times Literary Supplement,* September 12, 1958, p. 517. Rev. of *Psalms.*

Vidler, Alec. "Unapologetic Apologist," *Book Week,* I (July 26, 1964), 3. Rev. of *Discarded Image.*

Vinaver, Eugene. "An Arthurian Dialogue," *Manchester Guardian,* January 6, 1949, p. 3. Rev. of *Torso.*

Wain, John "Pleasure, Controversy, Scholarship," *Spectator,* October 1, 1954, pp. 403-5. Rev. of *Sixteenth Century.*

Walsh, Chad. "Back to Faith," *Saturday Review of Literature,* XXXIX (March 3, 1956), 32-33. Rev. of *Surprised.*

———. "C. S. Lewis on the Heavenly Goal," *New York Times Book Review,* September 18, 1949, p. 3. Rev. of *Weight of Glory (Transposition).*

———. "A Convincing Brief for Miracles," *New York Times Book Review,* September 28, 1947, p. 5. Rev. of *Miracles.*

———. "A Haunting and Lovely Ancient Legend Brilliantly Refashioned by C. S. Lewis," *New York Herald Tribune Book Review,* January 20, 1957, p. 3. Rev. of *Faces.*

———. "The Keynote Is Honesty," *New York Times Book Review,* March 1, 1964, p. 12. Rev. of *Malcolm.*

———. "A Toast to Dr. Slubgob with Some Pertinent Remarks," *New York Times Book Review,* February 21, 1960, p. 14. Rev. of *Last Night.*

———. "Whatsoever Things Are True," *New York Herald Tribune Book Review.* April 13, 1947, p. 5. Rev. of *Abolition.*

Whicher, G. F. "The Dignity of Poetic Truth," *New York Herald Tribune Books,* July 23, 1939, p. 8. Rev. of *Rehabilitations.*

White, T. H. "Psyche and Psychology," *Time and Tide,* XXXVII (October 13, 1956), 1227-28. Rev. of *Faces.*

Williams, Bernard. "That Our Affections Kill Us Not," *Spectator,* April 1, 1960, pp. 479-80. Rev. of *Four Loves.*

Williams-Ellis, Amabel. "Traditional Tales," *Spectator,* CVC (July 8, 1955), 51-52. Rev. of *Magician's Nephew.*

Wilson, P. W. "A Devil's Disciple at Oxford," *New York Times Book Review,* March 28, 1943, p. 3. Rev. of *Screwtape.*

————. "Prophecy Via BBC," *New York Times Book Review,* July 22, 1945, p. 8. Rev. of *Beyond Personality.*

Index

238